MANAGEMENT 2.0

DISCOVERY OF INTEGRATED ENTERPRISE EXCELLENCE

Jerry,
Thanks for the great inputs to my books, review, and spreading the word about IEE benefits!

Forrest 9-2-2020

FORREST W. BREYFOGLE III

OTHER BOOKS BY FORREST W. BREYFOGLE III

Statistical Methods for Testing, Development, and Manufacturing

*Implementing Six Sigma, Second Edition: Smarter
Solutions Using Statistical Methods*

*Solutions Manual, Implementing Six Sigma: Smarter
Solutions Using Statistical Methods*

*Managing Six Sigma: A Practical Guide to Understanding, Assessing,
and Implementing the Strategy That Yields Bottom-Line Success*

Wisdom on the Green: Smarter Six Sigma Business Solutions

*Lean Six Sigma in Sickness and in Health: An
Integrated Enterprise Excellence Novel*

*The Integrated Enterprise Excellence System: An
Enhanced, Unified Approach to Balanced Scorecards,
Strategic Planning, and Business Improvement*

*Integrated Enterprise Excellence, Vol. I: The Basics: Golfing Buddies
Go Beyond Lean Six Sigma and the Balanced Scorecard*

*Integrated Enterprise Excellence, Vol. II: Business Deployment: A Leaders'
Guide for Going Beyond Lean Six Sigma and the Balanced Scorecard*

*Integrated Enterprise Excellence, Vol. III: Improvement Project
Execution: A Management and Black Belt Guide for Going
Beyond Lean Six Sigma and the Balanced Scorecard*

*Solutions Manual: Integrated Enterprise Excellence
Volume III: Improvement Project Execution*

*Lean Six Sigma Project Execution Guide: The Integrated Enterprise
Excellence (IEE) Process Improvement Project Roadmap*

*The Business Process Management Guidebook: An
Integrated Enterprise Excellence BPM System*

Leadership System 2.0: Implementing Integrated Enterprise Excellence

TABLE OF CONTENTS

FOREWORD

A friend, who is a finance executive at a semiconductor company, told me he was involved with a cost-cutting initiative handed down from upper management. My friend's functional area of the business was a fabrication (fab) line at a plant in Texas. An examination of operating expenses showed a significant expenditure for air conditioning, especially in the summer. The building's current air conditioner setting was 71.3 degrees Fahrenheit. My friend asked the plant engineers about raising the temperature a couple of degrees to save some money. The plant engineers immediately called a meeting and showed him yield curves; for every 0.1 Fahrenheit degree of change, there would be a drop in yield at the factory. The cost of the yield drop would far exceed the savings in air conditioning costs. It is not unusual for semiconductor fabs to understand their processes that well, with this degree of precision.

Well, it turns out that there are tools for your business that can deliver real insights into precisely what your processes can provide, even if your business is distant from semiconductor fabrication. Organizations that can benefit from these business tools include healthcare, manufacturing, services companies, and virtually any other for-profit or non-profit organization, including school districts and government agencies.

You used tools your whole life; tools have enabled you to do things better or even allowed results that would be otherwise impossible. You used tools in your home shop and your professional career. Sometimes tools are physical things; other times, they are software-based.

Yet, many executives who have risen to their level often lead their organizations based on what others have done, and lots of digging through data and reports to try to figure out what is really happening in their business. *When the inevitable frustrations set in*, firefighting occurs, the pressure increases, and results are tentative at best. The core of the problem is the lack of practical tools for executives to understand the underlying capabilities of their processes and the steps needed to improve those processes.

Forrest Breyfogle, with his Integrated Enterprise Excellence (IEE) system, provides the tools every executive needs. Forrest has spent the better part of his career studying how business processes operate and which tools and techniques work and the limitations of each. He now offers a structured approach for use company-wide to identify and drive actions that get results. In this book, he introduces these concepts in a novel format. Four golfing buddies share insights from their respective industries and from the issues they face. This book is written with a backdrop of golf to increase the understanding of IEE concepts and benefits from the methodology. This book presentation approach lets Forrest weave in IEE concepts, also showing how lesser techniques fail executives.

So why not just publish a book that details these IEE techniques? Well, Forrest Breyfogle has written that book and several books on various aspects of the topic. The first book, initially released in 1999, *Implementing Six Sigma*, is considered by many a definitive book on the implementation of Lean Six Sigma concepts and is used as a textbook in many universities. Several other later published books provide the details of implementing IEE. However, this book is needed because too many executives don't understand that they require tools to run their organizations.

Executives may think that current management tools like red-yellow-green scorecards are sufficient, but these tools can lead to harmful consequences. Conversely, to produce the best results, one should have advanced tools and skills and know-how to use them appropriately and with precision. That brings the challenge of educating many top executives about these tools in an accessible way. This book fulfills the need by first presenting business challenges from different industries that every executive can identify with. He then illustrates associated frustrations from ineffective tools and their poor results. Forrest follows by demonstrating how to achieve success through the IEE Business Management System.

I have worked at two companies two decades apart, where each set a record for the fastest growth in the Fortune 500. Both were primarily engineering- and manufacturing-focused at the time. Many of the top performers started as engineers before they advanced to upper management. What became a common occurrence was that these engineers, masters of rigorous technique and expert users of tools, wanted to *wing it* as managers. Many of these managers failed in their new roles – they had been up-and-comers as they advanced through the technical-skill ranks but petered out when they went into management. These people were just as smart after promotion as they were before. The problem was that there was not a clearly defined set of tools for these new managers to use to analyze processes and lead their teams.

This book is that vehicle to help many in an organization understand that they need to use the right tools to improve their area of responsibility, just as they used the most effective tools when they started their careers.

For leaders such as CEOs, General Managers, Senior VPs, and Division Heads in any organization, the tools described in this book bring clarity and mechanisms to drive the right, efficient, improvement behavior to their core processes.

Once you've studied this book, in written or audio form, you will want to share it to help others understand and get excited about how IEE techniques can improve their company's performance while lowering the stresses from firefighting and unsatisfactory results.

Imagine thoroughly understanding what your processes are capable of, and the steps needed to address process improvement. Imagine knowing that if your people present this information to you, it means that they are productively involved with analyzing and improving processes. You will have a company that regularly improves, can see those results in real gains, and has operational productivity. And as a leader, you'll develop a culture based on objective analytics and tangible results.

IEE is the system that you need, providing the tools that get results. Enjoy this book and share it with your friends and colleagues.

Bob Ashenbrenner
President
Durable Mobility Technologies, LLC

PREFACE

Many well-respected companies such as Circuit City (Galuszka 2008), GE (Bloomberg 2019), K-mart (Egan 2015), and Sears (Colvin and Wahba 2019) have experienced a significant decline or completely collapsed.

Other esteemed corporations such as Dell (Hess 2010) and Wells Fargo (Wolff-Mann 2019) made news headlines because they set and gave focus to the achievement of organizational measurement goals that led to harmful behaviors.

Companies have replaced their CEOs with an expectation to improve the company's bottom-line but instead experienced problems, including a short-term tenure. (Sullivan 2007 and Wiersema 2002).

BP's Gulf of Mexico oil spill (Broder 2011) and Blue Bell Ice Cream's listeria contamination (Axelrod and Rand 2015) are two examples of the dreadful consequences, including death, which can occur when esteemed companies do not respond to operational issues in a timely fashion.

Why did I write this book? Management at these companies had good intentions and many highly skilled people. Still, they lacked an objective, repeatable, and focused set of processes that would have shown management the real state of their business. They had used either ad-hoc management or ineffective methods that did not deliver predictable business improvements.

There are some major *elephant-in-the-room* business management issues that no one seems to be addressing. In my opinion, this not-talked-about elephant is an underlying component of many past and current business problems. Presented in a story format, I discuss many over-the-years observed organizational practices. This dialogue includes resolutions to numerous unfavorable, if not destructive, methods commonly used in organizations.

This book provides a no-nonsense next-generation business management system that minimizes the risk of organizations doing bad things. Besides, the described methodology provides direction for establishments to move toward the achievement of the 3Rs of business; that is, everyone doing the Right things and doing them Right at the Right time.

This book, written as a novel, describes an enhanced business management system called Integrated Enterprise Excellence, which has an abbreviation IEE, pronounced I-double E. The IEE system offers much flexibility, including a means for effectively managing an organization remotely.

IEE provides a comprehensive 9-step system that CEOs, Presidents, General Managers, executives, managers, leaders, practitioners, and others can use to resolve *elephant-in-the-room* management issues such as:

- Business goals not being met.
- Scorecards leading to harmful, if not destructive, behaviors.
- Persistent day-to-day firefighting problems.
- Business strategies that are very generic and/or difficult to translate to organizational work environments.
- Lean events and other improvement projects that can consume a lot of resources but often do not offer a quantifiable benefit to the business as a whole.
- Lean Six Sigma process improvement deployments that have improvement projects, which are either not completed in a timely fashion or make substantial financial claims that are questionable.

Whether documented or not, an organization has processes for executing work. These processes have output responses (Ys) and inputs (Xs). This relationship can be expressed mathematically as $Y=f(X)$; that is, a process Y response is a function of the Xs that impact a process-output response. Organizations often give focus to managing the Ys without giving much attention, if any, to improve the Xs or the process that can lead to the enhancement of a process's output response. Y-Management can lead to very harmful organizational behaviors, including playing games with the numbers to make situations appear better than they are.

Leadership often has the desire to improve an organization's key performance indicators (KPIs) or to achieve its objectives and key results (OKR) quickly. This metric performance enhancement aspiration can lead to the setting of specific, measurable goals for a future time-period. However, often these measurement objectives are arbitrarily set with no mention about improving the underlying processes that can lead to performance measurement response enhancements so that there is long-term, business-as-a-whole benefit. A meet-the-numbers style of running a business is Y-Management and can result in many forms of unfavorable organizational behaviors and lack of sustainability. IEE provides a system for overcoming Y-Management issues.

This book follows four successful friends who met in graduate school while pursuing their MBAs. Now they meet for golf outings to continue their friendship, discuss their careers and compete in a friendly golf game for the price of a meal. The challenges they face in business and their personal lives are all too familiar. Golf provides an intriguing metaphor for the game of life, with its complexities and challenges, changing conditions, chances for creativity, penalties, and rewards. Moreover, golf is the game most often associated with the business.

Hank, Jorge, Wayne, and Zack share their experiences and pursuit of improvement in their organizations during golf outings. During these rounds of golf, they discover powerful new insights that help them see how they can improve their games, both in business and golf, through the IEE business management system.

BOOK OVERVIEW

Many traditional business practices give focus to the achievement of vague but well-intended executive-retreat-developed strategic statements that often have wording like 'expand production capacity' or 'develop global logistic capabilities.' Common-place business management methodologies that target the execution of hard-to-get-your-arms-around, organizational-handed-down strategies can lead to harmful, if not destructive, behaviors.

Everyone should be well aware that organizations need to improve and adapt to survive. Because of this aspiration, a business may undertake a process improvement program such as Lean or Six Sigma; however, often, these process improvement program undertakings are not long-lasting. The reason for this occurrence is that, when leadership undertakes a program self-assessment, they often find that they cannot see a tangible big-picture positive financial impact from the conducted process improvement program's efforts. Far too often, process enhancements from an improvement program occur in silos, where there is little if any positive impact on the big picture.

This book also describes organizational issues that commonly occur with tried-but-not-so-true techniques like strategic planning, the balanced scorecard, red-yellow-green scorecards, table-of-number reports, hoshin kanri, and Lean Six Sigma programs. There also is an explanation of fundamental issues with statistical control charting, process capability analyses, and acceptable quality level (AQL) sampling quality tools and what to do differently to address the problems.

The tools in an automobile mechanic's toolbox can be handy. However, a mechanic must know not only how to use their tools individually but also be able to apply the right tool correctly at the most appropriate time when addressing a vehicle issue. Similarly, many business management and process improvement tools can be very beneficial; however, not unlike an automobile mechanic, the people in an organization must know when and how to use specific tools for the management and improvement of an organization.

This book provides a roadmap for the wise utilization and execution of business management and improvement tools, both at the enterprise and process-improvement-project level. Described, for both manufacturing and transactional processes, is the use of traditional statistical and non-statistical techniques so that there will be whole-enterprise benefits.

Proven techniques for improving an organization's bottom-line and better addressing customer wants, needs, and desires include analysis of variance (ANOVA), analysis of means (ANOM), brainstorming, cause-and-effect diagram, design of experiments (DOE), 5 whys, Gemba Walk, general linear model (GLM), hypothesis testing, kaizen event, kanban, Lean, muda, Pareto charts, plan-do-check-act (PDCA), poka-yoke, regression analysis, scatter plot, total productive maintenance (TPM), value stream mapping, visualization of data, and wisdom of the organization (WOTO). Chapter 9 of this book provides a discussion between Jorge and Hank about the use of a web page. This page uses hyperlinks directed toward the application of these tools in an enhanced IEE Lean Six Sigma process improvement Define, Measure, Analyze, Improve, and Control (DMAIC) roadmap.

This book also describes the benefits and usage of the 9-step Integrated Enterprise Excellence (IEE) business management system. Among other things, IEE provides a means to create and report 30,000-foot-level operational and satellite-level financial performance metrics, which separate common-cause variation from special-cause events. When only common-cause variation is present in a process-output response, the IEE high-level 30,000-foot-level performance-metric reporting methodology utilizes data from the recent-region-of-stability of a process's output response to provide a predictive statement estimate. When a provided 30,000-foot-level futuristic statement is undesirable, this metric enhancement need *pulls* for the creation of a process-improvement project. This IEE approach for improving a Y response gives focus to enhancing the associated Xs and processes that impact the magnitude of a Y's response level.

Appendix A, Web page 13 provides access to software for creating 30,000-foot-level and satellite-level reports described in this book. The author intends to have a *no-charge* licensing fee for this software.

In Chapter 7, there is a discussion about the "Positive Metrics Poor Business Performance: How does this happen?" article (Reference Appendix A, Web page 2). Provided in this article is an overview of the IEE system. The article-described IEE value chain offers a means to structurally link, through hyperlinks, organizational 30,000-foot-level and satellite-level metrics with the processes that created them. Organizations can use the described Enterprise Performance Reporting System (EPRS) software to provide automatic updates to high-level IEE value-chain performance metric reports throughout the business.

This book presents a blended analytical and innovative approach for creating an enterprise improvement plan (EIP). An EIP graphic shows organizational 30,000-foot-level IEE value-chain metrics that, when improved, will enhance an organization's overall satellite-level reported financials. In IEE, all value-chain measurements have an owner who is responsible for the performance metric's response and associated process enhancement efforts.

IEE offers an operational excellence system for providing products and services. IEE provides a framework for orchestrating and support-ing systems such as integrated management system (IMS) and Quality, Health, Safety, and Environment (QHSE) management. IEE not only can work in conjunction with standards such as ISO 9001, ISO 45001, and ISO 14001 but also provide a holistic infrastructure that supports compliance and continual improvement for these programs. The IEE system can provide the framework for ISO 9001 certification and total quality management (TQM) implementation.

The IEE system offers a vehicle for implementing Deming's man-agement philosophy and achievement of the Baldrige Award and Shingo Prize. IEE can be used to enhance an organization's Toyota Production System (TPS) and quality management system (QMS) implementa-tion efforts.

Appendix A provides many website linkages that offer additional how-to information about the book described techniques. Included in this appendix is application software for applying the methodologies.

COMPARISON OF IEE TO OTHER SYSTEMS

Figure 0.1 provides a comparison of the IEE system to taught meth-odologies in a typical MBA program and traditional organizational deployments of Six Sigma, Lean, and the original balanced scorecard methodology.

Comparison of Systems

SELECTED ATTRIBUTES ++: Attribute included +: Partial/incomplete Inclusion -: Not included	Integrated Enterprise Excellence (IEE)	Typical MBA Program	Traditional Six Sigma	Traditional Lean	Original Balanced Scorecard
Defines process for improvements at operational/project level	++	-	++	++	-
Defines a process for improvements at enterprise level	++	-	+	+	-
Derives improvement projects from enterprise value chain metric performance needs	++	-	-	-	-
Uses DMAIC process to implement process improvements	++	-	++	+	-
Integrates enterprise scorecards, strategic planning, business improvements, and control using 9-step IEE system	++	-	-	-	-
Supports standardized graphical representation of selected data (dashboard)	++	+	-	-	+
Aligns enterprise level business metrics (satellite-level) and operational metrics (30,000-foot-level)	++	-	-	-	-
Includes process for definition of rational metrics that are aligned at operational and enterprise level	++	+	-	-	-
Includes process for distinguishing between "common cause" and "special cause" problems so as to eliminate firefighting	++	-	-	-	-
Uses a traditional approach for business management and/or making process improvements	-	++	++	++	++

Figure 0.1: Comparison of IEE to other Systems

This figure summarizes the benefits of IEE; however, as highlighted in the table, the IEE business management system is different. This book describes and highlights the benefits of these differences.

MAIN CHARACTERS IN THE BOOK

- Hank is one of the four golfing MBA friends. As a VP, he works at Hi-Tech Computers, which has been using its Lean program to execute kaizen events to reduce organizational waste.
- Zach is one of the four golfing MBA friends. As a VP, he works at Z-Credit Financial, which has been using the balanced scorecard to improve the execution of the organization's strategic statements.
- Wayne is one of the four golfing MBA friends. As a VP, he works at Wonder-Chem, which has been using Lean Six Sigma to execute improvement projects to reduce costs.

- Jorge Santos is one of the four golfing MBA friends. As a VP, he works at Harris Hospital, which discovered and successfully implemented the Integrated Enterprise Excellence (IEE) business management system.
- Janice Davis is the CEO of Harris Hospital. She has an MBA degree.
- Ron Wilson facilitates IEE deployments in organizations.

READER'S AND LISTENER'S GUIDE

For the audio version of this book, the book's figures, acronyms, glossary, and references can be downloaded from SmarterSolutions.com/iee-audio-book1-supplemental-material. Figures in this supplemental material are larger than those provided in this book. Readers of this book can use this additional information to examine a figure's smaller printed details more closely.

When explaining IEE and its benefits in this book, there are references to a few figures and web page links. To avoid disrupting the book's flow by referencing a figure number or another portion of this book for each reference occurrence, readers and listeners of this book can use the following to locate the referenced information.

- IEE one-minute video: Figures 7.1 and 7.2; Appendix A, Web page 1 (video link)
- IEE overview article, "Positive Metrics Poor Business Performance: How does this happen?": Figures 7.3 – 7.14; Appendix A, Web page 2 (PDF copy)
- IEE 9-step business management system: Figure 6.1
- IEE value chain in "Positive Metrics Poor Business Performance: How does this happen?" article: Figures 7.9-7.11
- EIP (Enterprise improvement plan) example: Figure 7.12
- IEE Define, Measure, Analyze, Improve, and Control (DMAIC) project execution roadmap: Figure 9.3

- Capturing Voice of the Customer: Appendix A, Web page 7
- Enterprise Performance Reporting System metrics (EPRS-metrics) software: Appendix A, Web page 13 (30,000-foot-level metric-reporting software)
- Enterprise Performance Reporting System IEE (EPRS-IEE) or (EPRS) software: Appendix A, Web page 14 (IEE system software that includes IEE value chain with automatic metrics updating)
- SmarterSolutions.com web pages for additional information about IEE methods: Appendix A, Web page 11
- IEE implementation books: Appendix C

This book references computer hyperlinks. Access to these links could be through a desktop computer, notebook computer, tablet touch screen, or smartphone. A *click of a mouse* or some other variation of the word *click* describes navigation through these hyperlinks.

AUTHOR COMMENTS

Process improvement and other business practitioners often state that IEE concepts look great, and they believe their organization could benefit much from utilizing the methodology. These individuals then continue saying that the problem that they have is that IEE concepts need to be presented to people much higher in their organization's hierarchy than where they reside.

To address this valid point, in addition to an e-book and paperback book offering, an audio-book version of this book is available that IEE proponents can suggest to others. Business leadership, executives, and others who have constraints for book-reading time might listen to this book on their commute to and from work or during exercise workouts.

Another frequent question is how to receive more information about implementing IEE. Appendix A provides more than twenty website links for additional information about the implementation of the

IEE techniques described in this book. Appendix C includes books that provide IEE, how-to methodology implementation details.

This book is a derivative work of *Wisdom on the Green: Smarter Six Sigma Business Solutions* (Breyfogle, Enck, Flories, Pearson, et al. 2001) and *Integrated Enterprise Excellence Volume I* (Breyfogle 2008).

The organizations, Harris Hospital, Hi-Tech Computers, Z-Credit Financial, and Wonder-Chem, presented in this book, are fictitious. As the author, I have created many situations that these four company's employees, Jorge, Hank, Zack, and Wayne, need to resolve smartly. The described circumstances may have fabrication in the book's storyline; however, I have observed all the basic presented scenarios at some point in time in my career.

Except for the four permission-granted organizational scorecards, randomly generated data were used to create the illustrative metric reporting figures.

ACRONYMS, GLOSSARY, REFERENCES, AND REGISTERED MARKS

The glossaries and acronyms sections of this book provide reference material for increasing the understanding of unfamiliar statistical and golfing terms. The reference section of this book offers additional resources for the reader or listener of this book.

Integrated Enterprise Excellence, IEE, Enterprise Performance Reporting System, Satellite-level, 30,000-foot-level, and 50-foot-level are registered service marks of Smarter Solutions, Inc. In implementing the programs or methods identified in this book, authorization is granted to you to refer to these marks in a manner that is consistent with the standards set forth herein by Smarter Solutions, Inc., but any and all use of the marks shall inure to the sole benefit of Smarter Solutions, Inc. Smarter Solutions is also a registered mark of Smarter Solutions, Inc.

AUTHOR

The author solicits your comments and improvement suggestions for this book. He is also available to discuss the application of the described techniques, which is his passion.

Forrest W. Breyfogle III
Smarter Solutions, Inc. (SmarterSolutions.com)
Forrest@SmarterSolutions.com

1 THE STARTING POINT

Author Note

There are some golfing terms in the first part of this book. The frequency of golfing-term usage decreases significantly after the first few chapters.

For the non-golfer who is either not interested or unfamiliar with golfing terminology, I suggest choosing one of the following options:

First option: 'Roll with the flow.' Scan over this book's golf-game dialog without attempting to understand the details. Focus on gaining an understanding of IEE techniques and their applications.

Second option: Look over the 'Glossary: Golf Terminology' section of this book before starting to read Chapter 1. This summary of golf terminology can help with the understanding of the golfing dialog presented in this book. This Golf Terminology Glossary is also available to audiobook listeners in their supplemental material.

MARCH

Hank arrived early at the golf course and was hitting some balls to loosen up. The sky was crystal blue, and the wind was still. The weather was perfect for eighteen holes of golf, but Hank was having a hard time getting his mind off work.

As vice president of operations at Hi-Tech Computers, his background in electrical engineering and an MBA had helped make him be a fast tracker. Hi-Tech was an aggressive, successful computer component manufacturer with plants in the southwestern United States and Mexico. Recently, however, the company had been facing new competition and pressures from its biggest customers to comply with growing regulations, to improve delivery times, to become more flexible, and to lower prices. Of course, they all wanted perfect products as well. Things were heating up. Hank again tried to concentrate on golf.

Hank was tall and muscular at 46 years old. He looked more like the former linebacker he had been in college than a PGA pro. Hank loved golf, but all attempts to improve on his 12 handicap seemed to fall victim to a few big numbers each round. If he could just eliminate those big mistakes, especially the penalty strokes for out-of-bounds lies, he was sure he could achieve his goal of consistently breaking 80. After all, Hank thought that he could hit the ball a long way and often made great shots. He had a hole in one and a flock of eagles on his resume, but he could also run into trouble on the very next ball. If he could just eliminate the double bogeys (and worse), he would be happy with his game. Hank forced a resigned smile as he vowed to practice more and to try harder this year. If work would ease up just a little, he could blitz this game. Hank loved to *grip it and rip it*, the exact opposite of his regular playing partner, Jorge, who thought his way around the golf course as well as in the boardroom at Harris Hospital.

Hank thought for a moment about the possible root cause of his big numbers. Sometimes he hooked the ball, sometimes he sliced it, but usually, he hit it pretty well. Every once in awhile, it was dead-solid-perfect. He was proud of his ability to scramble, to recover from trouble, both on the course and when fighting fires at work. He just wished for fewer of those big mistakes that cost him extra time, constant reorganizations at work, and penalty strokes on the golf course. Yes, the increasing pressure from Hi-Tech's customers, shareholders, and regulators was eating into his golf practice time. Recently, more *snowmen*, those nasty eights, were showing up on his scorecard than he cared to admit.

Hank was still engrossed in his thoughts when he saw his old college buddies, Jorge, Wayne, and Zack, walking toward the practice green. Their tee time was still twenty minutes away, so they caught up on family news as they practiced. Zack, always the serious one, was even able to slide in some business discussions about the latest investment model his company was developing that would produce a high rate of return with minimized risk. Meanwhile, he rolled in another long practice putt. Jorge was hitting a few of his magic chip shots from the fringe, while Wayne stretched and warmed up his smooth, rhythmic swing with his 7 iron.

As they approached the first tee, they agreed to their usual pairings: Hank and Jorge teamed against Wayne and Zack in a game of two-person best ball. The best individual score on each team determined who won the hole. The team that won the most holes could win the front nine, the back nine, and the total. Loss of two out of the three meant you picked up the lunch tab. Hank liked this game. He could play his ball and keep his score, make an occasional great shot, and still rely on steady old Jorge to carry him on a hole if he came up with one of those big numbers. The game had provided lots of camaraderie and good-natured competition over the years.

After winning the coin toss for honors, Hank stepped to the first tee and surveyed the 425-yard par 4. He didn't like this hole. It's not that he didn't want a challenge, but he preferred a simpler par 4 that gave him a chance to warm up a bit. This one was long and hard, demanding immediate execution from the very first swing. Closer inspection showed a Mexico-sized bunker guarding the next 75 yards along the inside of the dogleg about 150 yards out on the right side of the fairway. About 100 yards off the tee, a stream that today looked like the Rio Grande crossed the fairway. "Get those negative thoughts out of your head," Hank thought as he made his first swing. The muffled click told him immediately that he was in trouble. His new ball cleared the Rio Grande but disappeared weakly into the heart of Mexico.

Jorge was up next and hit a modest drive that ended up short but in play. Wayne stroked a beautiful 275-yard drive that successfully avoided the hazards that had befallen Hank, and then Zack hooked his drive into the light rough on the left.

With a smile on his face, Zack pointed at Jorge and Hank saying, "Looks like you guys will be picking up the tab for lunch."

As they rode to their second shots, Jorge said, "Hank, you'd better get rid of that slice. I know it's been a while since our last game, but I don't want to lose to these guys again."

Hank bit his lip. He didn't have a slice problem. He just wasn't warmed up yet. He changed the subject. "My mind is still at work and not on this lousy game."

Hank stepped out of the cart and selected a 3 wood. It was a challenging shot, but he was still 300 yards from the green, and on a long par 4 like this, Jorge would never be able to reach the green in two. Hank didn't want to start too far behind in this match. His mind was churning, and his swing was rushed as his mighty blow took mostly sand. The ball trickled only a few yards ahead, still in the trap. Hank's blood pressure rose as he hit the next two shots only a few yards each. Now he had done it—blown the first hole on his way to another 8 or worse. And, there were still 40 yards of sand in front of him. Hank took a deep breath and tried to ignore the barbs flying from the other golf cart as he stepped out of the trap and exchanged his 3 wood for his trusty 5 iron. It wouldn't make it to the green, but it should get out of the trap and get him back in play. A mediocre swing advanced his ball out of the trap, just barely to the point where he had expected to find his original drive. "Four strokes wasted—I've done it again!" Hank fumed to himself.

As he climbed back into the cart, Jorge calmly said, "Why didn't you just chip the first one sideways back out into the fairway and save yourself a few strokes and a lot of grief?"

Hank fought back the urge to snap at his partner just long enough to realize the wisdom of his advice. He did that too often—threw good strokes after bad, compounding his original mistake by blindly charging straight ahead. How could someone who hit the ball no better than Jorge play him almost even? On most holes, Hank thought, he easily out-played Jorge, but on a few holes each round, Jorge would take a scrambling par or routine bogey while Hank exploded to a double bogey—or worse. When the final scores were tabulated, Jorge was almost always closer than you would expect and sometimes even beat Hank. Was there a smarter way to play this game? Was Jorge on to something?

As Hank tried to reason it out, he forgot about the comments coming from Wayne and Zack and began to settle down. When they reached his ball, he hit a smooth 6 iron on the green and two-putted for another dreaded 8. Fortunately, Jorge had scraped the ball along, getting close in three, hit another great chip shot within inches, and made the tap-in for bogey. Meanwhile, Wayne and Zack seemed distracted and made bogey as well.

"Hank, you'd better get your head in the game, or we're gonna end up paying for lunch," Jorge prodded him.

"I told you that my mind is still at work," Hank responded.

"So, what's the problem?" Jorge asked.

Hank replied, "I've been pressuring my managers to increase profit margins. They did it all right, by shifting most of the connector assembly work to a couple of our plants in Mexico. The problem is that another manager discovered that our division had a component supplier inside Mexico with an even lower cost structure and decided to move half of the production to that plant."

Wayne, who had been listening in on the conversation at the second tee, empathized with Hank. "We're running into the same problems at Wonder-Chem. There's always constant pressure from Wall Street analysts to reduce costs and increase quarterly profits. Meanwhile, it seems like there's always another problem surfacing. For example, last month, we had a major yield hit, which held up delivery of our shampoo products to our northeast distributors due to a container defect. Our engineers were trying to cut costs with a new injection-molded container; however, the sidewall of one of the corners was too thin, and 300,000 shampoo bottles leaked all over our warehouse floor when a cold front moved through."

Hank continued his story. "After transferring the equipment and operations, they found out that the third plant lacks the necessary quality and safety certifications, and it's not even set up to ship product to the United States! It's been a colossal screw-up!"

"Why didn't these issues surface when your management was researching lower-cost alternatives?" Jorge asked as he lined up to hit his driver on the second tee.

Watching Jorge, Hank remembered how long it always took his friend to prepare for his shot. "We could be out here all day," he thought and decided to hold his reply until his partner finished. After all, there was a hefty lunch bill riding on the match.

Jorge waggled gently side to side, readjusting his stance, trying to avoid the inevitable. The driver had always been his weakest club, and it pained him each time he reached for it. As expected, Jorge didn't break any driving records, but the ball went 175 yards straight down the fairway.

"You need to get over your driver phobia if we're ever going to finish this round."

"Well, at least *I'm* on the fairway," Jorge responded with a slight smile.

"Whatever," Hank replied. "As I was saying, the management in Mexico assumed we knew about the certification and delivery issues. They were in the process of laying out a plan to ship products to a US plant using a certified freight forwarder that could ship between the US and Mexico. Can you imagine? They planned to use a middleman to ship product from Mexico to a plant in Oklahoma and then turn around and ship from Oklahoma to our customers!"

As he told the story, Hank began to burn with anger, "Our management team has spent the last two days developing a plan to meet current orders from our existing plants and move production back to the original two plants in Mexico. Instead of saving cost and labor, we've added millions to our expenses this year."

6

After sharing his story, Hank began to refocus on his golf game. With his obligatory 8 or "snowman" out of the way for one of the 18-holes that they played, he ended up playing pretty well, recovering to shooting 85. Jorge struggled on the long holes but teamed well when Hank faltered to finish with 89. Wayne was reliable as ever with his 76, just a few missed putts from shooting par. Zack used his wonderful putting stroke to stave off total disaster and finished with 96. Hank and Jorge lost the front side by one hole, but recovered to win the back nine holes by two and win the overall match. Later that day, as Wayne and Zack split the lunch tab, Hank re-lived Jorge's beautiful 20-foot putt on the 18th green, which sealed their victory.

He was even able to tell a version of the old golf joke on himself. "Hey, Hank, how did you make 8 on the first hole? I just missed a 30-footer for my 7!"

Hank's friends wished him luck in solving his production problems. They all knew that Hank was really at his best when fighting fires. The interesting part would be hearing about his solution to resolve the most recently identified problem *fire to fight*.

On the drive home, Hank thought about his good friends. There were many interesting similarities between them. They had played together for years, ever since they had met in MBA classes at the university. They were all competitive in golf and business, and Hank thought it was no coincidence that they had all advanced to the VP level in their respective companies. However, each had some unique traits.

Jorge was 47 and a senior vice president at Harris Hospital. Short and stocky, with a choppy golf swing due to an old soccer injury to his shoulder, he was good at keeping the ball down in the wind. He used his typical fade to great advantage as long as the shot did not require too much distance. His real trademark was his short game. Too often, it seemed Jorge was chipping on and one-putting while Hank was on in two- and three-putting or worse. It wasn't so much that Jorge was a great putter; he wasn't as good as Zack, but he just didn't leave himself very many long or hard putts.

Wayne was 45, and a VP of Research and Development at Wonder-Chem. He had leveraged his BS in Chemistry and MBA to manage product development successfully for the last few years. Wayne had the look of the former basketball player that he once was, even though he was not exceptionally tall. Fortunately, he had been a great shooter and a starting varsity guard in college. His conservative haircut, clothes, and bifocal glasses made him look more like an accountant than a scientist, but his precision golf swing was a thing of beauty. Ten years earlier, Hank had joked that he was going to invest for retirement by sponsoring Wayne on the Senior Tour when he reached fifty. Back then, Wayne had been almost a scratch golfer, but age seemed to be taking its toll. For several seasons Wayne had not putted as well, and his average had slipped into the upper 70s. That was good for the group competition; at least they didn't have to play 3 against 1 as they had in the beginning, but Hank wondered what had happened to Wayne's game.

For that matter, what had happened to his own game? He had slipped a few strokes as well, and now Jorge was beating him more often. He thought again about Jorge's "lesson" on the first hole today. It would bear more investigation.

Finally, there was Zack. Youngest of the group at 44, he looked even younger. He had the muscular build of a baseball player and the baseball swing to go with it. He was the most erratic of the group until he reached the green. Then the magic started. His eagle eye could read putts with the best of them, and he spent lots of time practicing on the putting green. No one drained as many putts as Zack. Fortunately for Hank and Jorge, he was usually already out of the hole by then.

Yes, it was a good group: good friends, good competition, and good people. Unfortunately, as Hank pulled in the driveway, he remembered his problems at work. He began to worry about what he would do next to resolve Hi-Tech Computers' manufacturing-plant issues.

2 THE MEXICO MEETING

ONE WEEK LATER

Things were happening fast for Hank. One week after the golf outing, he found himself on the way to Juarez, Mexico for a weeklong business trip. There would be many hours of meetings once he arrived, so he allowed himself a moment to relax and to think about the golf outing. Surprisingly, he had shot a pretty good score. It would have been terrific if it hadn't been for that eight on the first hole. Maybe there was a lesson in Jorge's comments. Still, hindsight is usually 20/20. Once you've wasted three or four shots in a bunker, it's easy to say you should have played a safe ball out of the trap rather than take a heroic chance with a 3 wood. Still, he could have made that shot. He'd done it before – not that often, but he had!

How do you know when to take a chance and when to play it smart? The odds of making the more difficult shot are lower, but the possible rewards are much higher. Did Jorge know the odds? Were the odds different for players with different skills? Should you always try to do what the pros would do, or should you sometimes take Jorge's advice and play it smart? Jorge was good at thinking his way around the course. He certainly did get more out of his limited physical skills than Hank. Did he just play more, or was there a smarter solution? Hank decided he should study this further, on the golf course, naturally.

Suddenly thoughts of the Mexico meeting played through in his mind. Not only did he need to find a solution to the current production

9

problems, but he also had to address the original business issues that had led to the plant transfer in the first place. The plants needed to reduce costs and increase throughput to stay competitive in their market.

On Monday morning, Hank met with his new manufacturing director, Karen Johnson, and the production supervisors from the Juarez and Mexicali plants, Juan Rodriguez and Carlos Silva. Hank wanted to discuss how to salvage the current situation. Karen was a manufacturing engineer who had become a good manager. He liked Karen and trusted her judgment.

Just a few hours before the meeting, Hank received an email that informed him that the move did not impact the Juarez plant's production. Operations at their second plant in Mexicali had been transferred to a plant in Mexico City.

He also discovered that the original plant in Mexicali was not completely shut down. During a five-hour marathon meeting, they decided that the best solution would be to transfer operations back to the Mexicali plant from Mexico City.

The complete waste of this undertaking was painful. Equipment transfer costs, lost sales, and set-up costs were just the tip of the iceberg in terms of damage to the bottom-line. In preparation for the plant's closing, they had also lost some of their best employees through layoffs at the Mexicali plant.

By Thursday morning, the operations meeting was complete, and the business unit review was set to begin. The other critical managers for the business unit flew in on Wednesday night.

Because of a reorganization, the members were all new; however, the least-experienced member had been with the company for ten years, so at least they weren't novices. The new members included John Jenkins, the supply chain manager; Ellen Simpson, the quality manager; and Andy Anderson, the marketing manager.

Hank opened the meeting with a clear plan in mind. "The purpose of this meeting is to define this business unit's problems and develop a plan to solve them. I want to know all of the important problems you're facing. Anything not brought up today cannot be used as a crutch for future poor performance. Let's start with marketing."

Anderson stood and walked to the front of the room like a fifth-grader who hadn't completed his homework. "Well," he stammered, trying to collect himself while plugging his laptop into the projector. "As you can see from this chart, we've gone from a 50 to 35% market share over the past year." To his surprise, Hank said nothing. Anderson was expecting some browbeating over the poor performance, even though the deficiencies were due to his predecessors.

Anderson collected his thoughts and continued, "This reduction in market share is due mainly to three new competitors who have entered the market. This competition has turned the sub-assemblies we make into a commodity item. Customers are no longer willing to pay a premium for our brand name."

Hank responded in an even tone, "I would challenge some of your conclusions; however, this meeting's purpose is to discover problems. Is there anything else?"

Anderson was thinking fast. He hadn't expected to get past the 15-point drop in market share, not with Hank's temper. Everyone was scared of Hank, so they didn't always give him the complete story, but his reaction hadn't been so adverse. Maybe he could tell him about the product delivery problem.

Here goes nothing, Anderson thought, as he advanced to the next chart and continued his presentation. "We're also losing customers because our delivery times aren't meeting their needs."

"Wait a minute," a shout came across the table. Rodriguez was on his feet in a flash. "That's not true! We've a near-perfect record of on-time delivery."

Anderson responded, "That's because our sales representatives tell customers our lead time is three weeks. Customers who need their product sooner don't order, or they're forced to wait for three weeks and then don't reorder with us. Our competitors have a shorter lead time and…"

Rodriguez interrupted again, "But why didn't you say something!" Rodriguez was beside himself due to what he considered an unwarranted attack.

"We did!" Anderson responded forcefully. "If you'd been listening…"

Hank interrupted them, "Okay, I see the problem. We'll work it out later. For now, we're just defining the problems. Let's hear from the supply chain next. John?"

Jenkins relaxed a bit as he stood. Maybe there would be no executions today, after all. He spoke from his position at the conference table. "We have supplier and delivery problems. Our suppliers sometimes run out of inventory when we have a big order, and at other times we have weeks of inventory. Due to the complicated bidding process for our suppliers, the purchasing group headcount has increased. Our delivery contractor can't seem to provide consistent delivery times and tends to lose orders on a fairly regular basis. Unfortunately, we're forced to use that particular contractor because purchasing negotiated a contract for the entire business unit."

"Is that it?" asked Hank. Jenkins nodded. Hank then asked Juan to summarize the critical production issues in Juarez.

Juan stood and started through his list of problems. It seemed as if Hank had heard them all before: large finished-goods inventory, a large amount of work in progress, not enough storage space, changing schedules, missing parts, and quality problems.

Finally, he finished, and Hank asked, "Is that all?" Juan nodded.

"Great, now how are we going to fix these problems, people?" Hank asked with a steady, even stare.

No one said a word. Hank decided to wait for an answer.

After three minutes of silence that seemed like an hour, Carlos spoke, "When working for my previous employer, we used a different production method. It was called Lean, and it seemed to address many of the problems we discussed today."

Hank had heard of Lean and had even read some on the topic. After further discussions, Hank decided that he would look further into Lean techniques, but for now, he was exhausted, and he knew it, as did every-one else in the meeting.

Hank was glad to be home. The trip to Mexico had been grueling but worthwhile. Now, all he had to do was learn how to implement a Lean system; he thought with a smile. He decided to take Sunday off—after all, those problems would still be there Monday. Today, he would keep his other promise to himself and work on his golf. Driving to the practice range, he thought back over his last few rounds and tried to remember his worst holes. He was sure that if he improved on those two or three nasty holes each round, even if they became bogeys, he could save two or three strokes on each lousy hole. The effort could quickly improve his round by five or six shots and get his average down close to 80. That would mean some rounds in the seventies. Look out, Wayne!

But how could he avoid those big meltdowns? If he followed Jorge's advice and always took the safe shot, he would give up any chance for the occasional great shot that got him a birdie or eagle. That seemed counter-productive, and not nearly as much fun. He paid for a large bucket of balls and decided that his driver set the stage for success or failure on most holes. An excellent long drive usually meant a chance at par or birdie, and it felt great when the others in the group "ooh'd" and "aah'd" over one of his massive hits. He smiled as he thought about last summer and the drive he had smoked 325 yards, followed by a beautiful 125-yard 8 iron, which fell for an eagle! They still talked about that one.

On the other hand, he often hit a bad one as he had on the first hole at the last outing, got in trouble, and quickly degenerated to a double bogey or worse. Maybe he should just practice more with his driver. As he set the balls down on the range, he reached for the *big dog* and started to work. It was his favorite club. He'd work it out.

After a few phone calls on Monday, Hank was able to contact Lean and Mean Manufacturing Consultants (LMMC) and, in a short time, was speaking with the president, Jason Sanders. Hank wanted to know more about Lean, and Jason was happy to give him a summary.

Jason started by talking about Lean production. "Lean focuses on the reduction of waste through the value stream. Even though the techniques originated in manufacturing, the techniques are also applicable for service or transactional processes. Even new product development can benefit from the methodology."

Jason continued, "Lean is a set of techniques used to reduce waste in business operations. The Toyota Production System, or TPS, as it's sometimes called, is a good example of Lean implementation. Toyota has been developing its production philosophy and implementation tools since the 1950s."

Hank took the following notes on some basic principles of Lean principles and Lean tools:

- Don't overproduce: Make sure that the customer gets it when he wants it. Timely production holds true both for internal and external customers.
- Define customer value: Root out non-value-added activity.
- Focus on the entire value stream, including the supply chain: It does no good to reduce the time it takes to produce a product if the delivery system accounts for 80% of the product delivery time.
- Convert from batch processing to continuous flow whenever possible.
- Synchronize production between process steps.
- Develop the ability to make your full product mix on any given day.
- Relentlessly pursue perfection.

Tools used to implement the Lean production philosophy include:

- Utilize 5S workplace organization method. The 5 steps of 5S are Sort, Set in order, Shine, Standardize, and Sustain.
- Store inventory close to where it will be used in production.

- Reduce setup time: Setup time impacts the ability to make every part every day, an objective of Lean manufacturing.
- Implement production cells: In cell production, the entire production process is split into small groups, where each of these cells is responsible for a complete unit of work.
- Utilize kanban workflow management. Kanban is a Lean scheduling system for just-in-time manufacturing.

What the Lean consultant told Hank made sense to him. He would delegate the details of implementation to someone else in the organization while he oversaw the progress. He made a note to contact his manufacturing director, Karen Johnson, to have her meet with Jason to start putting an implementation plan together immediately. Hank smiled to himself as he hung up the phone. He liked working with Karen, who was smart and efficient. They would attack this problem head-on and solve it together.

He relaxed for a moment and thought about golf again. Maybe Lean could help there, too. Could it help eliminate those wasted second, third, or fourth shots? Hitting the bucket of balls on Sunday had undoubtedly not helped much. Sure, some beautiful shots turned heads on the range, but deep down, Hank knew that at least ten percent of his drives were still unacceptable. That would have cost him strokes on the course. Then he thought about Jorge's advice again and could not erase the feeling that Lean techniques could help him reduce the number of strokes for a round of golf.

3 METHODS

Hank could hardly contain himself as he worked his way down the winding road from his house to the golf course. He was eager to tell his friends about the new program he had implemented to solve the manufacturing problems in Mexico.

As he traveled the familiar route to the golf course, he randomly thought about his business. How many reorganizations had occurred in the last three years? Was it four or five? Well, no matter; if the current leaders couldn't cut costs and increase throughput, he would just find someone who could.

To Hank, the business was a form of combat. The object was to create a winning strategy, deploy your forces, and execute a plan, thereby destroying the opposition. In many ways, it was just like football, Hank thought. After the fiasco last month, he had had to shake up his organization again. As he arrived at the golf course, his thoughts turned to the details of his current method of combat, the Lean Program.

Meanwhile, down on the practice green, Wayne watched the crowd collect to observe the spectacle that Zack and Jorge had created. They were betting on who could make the longest putt. They had started with five-foot putts and worked their way up to 15 feet. Jorge was focused entirely, ignoring everyone at the moment. He knew every break on this practice green, and a lot was riding on this putt. He had just bet Zack's leadership of the free world that he would sink this 25-footer.

Just as the putter started forward, Hank came down the hill, yelling greetings to his friends. Jorge's concentration was remarkable as he stroked the putt and watched the ball gather speed down a slight incline, and then break three feet left to right just as he had predicted. Upon reaching the hole, the ball caught the far side of the cup, executed a complete 360-degree wrap-around, and hung on the edge. A noticeable sigh rose from the assembled crowd. Then, just as everyone had given up on the shot, the blades of grass underneath the ball gave way, and the ball dropped into the cup.

Everyone around the green was cheering. Jorge was surprised at how much he enjoyed the accolades. As he smiled to himself, he thought, "Was it the putt or the fact that I've regained control over the free world?" It was the putt; neither he nor Zack had ever bothered to place an operational definition on what they meant by control of the free world. Jorge wasn't sure what he had won. In the end, he just enjoyed the competition.

"Great putt," Hank called out, "but save a few of those for our match, partner. Hey, you guys won't believe what's happened at work since last month!"

Jorge stopped him in mid-thought, "We're not going to start talking about work right away, are we? How about talking about my beautiful putt for now?" he said with a laugh. Hank agreed impatiently to hold shoptalk until later.

By the fifth hole, Hank's earlier excitement began to resurface. While waiting for Zack to find his ball in the thick rough down the left side of the fairway, Hank again started to explain what had happened last month. "After the fiasco, I reorganized the manufacturing group and brought in a new director. Then I had her initiate a Lean Program."

"From what I've learned about Lean, we should be able to respond more quickly to product-demand changes, reduce costs, and increase our throughput," Hank continued.

"I found my ball," Zack yelled. "Do you believe this rough? I almost needed a hedge trimmer just to get to my ball," he joked. At this point, the group wasn't paying any attention to Zack as talk had turned strictly to business.

Hank continued, "All kinds of problems have brought our business to the brink of extinction. To develop a game plan for saving the business, we held a management review and decided to start a Lean Program."

Wayne was getting interested. He had recently started discussions with his management team about what program they could initiate to help solve some of their company problems. Low yields, poor on-time delivery, raw material issues, and high costs were just a few of the chronic difficulties Wonder-Chem was facing. Wayne asked, "How will Lean reduce costs?"

Hank spent the better part of the ninth and tenth holes explaining what he had learned from Jason, his Lean Consultant.

Wayne explained that his executive team had heard a Lean Six Sigma presentation and decided to implement the program. He noted that Six Sigma and Lean Six Sigma are often considered a problem-solving project-based quality improvement program. He pointed out that the total quality management (TQM) initiative that Wonder-Chem had implemented some years ago was abandoned. Their slogan had been:

Wonder-Chem is committed to being a company of the highest quality in every aspect of its business activity.

There had been some good, isolated results from the TQM program, but not enough to capture upper management's attention or sustain the program.

In retrospect, Wayne felt the major problem they experienced with TQM was choosing the Quality Department to implement the program. Wonder-Chem's quality organization could be very hardline and uncompromising concerning how the Quality organization viewed problems. The department seemed to have no concern for overall business issues, with its total focus placed on quality. As a result, the Quality Department had a hard time getting operations managers to cooperate and allow their people to join Quality Improvement Teams. Wayne remembered one meeting in particular. During this gathering, the TQM program leaders demanded more top-management support and financial resources to address a long-range improvement, while ignoring the hard business reality that the funding they were requesting would severely impact production operations.

"This time, I'm going to do it differently with Lean Six Sigma," Wayne explained. "I'm going to hire a Lean Six Sigma trained program leader to drive the program. He or she will be responsible for achieving financial goals through the completion of projects."

"TQM was a good initiative," Hank interjected. "We went through TQM training some years ago and got some good results here and there. I heard that Lean Six Sigma was an improvement over TQM in that practitioners worked on projects that had finance-validated savings."

Zack walked up, complaining about his horrible shot. "This hole is going to ruin my round. This round isn't my typical game."

"Not your typical game?" chided Wayne. "Every time we play, you run into several holes that kick your butt. Maybe you need a new driver, one you can keep in play," he said with a sly grin.

For an instant, Hank was distracted from the business discussion. Zack had lots of flaws that cost him strokes; what he needed was a new swing. He thought for a moment about his own game. Maybe one of the new over-sized titanium drivers would be just the cure for his bad hole or two each round.

Then Zack switched topics to offer his perspective on the business discussions. "One of our directors heard about a concept called the balanced scorecard, and has been very excited about the prospects, so I decided to look into the methodology."

Hank responded, "We use scorecards, and dashboards too. I understand that a scorecard focuses on a given metric and compares it to a forecast or target, whereas a dashboard can present multiple numbers in different ways. I've heard of the balanced scorecard, but Hi-Tech Computers has not looked into the methodology. Please educate me."

Zack answered, "In the early 1990s Kaplan and Norton wrote a *Harvard Business Review* article (Kaplan and Norton 1992), which became the stimulus for many organizations to use the balanced scorecard in their company. This article describes how balanced scorecards track the business in the areas of financial, customer, and internal business processes, as well as in learning and growth. The organization's vision and strategy formulate these metrics. Each category is to have objectives, measures, targets, and initiatives. We're following the basic balanced scorecard methodology described in the original article."

"How do you know how well a metric is doing relative to its target?" Wayne interjected.

"The balanced scorecard uses red, yellow, and green colors to describe the current performance level.. If the color is green, the metric performance is satisfactory relative to achieving its target or plan. If the color is yellow, the current level of performance is marginal. If the color is red, the current level of performance isn't satisfactory, and corrective action should be taken. Tables or graphs also present the current metric status."

Wayne interrupted, "That seems simple; however, I've concerns about creating metrics from strategies. I don't know about your company's strategies, but ours often appear to be simply a bunch of words. Besides, these words could have multiple interpretations and can change significantly between years."

"Yes, I've had that same concern," Zack said. "Everyone was excited that this methodology could be a means to implement our strategic plan. From the metric color, we should know when corrective action is needed. However, I'm not so confident in our current strategies. We could be having people react to things that aren't real or important. Also, since leadership establishes our targets annually, it would seem that we could get a metric disconnect each year."

Wayne interjected, "I've never felt terrific about the wording of our strategic plan statements. We typically assess and make wording adjustments annually. In these sessions, it seems like the person who has the most authority or yells the loudest gets his or her way. Also, the last time we had a new CEO, our strategy changed a lot, which caused havoc for some time."

Zack continued, "Know what you mean. Our company's strategic plan appears to be just a bunch of words that any company could be writing. Also, you know only a few people are involved in setting the strategic course for the whole company. What if the chosen direction is wrong? That could be bad news for the company. We're not analyzing our enterprise data so that we gain true insight into where we should focus our efforts. Perhaps we should have some analytical folks look at the situation differently so that we gain a new perspective before creating these strategic plans. I'm concerned that we're directing everyone's measurements and activities to these statements, which aren't specific and might be harmful to the business."

As the others continued to talk about their programs and the promise they saw for improvements, Jorge said nothing. He thought that his company didn't need any process improvement or any other program. Jorge believed that his people had a lot of experience and worked hard. He also thought his rapport with his entire management team allowed him to handle problems on a personal level. And he certainly had some issues to work on.

Reduced medical payment schedules had forced Jorge to develop a cost-reduction program within his hospital. After hearing about Hank's problems with his plants in Mexico last month, he had carefully pointed out to his managers that they needed to protect the patients' interests during any cost-reduction initiative. He was confident that the cost reductions wouldn't pose any problems. He had a vast pool of talent on his management team, and they were all very committed to their patients.

As they approached the green, Jorge was farthest from the cup. He strode across the green, feeling the springy *give* under his feet that you get on well-maintained golf greens. It was like those rubberized surfaces used for running tracks. He wondered who came up with that idea of combining crushed tires with asphalt to create those spongy track surfaces. He was always fascinated by such creativity. He was always look-ing for someone with that spark to add to his team.

"Okay," he thought to himself, "back to golf." As he read the break of the green, Zack called out another leader of the free world challenge. If Jorge sank the putt, he could maintain his rule. If not, Zack had an opportunity to become supreme commander on his next putt. Once leadership changed hands, the other could regain power only through another challenge. Jorge was always up for a challenge, especially around the green.

After sinking the 25-footer, Jorge gave Zack a good-natured ribbing for even thinking he could challenge the master. Zack conceded that Jorge was master of the green, for now anyway.

While waiting for the others to putt out, Jorge wondered why Zack never challenged Hank or Wayne. Maybe it was because Jorge and Zack were acknowledged as the best putters in the group. Hank and Wayne were long-ball hitters. They were always giving each other a hard time about a short or missed drive.

It occurred to him that they all seemed to focus their practice on their strengths. Hank and Wayne rarely showed up early on the putting green. They were always at the driving range practicing with a driver or a long iron. Likewise, when he went to the driving range, he gave focus to his short irons. After thinking about it, he decided that the best way for him to take strokes off his score would be to practice the part of his game that offered the most opportunity for improvement. For him, it wasn't just how far he could hit the ball; it was positioning the ball on the fairway. He had an excellent short game, but most of his skill went to overcome the poor ball position after his tee shot.

Later, Wayne ruined a routine par-hole opportunity with an agonizing four-putt and complained, "I think I'll go buy one of those new one-shot putters that I saw at the clubhouse. I haven't four-putted in years."

Jorge just smiled, remembering some years ago when they were playing regularly. Wayne had bought three new putters in one year to help "fix" his putting. He was still at it.

Just then, everyone jumped when Jorge's cell phone rang. After a brief but animated conversation, Jorge returned to the group. "What's going on, Jorge? I've never seen your face so red," Wayne asked with real concern.

Jorge had a hard time collecting his thoughts. After a moment, he was able to explain his panic coherently. "There has been a major problem at the hospital. A change in saline bag labeling and sizing caused a whole floor of patients at the hospital to be over-medicated."

He went on, "Doctors are on their way, and I have to head over to help organize our patient protection plan and notification of appropriate government agencies. So far, everyone's okay, thank goodness. However, there are notifications and paperwork that have to be handled very carefully to avoid any further allegations of incompetence and cover-up."

Jorge jumped into his cart and headed for the clubhouse as his friends wished him well. They headed for the next tee a lot more somber than they had been just moments ago. Their match was suspended, and they would finish the round without much enthusiasm.

Driving back to the clubhouse, Jorge began collecting his thoughts. He was greatly relieved to hear that none of the over-medications was life-threatening. Still, this was a severe problem. How could something like this happen? Who had dropped the ball? Jorge thought long and hard on these questions. Was it his fault for pushing for cost reductions? Was it the administrator's fault for notifying only the supervising nurse of the first shift? Was it the nurse's fault for leaving town in the middle of the night to be with her husband, who had suffered a heart attack? Was it the inexperienced nurse who selected the wrong size bag due to a change in labels?

Jorge made it to his car on autopilot, but he was still trying to sort out just what had happened. It seemed like such an unlikely string of events. Why?—How?—he couldn't seem to decide. He was in a painful loop of self-doubt and managerial rage. He decided to put it out of his mind until he got more information at the hospital. After all, there would be plenty of time to try to recover from this mess in the coming weeks.

Jorge tried to focus on the oldies' radio station rather than his current problems. Too bad the music he grew up with was now known as oldies. He started thinking about all the musicians he used to listen to as a young man. It was amazing how many musicians began and how few found their big break. And for the bands that made it, there was always some exciting story about their hardships along the way.

Didn't all musicians think that they were talented and hard-working? And believe that they would make it? But most hadn't done so. It seemed like it was almost the luck of the draw. With so many bands starting, one had to get a break.

Then it hit him like a 300-yard drive right between the eyes. The over-medication was not a fluke event. Having some problems is inevitable; it's just a matter of which problem occurs. There are thousands of potentially deadly events that can happen every day in a hospital. All operations, medications, and critical information transfers are like potential musicians trying to get their big break. Some problems will occur sooner or later by chance.

Jorge then thought about the source for the issues and recalled how he had heard that aircraft safety experts say there are three causes of accidents:

- Pilot error
- Equipment failure
- System failure

Jorge then realized that Harris had now suffered from a *system failure*.

For any critical activity, there are numerous chains of events that can cause some horrible outcomes. Given so many possibilities, even good people doing their jobs well can have problems unless processes are designed to be mistake-proof and robust to the normal variation from its input variables. Of course, whenever issues are later reviewed, the chain of events looks so specific and unusual that everyone believes they were unique occurrences.

Often, we do not recognize that it is the system that allows the failures to take place. The better the system, the less likely a failure will occur. Jorge chastised himself for not realizing this before. He had presided over task forces that had solved many specific problems. Upon completion of a task force, the members patted themselves on the back for fixing the problem. They then handled the next challenge as though it were an independent issue, missing the system connection between them.

Furthermore, the way the process was set up, all of the prominent high-risk areas had backups. He wondered how many times the backup systems saved a life with no recognition that the backup procedure was even used. After all, if the backup saved someone's life, technically, that was still a failure of the original system, costing time and money. Then, with enough failures of the initial process, even the backup systems were likely to fail at some point. Other potential issues might not seem as deadly on the surface, but if you combined several failures for these secondary issues, the result might be fatal.

Jorge's revelation helped ease his anxiety somewhat; however, having this understanding was still not enough. How could this have been avoided? He kicked himself for not having implemented some type of improvement plan like those of his friends. He hadn't thought he needed it. His problems were different; they were information-related.

Now he knew he did need something, but what? The programs his friends were talking about seemed a lot like Wayne's new putter or Zack's modern driver. They reminded him of his discussions with his managers: isolated efforts to solve disconnected problems. What he wanted was to change the process of how people did their jobs. That was the only way to head off all the potential failures in the system.

As Jorge pulled into his parking space, he realized he was shaking. This building was his hospital. These patients were under his charge, and he was responsible for their well-being. He had almost had a catastrophe, the magnitude of which he didn't want to contemplate.

"All right," he told himself, steadying his hands as they rested on the steering wheel; it ends here. We will change how we do business. Patients won't have to fear for their health when they enter our hospital. And we will still reduce our costs so that we can provide affordable care." Just how this was going to happen, he wasn't sure—but it would.

As he climbed out of the car, some doubt started creeping back.

4 INITIAL ISSUES

MAY

It was mid-morning on a beautiful Saturday. Wayne was sitting outside the Pro Shop at a picnic table, enjoying the cool morning breeze and a cup of coffee. He had arrived at the golf course early to hit some balls at the driving range, and his swing was in fine-tune. Now he was just waiting for his friends to arrive. That was the good news. The bad news was that every golfer in the state, it seemed, was either already on the course or in line in front of them. Wayne tried to prepare himself mentally for a long day of slow play. Concentration would be a challenge today. If they had not all been so busy at work, they could have played during the week.

It had been a long week—a long month for that matter. Wayne's management team was working hard to get the Lean Six Sigma program established. They had the newly hired Lean Six Sigma Director start putting together some material from their previous TQM program and developing a new training plan.

He had high hopes for Lean Six Sigma and was disappointed at the response the program generated during its initial six weeks. Earlier in the week, he had visited some of the Lean Six Sigma training sessions unannounced and found only half of the scheduled managers present.

Engineers and other employees who were required to attend were unhappy about middle management not buying into the program. They expressed their concerns openly, worried that their managers wouldn't know how to utilize Lean Six Sigma techniques nor understand the time burden the program's execution placed on their employees to complete assigned projects.

Wayne agreed with his employees' concerns, and the next day instituted a sign-in sheet for management. He couldn't believe he had to resort to this, but attendance did pick up as a result. However, Wayne wondered if this was really a long-term solution, or if managers were just going through the motions by attending the sessions. He certainly hoped his managers were committing to the program; the company needed to cut costs and improve the performance of their over-the-counter health care products. In the long run, they also needed to reduce development times for their prescription drugs.

Wayne contemplated his company's loss of market share over the past couple of years. Marketing had not been able to reverse the decline, giving excuses that prices were too high.

Jorge and Hank showed up five minutes before their scheduled tee time, interrupting Wayne's thoughts of future cost-revduction and improvement ideas. No one had heard from Zack, and rather than giving up their tee time, they proceeded without him, hoping he could join them later.

An hour later, Zack caught up with his friends who were waiting to hit on the fourth tee and were engaged in an agitated conversation. Wayne was gesturing wildly, as Zack arrived just in time to hear the trailing part of his sentence, "… and the managers weren't even showing up to the training!"

"Hey, Zack," Jorge called out, grateful to change the subject, "Where've you been?"

"I went to the office to take care of some documentation," Zack replied. "We've been working to implement the balanced scorecard system throughout the company so we can determine where to focus improvement efforts. It's taken a lot more effort than expected. Not only that, I think that our fundamental approach is flawed."

Zack continued, "Let me describe what I mean. A while back, our executive team developed strategies from our corporate vision. From these strategies, we were to establish organizational metrics and goals for these measurements. Let me pull out my strategies cheat-sheet, so I can better show you what I mean" (See Figure 4.1).

Z-Credit Financial
Strategies

- Develop strategic relationship with industry leaders.
- Focus on the development of global logistic capabilities.
- Expand production capacity.
- Achieve further vertical integration.
- Maintain technologically advanced and flexible production capabilities.
- Develop new products.

Figure 4.1: Company Strategies

"What do you think about each of these statements? I'm having difficulty getting my arms around what we should be doing correctly relative to these directives.

"Look at the first listed statement: 'Develop strategic relationship with industry leaders.' Shouldn't we always be considering the establishment of strategic alliances, not just next year?

"What about the second statement: 'Focus on the development of global logistic capabilities?' It seems to me that we should've been doing this for years as part of the execution of our standard processes since we started going global about ten years ago.

"To me, the third statement, 'Expand production capacity,' is interesting. Is it a good thing for our company to expand capacity for all offerings? I doubt it. Some of our products are approaching the end of life, and we should decrease capacity, if anything.

"Let's examine the fourth statement: 'Achieve further vertical integration.' What implication does this have for the size of our company? Are we to give focus to acquiring suppliers throughout our company? In a general sense, this would probably be a horrible thing to do that could negatively impact our financials.

"What about the fifth statement: 'Maintain technologically advanced and flexible production capabilities?' Geez, looks like an American *motherhood and apple pie* statement to me.

"Now, statement six: 'Develop new products.' What more can be said about this directive than duh."

While waiting for their turns at the tee, Wayne and Hank glanced at the pocket-size plastic-coated card. Then Wayne said, "Zack, I agree with you. These statements could just as easily have been written for my company."

Wayne stopped mid-stride as he was finally stepping onto the tee box, turned towards Zack, and proclaimed, "Just had a thought! It's time to exhibit some leadership and get to classes and some of the Lean Six Sigma project team meetings. Then my managers would know I'm serious about our Lean Six Sigma program."

Wayne launched a slight draw long and down the middle of the fairway. Zack continued, "Our Z-Credit Financial Company could benefit from red-yellow-green scorecards in that we would have a system where managers throughout the organization react to measurements that are not consistent with our plan. Do you think this could have helped you take care of the type of problem you had last month, Jorge?"

Jorge wasn't listening. Instead, he thought about how this particular hole was easy to play, with a wide fairway that would accommodate the variety of slices and hooks that their foursome usually produced. As luck would have it, he hit the ball straight and long, with just a hint of power-fade.

"Zack, what do you mean robust?" Jorge asked with a smile, obviously pleased with his shot.

"You should have built a balanced scorecard that would highlight that the change control process for patient medication was not mistake-proof. The only difference between your processes and ours is that ours deal with customers in the financial services industry. In contrast, your organization deals with medication and patients," Zack explained while lining up to swing.

After Hank and Zack had also hit good shots, they all congratulated each other and started down the fairway. Jorge thought about the unusually good outcome and how many times the four had teed off together over the years. Sooner or later, they were all bound to hit the ball long and straight on the same hole—this was a rare moment.

Zack continued as they headed down the fairway, "In each of the three divisions where we started this process there's been a lot of complaining. However, we keep telling people we need to understand where to improve so that customers are satisfied, and we meet our strategic goals."

"Have you noticed any improvements yet?" Jorge asked as he walked towards his ball.

"Improvements could take time. We're trying to get our minds around building balanced scorecards and setting targets for each of them," Zack responded.

Jorge intently listened as he selected a 9 iron to travel the 100 remaining yards to the green. His compact swing was ideal for short-iron play and produced a near-perfect shot with ample backspin that covered the pin placement cut on the front of the green. Jorge's ball landed ten yards beyond and slightly left of the hole, bit on the soft green, hopped backward five feet, and rolled back right towards the pin. Hank yelled, and Wayne ran to get a better look. The ball stopped four inches short of the cup. Zack congratulated Jorge while Hank and Wayne both agreed that the ball should have gone in.

Jorge was pleased. An eagle on a par 4 would have been a career shot, but he hadn't hit the target. Still, his shot was close, and that was a success to him. He would happily settle for an easy birdie.

After his excellent approach shot, Jorge was able to carry some momentum through the next two holes, where he recorded a par and another birdie on a par 3. He wondered why he was doing so much better on the last few holes. He was wondering if it was luck or real game improvement when a bogey and a double-bogey on the next two holes provided his answer.

With the excitement of golf greatness over, Jorge's thoughts wandered from the game back to work. He wondered why his friends hadn't asked him about the problem that forced him to leave early last time. Perhaps they were each consumed with their work problems.

Jorge then asked, "So Hank, you haven't spoken much about the Lean Program you started. How's it going?"

Hank replied, "Lean looks at the whole value stream. So, if your supplier is the reason your deliveries are late, you fix the supplier rather than try to speed up the manufacturing cycle time."

"But to answer your question, it's not going as well as I'd hoped. Lean has all of these great tools and approaches. We should be able to use them to reduce costs and lead-time, but I do not see results. I even hired a director of Lean and appointed a steering committee. We recently held a site-wide meeting at the manufacturing plants where this deployment is occurring."

"You're up, Hank," Wayne said, prodding the group to keep moving. It was easy to get sidetracked when play was slow, he thought.

Hank pulled his driver from his bag, as he explained to his friends some of the problems he was having with Lean. "I went to some training classes and had an experience similar to Wayne's: half the managers weren't in class; they were off fixing problems. When I asked why, they said the training was nice when you've time, but they had real work to do." In addition to the buy-in issues, Hank explained, there were problems with spotty implementation. Even where some application had taken place, he couldn't see any tangible results.

Wayne grew impatient while waiting for Hank to swing, but Hank continued to discuss the issues he was experiencing with Lean Enterprise. He spoke of the results of various teams. One team conducted some 5S workplace organization activities, with no visible results. Another group did some short-duration kaizen event improvement projects that had specific intentions for improvement. Although this had produced some localized benefits, Hank could not confirm how the claimed results would impact his business metrics. Optimistically, he told his friends that it would just take some time and that some of the advanced techniques would have a more significant impact.

The 16th hole was a wicked 527-yard par 5 with a double dogleg and a creek that crossed the fairway twice. Trees on both sides of the tight fairway gave weekend golfers plenty of chances to shed old golf balls.

While the group waited, Zack noticed that Jorge was about to tee off with a 3 iron. When asked why, Jorge answered with a sly grin, "I haven't hit a driver all day long!"

"But what about that great drive on number 4 that set you up for the birdie?" asked Hank.

"That was my 3 wood," Jorge smiled. "I'm tired of fighting my game. I don't want to have to make difficult second shots continually to save a hole after a bad tee shot gets me in trouble. I used some 'wisdom of the organization' to list out the reasons for my bad holes and decided that it was my erratic driver."

Wayne laughed, "Wisdom of the organization? What's that?"

Jorge replied, "Wisdom of the organization (WOTO) is a term I learned from our Integrated Enterprise Excellence consultant with whom I've been having many discussions at work. An abbreviation for this business management system is IEE, or I double E.

"If you recall during our last golf outing, I hastily departed because of a problem at Harris. At our hospital, a change in saline bag labeling and sizing caused a whole floor of patients at the hospital to be over-medicated, but fortunately, there were no injuries.

"This incident hit our CEO, Janice Davis, like a two-by-four. From this incident, it was apparent that our organization needed to do something different to avoid future similar issues. To make a long story short, I did some research and discovered the IEE system. Now Ron Wilson, an IEE consultant, is coaching me. Initially, Ron and I had a conference call where he had me watch a one-minute video that described IEE and walked me through an article that provided highlights of the IEE business management system. I ended up getting Janice's buy-in through a similar conference call with Ron. We're now undertaking the implementation of IEE at Harris.

"One thing that Ron is ingraining in our organization is the concept of high-level organizational common-cause and special-cause variation. To illustrate this point, consider hitting a golf ball. The result from a golf swing won't be the same every time we impact that little object for a particular situation. This variation is the result of our process for striking the ball.

"The variation in the lay of our golf ball for a given position can be the result of both common-cause versus special-cause variation in our swing. An example of common-cause variation is typical distance inconsistencies experienced for a given club from our golf bag; for example, a driver. A couple of examples of special-cause responses are the result from a wicked slice that's worse than usual or a driving-club impact that's a straight drive with a slight draw that's 25 yards longer than our average maximum stroking distance.

"Ron is a broken record, stating that if a common-cause variation is undesirable, the process needs an enhancement.

"What Ron also taught us is how the wisdom of the organization (WOTO) can be one of the first steps for guiding what to improve in our process. WOTO comes intuitively from process execution experience.

"At work, we use WOTO to come up with ideas on how to improve our business processes. I just evaluated my golf game using my own WOTO based on experience. My biggest problem seems to be my tee shots. Bad tee shots are killing me. It doesn't matter how good my short game is; too often, my drives are bad enough that I can't recover. I decided to leave my driver in the bag today, and I've had only one double bogey."

Zack questioned, "But Jorge, you hit some good drives, too."

Jorge elaborated, "Zack, you included the word *some* when describing my golf-driving process. Yes, I do have some special-cause so-called *good drives*. However, there would be a more positive impact on reducing the number of stokes for my overall game if I give focus to improving the common-cause variation from my golf club selection and usage process.

"To address the reduction of my common-cause golf swinging process, I examined the distribution of my drives in both distance and accuracy. Over the last ten years, I've played over 300 rounds of golf. When

I thought about it, fewer than 20% of my drives are excellent enough to get me in a position to make par or birdie. About two-thirds of them leave me in some degree of trouble, and on about half of them, I can salvage a par or bogey with my good short game. The other half of the time, I have to struggle just to save bogey. The rest of my tee shots are so bad that even my short game can't save me, and I'm facing double bogey or worse. By making smarter decisions on my tee shots, I may be a little shorter off the tee, but I'm more predictable. I can plan my attack better and reduce the chances of falling apart on a hole. I guess you could say that I've reduced the common-cause variation from my swing and made it more robust."

Zack said, "What do you mean? Have you been working out?"

Jorge laughed and said, "No, I guess you could say I'm just working *smarter*. The term *robust* refers to the concept of picking a process; in this case, the club I hit has a typical variation pattern well within the allowable limits for the task. You are familiar with mistake proofing, of course. Well, when we can't wholly mistake-proof the process, the next best thing is to be robust. In golf, that means club selection that has the highest probability of landing in a pleasant spot, concerning both direction and distance. If my 3 iron has a 90% chance of keeping me in play for par, and my driver only has a 30% chance of doing that, my process for making good drives is more robust with the 3 iron. Even if the driver gives me a slightly better chance for birdie by going farther, it has a much higher chance of going into a hazard or out-of-bounds. *Course management* is at least partially *risk management*. It depends on the situation."

With that, Jorge hit his 3 iron off the tee, 175 yards down the middle, just short of the creek, in a good position for his second shot.

Zack looked incredulous, "You need to tell me more about this IEE stuff."

Wayne interrupted, "I want to get educated, too."

Jorge responded, "Wayne, you're now implementing Lean Six Sigma, right?"

"Yep," Wayne responded.

Jorge then asked, "Hank, you're implementing Lean, right?"

"Sure are," Hank responded.

"Zack, you're building the balanced scorecard system from your strategies, right?"

"Yes, we are," Zack replied.

Jorge continued, "There are aspects of all these systems that are great. For example, having a performance metric reporting balance is what you want. Concentrating on profits and disregarding customer satisfaction can lead to disaster. Performance metric reporting balance should address both the profit and Voice of the Customer (VOC) and not merely track against goals that are often only arbitrarily set. If Hank would focus solely on making on-time deliveries but ignored work in progress or WIP, his company's inventories could go through the roof, causing significant financial issues. Hank's organization should have a performance metric reporting balance that addresses both on-time delivery and WIP. Care needs to be exercised not only in defining but also in monitoring the performance metrics responses from a process-output point of view. Some organizations create balanced scorecard metrics through a strategic plan that does not formally address their organizational value chain, where an IEE value chain describes what their organization does and how it measures what is done. This disconnection can lead to metrics that drive the wrong kind of behavior."

Hank interjected, "I can relate to that. Our metrics regularly lead to unfavorable, if not destructive, behaviors. Didn't Michael Porter in the 1980s introduce the *value chain* concept?"

Jorge continued, "Yes, Porter was an economist and Harvard Business School Professor who introduced the term *value chain* and described the methodology in his book *Competitive Advantage* (Porter 1985). Porter's value chain has five primary activities, which are inbound logistics, operations, outbound logistics, marketing & sales, and service.

"An IEE value chain builds on the concepts of Porter's value chain:

1. Porter's value chain gives focus to the execution of its five primary and support activities. An IEE value chain enhances and expands this thinking by providing attention to what an organization does and how it measures what is done.

2. The layout of an IEE value chain differs from Porter's value chain in the presentation of activities. The structural flexibility of an IEE value chain makes the methodology a natural fit for a team to create an IEE value chain in a variety of organizations. The type of organizations that can benefit from IEE techniques includes government agencies, schools, non-profit groups, hospitals, insurance businesses, service establishments, mining companies, software firms, and manufacturing.

3. IEE value chain metrics are unique in that they provide a high-level performance report, which describes how a process is performing. An IEE value chain performance metric response is often predictive, where if a predictive statement is undesirable, the process associated with this metric needs enhancement.

4. The IEE value chain is only one aspect of the 9-step IEE system for the management of the business as a whole and implementing improvements so that both an enterprise's financials and customers benefit, noting that even government agencies and non-profits have monetary issues and constraints to manage.

"IEE takes Lean Six Sigma and performance reporting techniques to the next level. IEE value chain metrics are to be selected so that there's an overall performance metric reporting balance across organizational functions that encourages the most beneficial behaviors for the enterprise as a whole. However, to reiterate, the IEE system for tracking these metrics is different. One benefit of the IEE performance metric tracking system is that this tracking methodology can reduce organizational firefighting.

"Let me give you a little background about the overall IEE system. As I'm sure that Wayne's deployment pointed out, Six Sigma was started by Motorola and made popular by GE in the 1990s. Some companies have dramatically impacted their bottom-line through the completion of projects. The people who drive these projects are called Black Belts."

"Black Belts? Is this some kind of martial art?" Zack interrupted again. He grinned as he noticed that Hank seemed to like that idea.

Jorge continued, "No, the term *Black Belts* is to describe Six Sigma and then Lean Six Sigma practitioners, who through their training, learn how to work with teams and tackle process-improvement problems systematically. An IEE Black Belt (IEE BB) has a similar role to traditional Lean Six Sigma Black Belt; however, there're some very significant differences, which we can talk about later.

"After the over-medication problem we had last month, I knew we had to do something different. I had read some articles about the benefits of Lean Six Sigma and decided to do some investigating. There has been a lot of pros and cons discussion about the success of Lean Six Sigma. Even the cartoon *Dilbert* gives Six Sigma a blow from time to time.

"In an internet search, I discovered an IEE alternative that integrates the strengths and downplays the weakness of many techniques, including Six Sigma, Lean, and the balanced scorecard."

Jorge calmly stood over his second shot and split the fairway a second time with another beautiful 3 iron that went 170 yards, stopping well short of the second creek crossing, right in the opening of the dogleg for his approach to the green.

"Are you doing this on your own or having a company help with your deployment?" Wayne asked.

"As I mentioned previously, we're using an outside company to help with our deployment."

Wayne quickly interjected, "You're smart. We were penny wise and pound foolish when we tried hiring someone who was trained in Lean Six Sigma and then tried to implement the system ourselves. You should be able to get things going a lot quicker using the resources of an organization outside your company. It's important to partner up with a provider that fits well with your company. This partner-selection process isn't the right time to try to save money by selecting someone local or using a university course."

Jorge continued, "I found a couple of books that had a step-by-step process for IEE implementation. Like Wayne, at first, I thought we could use these books to implement IEE on our own. After further investigation, I realized we needed expert advice to get started. The company we went with did not simply focus on doing projects. It focused on how to create an overall business system of measurements and improvements that helps organizations move toward the three Rs of business: everyone doing the Right things, and doing them Right at the Right time. Besides, it furnished the detailed roadmaps to accomplish this. This overall system could be used by executive management to improve organizational governance."

When they reached Jorge's ball, he hit a third perfect 3 iron to within a few yards of the front of the green. After some delay looking for Zack's ball in the left rough, they finally made their way to the green.

When it was Jorge's turn, he smoothly chipped his 7 iron into the front of the green and rolled it to within eight inches of the cup. Hank, who had hit a monster 285-yard drive, had hooked his approach shot into the trees and scrambled for a bogey. Wayne hit two beautiful shots and a half wedge onto the green before three-putting again for a bogey. Zack's ball went unfound in the trees, and with the penalty strokes, took an eight.

As they waited on the 17th tee, Jorge finished his story. "When I decided to go with IEE, I learned that success is dependent upon organizational understanding and buy-in at all levels. Our IEE implementation consultant provided a system to accomplish our goals. The IEE system of measurements has many advantages over the red-yellow-green scorecard or table-of-numbers approaches that give focus to the tracking of a metric against a goal that's often arbitrarily set. Also, there's a structured enterprise analysis phase that leads to the structured building of strategies and projects that are in direct alignment to overall business goal objectives. This system offers the framework for true integration of analytics with innovation.

"Defining and scoping-out improvement projects are essential. In a traditional Lean Six Sigma deployment, management might simply decide what it thought were the significant functions that were most important to improve.

"These managers might be right, or they might be wrong. Some organizations have claimed 100 million dollars in savings, but nobody can seem to find the money. The IEE system has a different approach where IEE value-chain-metric-improvement-needs *pull* for project creation.

"As with every new approach, there can be some buy-in problems. Ron said that it's important to get the CEO's buy-in upfront, which we did. The IEE system is transitioning our organization from firefighting activities to fire preventive actions. This transition is uncomfortable for some people since their rise to the organization's top was because they were good firefighters. The cultural transition to being more data-driven will be healthy for us."

As the group waited on the 18th tee, Hank thought for a minute, and then said, "Maybe I should leave my driver in the bag, and avoid my double bogeys, too."

Jorge smiled and said, "All of our games are different. Before you decide on your game improvement method, you need to measure and analyze your own game. I'm sure you'll find that, on many holes, your driver is a formidable weapon. You just need to understand the percentages."

Then Hank said, "At least, I think I'll check out your IEE methods. Can you get me started?"

"Sure," Jorge responded.

On the 18th green, Jorge snaked in a ten-foot side-hill putt for 79! It was his best score in several years, and his driver had never left the bag. He even beat Wayne, who shot 80.

Jorge said, "I want to get something out of my car. I'll catch up with you in the clubhouse. Hold off ordering drinks until I get there. I want to buy the first round."

Jorge hurriedly walked to his car. He opened the trunk and selected a folder from inside his briefcase. Before meeting his friends at their favorite table, Jorge stopped by the bar and gave the bartender the folder.

Jorge bought a round of drinks and said, "Ron led me to a couple of Lean Six Sigma background articles that I think you'll find very interesting."

Just then, the server returned to the table and said, "Sam, the bartender, wanted me to give you these copies."

Jorge responded, "Thanks."

As Jorge handed an article to each friend, he said, "Take a look at this article, 'Beyond Lean Six Sigma: Why Lean and Six Sigma Deployments

Fail and What you can do to Resolve the Issue' (See Appendix A, Web page 9). Some have stated, among other things, something like 'My organization started its Lean Six Sigma deployment five years ago, and now we're having difficulty finding projects, especially projects of value.'"

Hank interrupted, "This does not seem possible."

Jorge continued, "Know what you mean. However, I understand that when companies push or use a hunt-for-projects-to-create approach, it's not uncommon for this situation to occur. I've discovered that the IEE system not only addresses these issues but is also much more than a project-driven methodology, like Lean Six Sigma. IEE is an overall business system for both organizational measurements and improvements.

"I'm giving you this article now to set the stage for our later discussions. I hope that you'll look over this material before our next get together.

"Ron said that IEE and Harris's deployment of the system would address our hospital's current business management and improvement issues. The jury is still out on what Harris's IEE implementation will look like down the road since we just started, but I'm optimistic. I'll share with you what happens in our next golf outing."

As they were getting ready to leave, everyone agreed that it had been a very long day, almost a six-hour round, but somehow, everyone felt that it just might have been worth it.

5 CONTINUING PROBLEMS

AUGUST

It was late on a hot, muggy Friday night in August, on the eve of the monthly golf game. Zack sat sulking in his office. Why couldn't he figure out why customer complaints were still going up? True to his nature, when things started going badly, Zack took personal responsibility for fixing the problem. However, it seemed as if every time he and his team fixed one problem, several new ones would appear to take its place. It was as if he were trapped watching continuous reruns of the old movie *Gremlins*. Every time they killed off a defect, several unpleasant little relatives seemed to reappear. The thought of skipping the monthly golf outing with his old college buddies crossed his mind, but he hated the idea. Because of vacations and weddings, the foursome hadn't met since May, and he was way past ready for a little break.

Z-Credit Financial had recently developed a system to capture customer complaints and respond within 24 hours with an action plan for closure. Then, when complaints continued to come in, Zack dove into the details of the tracking system. He was trying to assess whether people had been conducting root-cause analysis and were following up on action items. It seemed that employees were following the proper procedures, and yet wrong addresses and incorrect balance transfers were still frequently occurring defects.

Zack wondered why his implementation of the balanced scorecard program hadn't led to fewer customer complaints. There was always something else going wrong, and overall, things were not improving. At one in the morning, he found his coffeepot empty and decided to give the investigation up for the night. He tried to think about how he could start fresh in the morning and knew for sure that he would be missing another round with his friends.

On the drive home, Zack's mind wandered toward the golf game he would be missing tomorrow. Jorge's magical round was the last real success story he could remember. Maybe Wayne was wrong. Perhaps he didn't need a new driver. Possibly he should change the way he approached the game, and leave the driver in the bag like Jorge. But what about all the other shots that got him in trouble? Whenever he worked on one part of his game, defects popped up in other areas to kill his round. What had Jorge said to Hank at the end of his round? He said something about each of them having different games and the need to analyze their rounds of golf before deciding on an improvement strategy.

As Zack entered the driveway of his home, he noted that the lights were out. Georgia and the kids had finally given up and gone to bed. The cold supper in the fridge and the dark house didn't seem like the payback he was hoping for. Maybe if he got started early tomorrow, he could still salvage some time with his family on Sunday.

During the last two months, Hank had also been experiencing problems with his Lean program. One implementation team was able to reduce batch size on one of the manufacturing lines. Still, defects caused confusion and challenges to the point that there was more work in progress (WIP) inventory than when they had started. There was an improvement in some process-cycle times. However, the overall cycle time to get a part through the system has increased considerably. Several of his key customers were now reminding him that the real business metrics were established and measured by the customer.

On another process, a kaizen event gave focus to the reduction of manufacturing costs for a particular product by addressing the setup time for a sheet metal punching operation. The team was able to reduce setup time from an average of two hours to 15 minutes by setting up the punches outside the press. Even though there were hidden problems with increased labor costs, the team truly believed that they were successful because there was a reduction in setup time. Hank knew that the overall business improvement was negligible so far, but he hoped that even a perceived success might motivate his team.

Hank felt as if he were back calling the defensive plays in college again. Whenever he moved people up to stop the run, the opponent would pass. When he dropped back into coverage, the opposition ran over them. When Hank decided to blitz from his linebacker slot, they would dump a screen pass over his head. He needed a better system then, and he needed one now. He hadn't been able to talk to Jorge since their last round, but now he was eager to know more about Jorge's systems approach to improvement, both for business and for golf.

Meanwhile, Wayne had growing concerns about his Lean Six Sigma deployment as well. The completion of two projects and the reported financial savings were decent, but he was not sure that the problems they had solved impacted the overall company's financials. A lot more projects were coming up, but he was not sure of their business value either. Overall, customer satisfaction had not improved, and teams were not spending enough time on their projects. Wayne had been burning a lot of midnight oil trying, in vain, to determine why Lean Six Sigma had not given him the results he expected. The teams were well organized and seemed to be motivated, but they just couldn't seem to see the critical relationships between the processes that they could control and the business outcomes they needed.

Wayne removed his glasses and rubbed his eyes. On these long days, he could hardly read the detailed reports, let alone see any key process relationships. Wayne was getting a headache. Maybe he needed new glasses. Ellen had been pestering him about having his eyes checked. He'd make that appointment as soon as he got over the hump at work. Too bad he didn't know anyone who could give his Lean Six Sigma program a vision check.

Wayne's mind drifted toward his family. Ellen was a great mom to Henry and Shelly. It was amazing how she could juggle being a mom and still be a partner in a consulting company. It was more comfortable now for them that their kids are teenagers and in college. However, he needed to be able to spend more time with Ellen and the kids when they were available. He needed to get this Lean Six Sigma program running under its identifiable power. Wonder-Chem needed more results, and his family needed more of him.

Unlike his friends, Jorge was making significant progress with his IEE business management system. Monthly status meetings now had metric reports that meant something. He found that their past efforts had wasted much time fighting phantom issues. Several of the teams had found some unexpected low-hanging fruit opportunities for improvement. Even better, these projects were well aligned with the financial business goals, making the project benefits even more visible. This project-work seemed to excite and motivate other teams to work even harder on their projects as well. Some real momentum was building.

Personally, Jorge was elated with the results. He learned that some of the statistical analyses his teams were doing had indicated there were many common-cause issues intrinsic to their processes. Previously, these issues would probably have been considered special-cause events, unusual to the process. Firefighting would have ensued, and often the almost random fixes would have masked real root causes and may have made overall system performance worse. Now, his teams were able to pinpoint those areas where overall system improvement was needed. This effort then led to a better perspective on how to proceed. Jorge's organization was creating metrics for Harris Hospital that separated the common-cause variation from special-causes. Now his teams were learning how to make long-lasting improvements through fixing the process, not just firefighting the problem of the day.

Jorge leaned back as he reflected on the application of an IEE-perspective to areas of his business besides operations. He could see the way that improvements through projects were affecting how his people viewed their processes in terms of the overall business results. The benefits of expanding IEE throughout the business had been exciting. Jorge had always been a systems thinker. IEE techniques had provided the vehicle for implementing systems thinking into Harris.

Jorge stretched and relaxed for a moment, thinking about dinner tonight and golf tomorrow. He deserved a break, and tonight's dinner with Sandra should be a great start to a good weekend. He was taking Sandra to their favorite place, a quiet little restaurant they had found when they first met. Thinking about Sandra made him smile. She was a beautiful lady and a very successful career woman in a non-profit. He'd learned so much from her. When he was studying, he had learned to reason in the logical/analytical style of a scientist. Later, his MBA classes taught him to think in terms of business systems. But when he met Sandra, he was amazed to find her to be very successful even though she seemed to rely almost entirely on her powerful intuition and understanding of human nature. Over the years, their discussions had taught him that his logic did not always lead to the right answer and that Sandra was right at least as often as he was. Now he relied on her incredible intuitive senses to augment his logic and systems thinking. Together, they made quite a team.

His mind wandered a bit further, thinking about creativity and wondering if that was what *thinking out of the box* was about: suspending traditional logic and analyses long enough to consider possibilities that did not seem to compute logically. He thought about the many times as a scientist and businessman that he had seen long-accepted theories disproved in favor of new illogical arguments. Yes, he decided, sound business management is a combination of science and logic, business and finance, and people's creativity and intuition. The trick was to treat it as a system.

6 THE DISCUSSION

AUGUST

Hank and Jorge stood alone near the first tee early Saturday morning. "Too bad about Zack and Wayne," Jorge lamented. "At least these two fellows they paired us with look like they can hit the ball."

"You would think Zack and Wayne could get out for a round of golf," Hank replied sarcastically. He didn't know if he was mad at them for not showing up or for working while he was playing. He worried about the time away from the office and wondered if he should be working as well.

As they waited to tee off, Hank started thinking about IEE. He was impressed with Jorge's success with the program and was wondering if it might complement his Lean program. Hank remembered what Jorge had told him at the last outing, specifically that the IEE system was not a program, but a statistically-based business system and improvement methodology, which advanced how operations are measured and improved. Jorge was emphatic about IEE's emphasis on how people *should* do their jobs, especially at the executive level. Since the last outing, Hank had been doing his homework and had a lot of questions for Jorge.

"I gained much insight through the article that you gave us. The article's content lived up to its title, 'Beyond Lean Six Sigma: Why Lean and Six Sigma Deployments Fail and What you can do to Resolve the Issue' (See Appendix A, Web page 9). I've done some additional reading and now see what you mean by saying that IEE has many Lean Six Sigma components. It seems that many are still saying, after all these years, that Lean Six Sigma is for operational processes and not the back office in companies. For example, Lean Six Sigma is for engineers to reduce defects, inventory, or lead times of manufacturing processes. I would think that these process measurement and improvement techniques should apply everywhere in an organization. Right?"

Jorge responded, "Agreed."

I've a second question about Six Sigma and its overall objective. Is the primary goal of the Six Sigma component to achieve 3.4 defects per million opportunities or something called DPMO? Is this also the goal of IEE?" Hank asked.

Jorge responded, "The DPMO metric is what you often hear about Six Sigma. Engineers created the DPMO metric. When Six Sigma became popular in the 1990s, each project problem statement was to have a defect definition for improvement through the execution of an improvement project. A process that has a 3.4 DPMO rate is said to be at a six-sigma level or six-sigma-quality level.

"One difference between IEE and Six Sigma is that IEE does not require a defect definition for projects. This no-defect-definition requirement is one of the fundamental distinctions between IEE and Six Sigma. Think about a project that's to reduce invoice days-sales-outstanding or work in progress (WIP). What's a true defect definition for these two situations?"

Hank said, "For these situations, there can be only the setting of goals. There're no precise specifications like the dimension on a part."

Jorge then said, "Agreed. Establishing goals so that you can calculate a defective or DPMO rate makes no sense for these situations. I don't like it when measurements have subjectivity like this. The practice of setting an arbitrary goal and tracking conformance to the created objective can lead to playing games with the numbers. For example, if someone wants to improve a sigma level, and there're no specifications, one could simply adjust the measurement's goal.

Jorge responded, "IEE includes most, if not all, of the Lean tools and techniques that you're now using in your deployment. IEE includes the utilization of Lean methods at both the enterprise business management level and the execution of improvement projects. Statistical measures and methods are also applied at both of these levels, equally in manufacturing and transactional situations. These statistical tools and methods help organizations improve business measures, prioritize what's important, better understand important current processes, evaluate potential solutions, and make sure that the process improvement changes are maintained."

"What role do managers play in the success of IEE?" Hank wondered aloud.

Jorge responded, "As part of analysis at the enterprise business-management and the creation of an overall organizational enterprise improvement plan (EIP), there's an establishment of improvement targets for various manager-owned processes. For example, a business goal to improve profit margins by 1% could lead to a plant-manager-owned-metric of a defective rate that's to have a reduction targeted objective of 10%. This manager would then assign an IEE Black Belt to this IEE value chain improvement metric. This IEE BB then works with a team to improve the process that's associated with this metric. In time, a reduction in the over-time-series-tracking of a process's non-conformance rate will demonstrate the value of the process changes.

"Management's task is to create the infrastructure, remove barriers, and make improvements happen," Jorge continued. "When you asked the computer components group to cut costs, you expected the individual managers to reduce their expenditures, reduce headcount, cut discretionary spending, and reduce inventory. Standard stuff, right? With this type of thinking, failure sooner or later will, unfortunately, occur in the organization. With this approach, people work independently within their responsibilities, trying to solve the problem. Nobody was looking at the bigger picture, which resulted in havoc for your Mexico operations."

Hank thoughtfully listened as he took his driver from the bag. He settled into his pre-shot routine and made a smooth but powerful swing. The results drew positive exclamations from Jorge and the two new partners, as a long drive with just a hint of draw pierced the fairway.

Hank worried silently for an instant that he might have hit it too well, and gone through the slight dogleg into the first cut of rough.

"A team approach for resolving this system issue would have resulted in a more effective solution. The problem may have been prevented instead of corrected after it occurred. A broader picture could have offered a bigger and more permanent solution. The training of IEE Black Belts begins with a comprehensive view, and they then work their way toward the details," Jorge continued as they approached Hank's drive.

"I don't believe it!" Hank yelled from a couple of feet away.

"No, it's true," replied Jorge, astonished at his friend's harsh reaction.

"Oh no, no," laughed Hank. "I was talking about the lie of my ball buried in this rough. How can the first cut be this thick?" He pulled a 5 iron from his bag as he said, "If I can get out of this rough in one stroke, it'll be a miracle. I'm interested in hearing the rest if you don't mind my stealing your ideas."

"Why did you pick that club?" Jorge asked, seemingly more interested in Hank's club selection.

Hank responded, "I'm about 170 feet from the pin. My 5 iron normally goes a bit farther than that, but I expect to have trouble getting out of this buried lie."

"Yes, don't you normally hit your 5 iron more like 185 or 190?" Jorge questioned. Without waiting for an answer, he continued, "Remember my decision to leave the driver in the bag last time? I did that to minimize the variation in my tee shots, so I could predict where I would land more accurately. Through better club selection, I can make my shot process more robust to the normal variation in my swing. With this approach, I could depend on good ball positioning to make pars or save bogeys. If you hit that 5 iron cleanly, you'll go over the green into the trees. If you don't, you won't reach it anyway, and you'll land in one of the first sand traps."

"OK," Hank said with a flash of interest, "what do you suggest?"

Jorge offered, "If you hit a 9 iron, you'll almost certainly get out of the rough and land in the open area just in front of the green. Then pitch on close to the hole and make your putt for par. You're looking at a tap-in for bogey five, worst case. But if that 5 iron shot goes in the rough, or you pull it into the trees, you're on your way to another eight. What do you think?"

"Or maybe I should have hit my 3 iron off the tee, stayed short of the dogleg, and hit my 5 iron to the green in the first place?" Hank added.

"That would have been good, too, but now that you're here, make the best of it. Plan and keep the overall goal in mind. It's not always about maximizing the current shot at any cost. Remember, the score-card does not ask how at the end of the day, just how many." said Jorge.

After Hank hit a solid 9 iron to within 20 yards of the front of the green, Jorge continued, "I was thinking about the problems you had in Mexico. An IEE solution wouldn't even have started with your state-ment that you wanted to reduce costs by moving operations.

"First, you start – better yet, let me show you a couple of sheets of paper that Ron gave me that I keep with me and use as an IEE system cheat-sheet. But, before I do that, I want to talk about IEE performance metric reporting.

"In IEE, there's a unique approach to present time-series, pro-cess-output data. 30,000-foot-level is a reference for this form of report-ing, not unlike a high-level view of the earth below looking out the win-dow of an in-flight airplane. What this form of metric reporting does is separate common cause variation from special cause events.

"I think that it would be best for me to now read from my cheat sheet the *first portion of a 30,000-foot-level metric glossary definition*, which is: 'Reporting of a process output response or business metric from a high-level viewpoint. In this elevated performance report, short-term varia-tion from the natural variation of input variables will result in an indi-viduals chart or charts that view these fluctuations as common-cause variations. This metric has no calendar boundaries, and data from the latest region of stability are used to provide a predictive statement for stable processes. An undesirable 30,000-foot-level prediction statement suggests that the associated metric's process needs improvement.'

"I hope that this 30,000-foot-level metric description gives you a good overview of this performance reporting methodology. I will be making many references to 30,000-foot-level reports; hence, a basic up-front understanding of this measurement reporting concept is essential.

"I do want to elaborate more on another term that I will mention frequently; that is common cause variation. Simply stated, common causes of variation are those causes that are part of the process as currently designed and deployed. A chart-identified special-cause event occurs when a response is outside the range of typical process output responses, as it's currently defined, or something has changed with the process's execution. Special causes typically result in variation beyond a pre-determined statistically calculated upper control limit (UCL) or lower control limit (LCL) boundary. But special-cause conditions can also cause patterns, such as trends or shifts, in the variation shown on an individuals control chart. In IEE, 30,000-foot-level reporting tracks organizational, functional output metrics; however, in IEE, there's an additional metric reporting. This other IEE performance metric is satellite-level reporting, which tracks financial metrics and has a formation process that's similar to a 30,000-foot-level report."

Hank then said, "We've used control charts in our manufacturing operations."

Jorge said, "30,000-foot-level and satellite-level metrics are different from traditional control charting. I'll get into the details of the differences later. Still, for now, one major difference I should point out is that a 30,000-foot-level reporting objective is not to *control* a process but instead provide a high-level view of the process-output response.

"If a 30,000-foot-level performance metric from a process is considered stable, that's an indication that the process, from a high-level perspective, is only experiencing common-cause variation. When only common-cause variation is present, this chart will utilize all the raw data from its recent region of stability to provide a prediction statement. If this best-estimate predictive statement is undesirable, the process needs enhancement. When there has been a successful process improvement, and this change impacts its 30,000-foot-level performance metric, this IEE metric reporting will show this change statistically and provide a new prediction statement, if the new process output response is considered stable."

Hank commented, "Yes, Jorge, I see that 30,000-foot-level reporting and its objective is different from traditional control charting."

Jorge then said, "Great, Hank. Let's get back to our sheets of paper.
One sheet of paper shows the 9-step IEE system, while the other sum-
marizes each step. You look at the figure on this sheet of paper while
I read a description of each step from the second sheet of paper" (See
Figure 6.1).

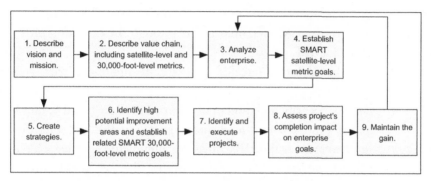

Figure 6.1: Integrated Enterprise Excellence (IEE) System

Jorge started reading a description of each step, saying:

- "Step 1: 'Describe your vision and mission,' which should be
  the guiding light for executing the following steps.
- Step 2: 'Describe value chain, including satellite-level and
  30,000-foot-level metrics.' An IEE value chain describes what
  an organization does and how it measures what's done through
  the functions of an organization. Satellite-level metrics track
  financial measures. 30,000-foot-level metrics track operational
  metrics. Both reports provide tracking from a process-output
  point of view. An organizational IEE value chain maintains basic
  structural consistency over time, even with different leadership,
  changes in the economic climate, and increased competition.
  IEE process improvement efforts give focus to what could be
  done differently in IEE value chain processes to enhance the

financials through process improvement and doing something fundamentally different.

- Step 3: 'Analyze enterprise,' suggests the use of many Lean Six Sigma tools to gain insight on where to focus our organizational process improvement efforts.
- Step 4: 'Establish SMART satellite-level metrics.' An example of satellite-level goals that are specific, measurable, actionable, relevant, and time-based is the enhancement of mean monthly profit margins by one percent in nine months. The actionable piece of this SMART objective is through the execution of the following IEE steps.
- Step 5: 'Create strategies' that are in alignment with step 4's goals.
- Step 6: 'Identify high potential improvement areas and establish SMART 30,000-foot-level metric goals.' In IEE, an enterprise improvement plan (EIP) shows the alignment of strategic identified performance metrics to improve through the execution of process improvement projects. Each performance metric to improve has an owner. If possible, the IEE measurement determined to enhance is within the organization's IEE value chain.
- Step 7 'Identify and execute projects.' In IEE, there's no emphasis on the types of tools or roadmap used when making process improvements. The focus of IEE is to make improvements such that the project's 30,000-foot-level metric transitions to an enhanced level of performance.
- Step 8 'Assess project's completion impact on enterprise goals.' An organizational EIP shows an alignment of the project's metric improvement to Step 4's financial objectives. Staging in a 30,000-foot-level metric report to an enhanced performance level provides a statistical indicator of process improvement, which can be quantified.
- Step 9 'Maintain the gain,' which is what an adequate control system offers. Step 9 loops back to step 3, forming a closed-loop for the entire system's on-going execution."

Hank had an amazed look on his face. His response was, "Wow, IEE is great!"

Jorge continued, "Note how this 9-step system describes an entirely different approach from the balanced scorecard approach used by Zack, which often starts with the creation of strategies. With the balanced scorecard approach, executive-created-strategies are to lead to metrics consistent with defined strategies.

"In IEE, the value chain in Step 2 describes what a company does and how it measures what's done. High-level value-chain metrics explain how an organization is executing, in a time-series fashion, functional process outputs measurements. For this tracking, there's a separation of common-cause variation from special-cause occurrences. In IEE, a 30,000-foot-level terminology references this high-level form of performance-metric-response reporting. 30,000-foot-level reports provide a high-level view of process performance, not unlike a picture of the terrain below when viewing from an airplane in flight. It's important to note how the creation of these metrics isn't dependent upon created strategies, which can change over time.

"Jim Collins describes in *Good to Great* (Collins 2001) the term Level 5 as referencing the highest level in a hierarchy of executive capabilities. The book states that a Level 5 Executive 'Builds enduring greatness through a paradoxical blend of personal humility and professional will.' 'Level 5 leaders channel their ego needs away from themselves and into the larger goal of building a great company. It's not that Level 5 leaders have no ego or self-interest. Indeed, they're incredibly ambitious-but their ambition is first and foremost for the institution, not for themselves.'

"Collins' book stated that, in a gathering of senior executives, someone who had just become a CEO, asked the question: 'Can you learn to become Level 5?'

"Collins' response to the question was that there are two categories of people. One type will work first and foremost about what they can get. The second category, suspected to be the larger group, consists of those who have the potential to evolve to Level 5.

"Ron stated that he agreed with Collins' statements about a Level 5 leader and the two general categories of people; however, Ron added some additional thoughts. Consider that a CEO has a profile consistent with the described second category. The question is, 'How would this pursuing Level 5 individual approach the task of not only becoming Level 5 but also of implementing Level 5 thinking so that the business as a whole benefit?' Plus, how could this individual create a system that's long-lasting beyond his or her tenure as the company's CEO? This objective would be no simple undertaking when the fulfillment of this desire is left just to the resources that the seeking Level 5 individual happens to possess. There's a solution to this dilemma for the person who has the Level 5 skill set and wants to channel her efforts into the goal of building a great company.

"IEE provides the roadmap and structure for someone who wants to do the right things for the company as a whole. The IEE methodology could be considered a Level 5 System, which is long-lasting beyond the tenure of any individual.

"Ron then asked a question which appeared to show that he was switching gears. 'Do you think that your organization's strategy would change if there were different leadership?' What do you think, Hank?"

Hank's response was, "Of course."

Jorge then responded, "I agree."

Ron then asked, "Wouldn't it be reasonable to conclude that it would be tough for an organization to create a Level 5 System when the primary guiding light for the organization is an executive-retreat created strategy, which can change with new leadership? What are your thoughts, Hank?"

Hank responded, "Makes sense to me."

"When executing the IEE system, IEE value chain improvements occur over time; however, the fundamental IEE value chain structure and its metrics are independent of the organization's strategy. In IEE, the development of strategies occurs after the formulation of the organizational IEE value chain, its performance measurements, and enterprise analysis. Because of this, the overall organizational structure can maintain continuity between leadership changes. The IEE business management system can provide the enabling roadmap to create a Level 5 organization.

"In the IEE system, your team wouldn't start to reduce costs by studying the individual budgets of the groups involved. Rather, team members would ask several questions: How do we define and measure cost? What's the nature of variation within our cost structure? What categories make up the entire cost structure for production in this division? What categories offer the greatest opportunity for overall cost reduction? For a given category, what components add to that category's total cost?"

Hank thought carefully about what Jorge had just said. "I've been thinking about all the times I told my people to solve some huge problem and didn't give them this kind of process to make the job doable. Think of all the opportunities for huge returns if we get some of these teams on the chronic problems we've been firefighting forever."

Hank was good with his wedge. It was a strong point in his game. He hit a pretty pitch shot that landed on the front of the green and rolled to within four feet of the flag. With his confidence up, he drilled his par putt and then asked Jorge the big question, "So I should start teeing off regularly with my 3 iron?"

Jorge laughed, "Of course not. Your big drives are a great weapon in your arsenal. But, golf is a target game consisting of distance and direction. Think about the target area that you need to hit with each shot. What are the limits of acceptable errors in distance and direction? Then pick the best club to hit, not by the longest distance you've ever hit it, but the range of distances you normally hit it. And don't forget the range of direction errors you normally make. For your driver, I'd bet most of your shots travel 230 to 270 yards."

With this, he pulled a sheet of paper out of his pocket and, handing it to his friend, said, "Hank, this is a graph that I created on my computer last week to provide my estimation for your drives pictorially."

The graph that Jorge showed Hank was the familiar normal distribution with a mean at 250 yards and a standard deviation of 15-yards (See Figure 6.2).

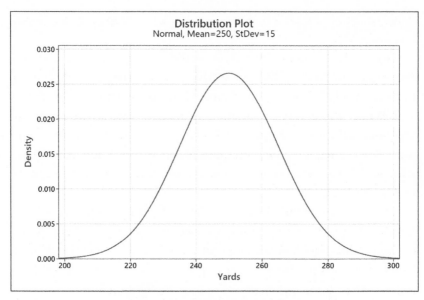

Figure 6.2: Distribution of shots

Jorge then said, "Plus and minus two standard deviations or sigmas only cover about 95% of your drives. Plus and minus three sigmas cover about 99% of your drives or 205 to 295 yards. Your 370-yarder last year was a pleasant *outlier*. These are just estimates, of course. You can refine them with measurement and analysis. But if you had thought about the likelihood associated with various driving distances, you might not have selected a driver back there where the far side of the dogleg was only 260 yards away."

"Of course," Hank's insight flashed. "I should think of my golf swing as a process where key process outputs that I want to control are distance and accuracy. A key process input variable to this process is the choice of clubs. For my swing, each club produces a distribution of shots with a range of distance and directional accuracy. I should pick the club most likely to give the best response for each operation; I mean shot."

"Now, you've got it," smiled Jorge. "There'll be times when you have plenty of open space, and your driver will be a terrific weapon. Just pick your spots wisely.

"Before we leave this topic, I want to illustrate how your shot distances could appear in a 30,000-foot-level performance metric report. As discussed earlier, a 30,000-foot-level report tracks the output of a process over time to assess process stability. If a process is stable, then a prediction statement is provided in the report.

"For a representation of your driver-shot distances, I again randomly generated 100 data points from a normal distribution where the mean was 250 yards, and the standard deviation was 15. I considered that the generated data were in time sequence; that is, the first generated point was the first shot, while the hundredth was the last."

With this, Jorge pulled another sheet of paper out of his pocket and, handing it to Hank, saying, "Hank, this is the 30,000-foot-level report that I created for your drives" (See Figure 6.3).

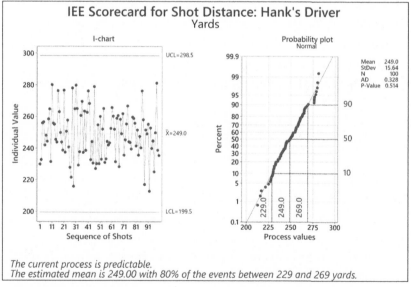

Figure 6.3: 30,000-foot-level report of Hank's driver shot distance

"For your shot-distance response, the individuals chart on the left side of this 30,000-foot-level reporting tracks the stability or consistency of your shot distance over time. When there's no points beyond the chart's UCL and LCL statistically-determined horizontal lines, the response is considered consistent or stable, and a prediction statement is provided from the best-estimate line in the probability plot on the right side of the report. Since there are no specifications for your shot distance, this 30,000-foot-level report provides a best-estimate mean shot-distance response with an 80% frequency of occurrence expectation. From this 30,000-foot-level reporting of randomly generated data, the estimated mean distance for your shots is 249 yards with 80%, or four out of five shots, between 229 and 269 yards.

"If you do not do anything differently with your current shot process, this prediction statement provides an expectation for your shot distances. If you're not pleased with this shot-prediction, you need to do something differently in your shot process. If you made, over time, an enhancement or detriment to your shot distance, there'd be a staging of the individuals chart, and the probability plot would reflect a new prediction statement for a recently created stable-shot response."

Hank responded, "Jorge, this 30,000-foot-level metric reporting format looks great! I think many Hi-Tech Computers measurements would benefit from this high-level reporting format."

As Jorge approached the tee box, he said, "Hank, that's great to hear."

Later, Jorge said, "In IEE, there're a couple of underlying principles that all employees can use within their job to improve their efficiency. First, they need to understand the big picture. Next, they need to know what the customer, both internal and external, wants. They also need to reduce variation and drive to target the output of processes."

"Didn't you say something about this is the way people should do their jobs? Until now, we've been discussing teams that go after specific problems. Where does the continual improvement come in?" asked Hank.

"These ideas can be used to improve your company's processes on an ongoing basis without causing chaos as you experienced in Mexico. The manager didn't understand the big picture or the Voice of the Customer when he decided to change plants based on component cost alone. He had thought the only goal was reducing cost. That's how you get silos."

Hank agreed. As they approached the next tee, Hank examined the 30,000-foot-level report on the sheet of paper that Jorge had given him. He then looked down the fairway at the hole and saw a small landing area for the drive that was only about 30 yards in diameter, about 200 yards from the tee. He reached for his 4 iron as Jorge smiled.

"Take my business," Jorge continued. "Our customer service representatives (CSRs) are supposed to keep track of patients' billing records. Historically, we had CSRs separated by functional area: Each would work in an emergency, hospital, or physical therapy. It seemed like a natural way to do it because each CSR would become familiar and efficient with the area-specific procedures. After experiencing IEE, one of our less-experienced CSRs suggested we combine CSRs into one functional area. This one-function-combination would allow all CSRs to see how each area addresses issues, allow us to back each other up, and reduce headcount by five employees."

"That's amazing!" Hank commented. "Why would someone make a suggestion that could put him out of work?"

"Because upfront, we assured everyone that any improvements wouldn't result in the loss of jobs. We explained we would retrain displaced workers to enhance their skills. Job reductions would only occur through normal attrition. The worker that made the suggestion was re-trained for an area we knew was going to need people soon."

"This sounds great, Jorge, but you haven't told me how this works. I would need to hear more of the details about the infrastructure and how the project teams function. And what about Lean? Was that a waste of my time? How about TQM, Baldrige Award assessments, and ISO 9001, for that matter? How do these techniques fit into this effort? What do you know about the theory of constraints or TOC? Does that fit within your IEE system too?"

"Tell you what, Hank. I'll explain the IEE connection with other programs while I take you on for the rest of the round. During lunch, I'll lay out some of the basics of the IEE infrastructure and project execution. Remember, I've only been at this for about three months, so I don't know all the details, but I can give you the big picture."

"Sounds great," Hank said. "Now, what about the connection between Six Sigma and Lean?"

"Hank, I've heard different answers to this question. It depends on whom you ask. Most companies that start with Lean believe that you do Lean first, which leads to the application of Six Sigma tools to reduce defects. Six Sigma proponents often say it works the other way round. They tend to believe that after the implementation of Six Sigma, you can address workflow issues using Lean methodologies.

"IEE has a different spin on things. The IEE system provides a high-level performance metric reporting system for business financial and operational metrics, which has no calendar boundaries such as quarter or year. Satellite-level metrics offer the tracking of business-financial measures. A 30,000-foot-level metric tracking approach provides an excellent high-level view of the performance output from operational processes and improvement-metric-enhancement efforts.

"Using an IEE satellite-level metric tracking strategy, businesses' time-series, tracked financial measures, like profit, would be monthly. While, as part of this methodology, 30,000-foot-level metrics could track project or operational parameters such as defective rates, work in progress (WIP), or lead times on a daily or weekly basis. The 30,000-foot-level performance metric tracking methodology can get organizations out of the firefighting mode."

Hank responded, "Sounds great!"

Jorge continued, "The purpose of the 30,000-foot-level chart is to view a process response from a high-level, an airplane-in-flight-out-of-the-window view, first to assess whether a process is stable. For a stable 30,000-foot-level output response, variation is considered common-cause, and the process-output is said to be predictable. If a futuristic estimate of the process-output response is unsatisfactory relative to the desired level, a process improvement project would then *be pulled* for creation. That is, you need to systematically improve the overall process, rather than chasing daily problems. The tools you select to fix the process depend on your situation. We want to avoid the Maslow's "Law of the instrument" phrase, which is, "when all you have is a hammer, everything looks like a nail." Both Lean and Six Sigma zealots need to consider the complete set of available tools for addressing a situation, not just the tools that they're accustomed to using. If the problem were from waste or muda, one might first look into the utilization of Lean tools. Other situations require Six Sigma tools, and some require both."

"What about kaizen events?" Hank asked.

"People often include kaizen techniques in their Lean implementation. Ron described one company, which said that they did a kaizen event every other week and saved $10,000 per event. This level of kaizen event activity might initially sound impressive, but do you think it's real?"

Hank paused for a moment, "If the boss told me to save $10,000 per event, I bet I could make it look like I did."

Jorge responded, "Exactly! However, what happened during the kaizen event might be detrimental to the entire system. For example, one cell could have improved its efficiency and piled excess inventory in front of the next cell of the process, creating a bottleneck. This localized gain degraded the overall system.

"The 30,000-foot-level metric view of a process can lead to process improvement kaizen events. A process for executing organizational kaizen events is within step 7 of the IEE 9-step system, which I earlier showed you. This approach keeps organizations from investing a lot of time and money on kaizen events that don't benefit the overall business."

Hank persisted with his questions, asking, "Where does TOC fit in?"

"Theory of constraints is part of step 3 of the overall 9-step IEE system. Step 3's execution provides an analysis of the overall enterprise. TOC can identify and model constraint areas that need improvement through projects in step 7 of the overall roadmap. Have you considered the impact of identifying organizational constraints and taking action on them?"

After a moment's hesitation, Hank said, "I have been so busy fighting fires that I haven't had a chance to do much of anything."

Jorge continued, "Consider that a manufacturing operation can sell everything that it can make. If you can identify a constraint and improve its operational capacity by three percent, all the gross revenue from additional product sales, less raw material costs, goes directly to the bottom-line since fixed costs are already covered. "

Hank responded, "Wow! When you think about it that way, that could be big bucks. It sounds like we could also use IEE to meet our ISO 9001 requirements as well. ISO wants us not only to document but show that we're improving processes."

"The question is, what do you do? Do you need to improve all your processes to address this ISO 9001 certification need or just the critical ones?" Jorge asked.

"I certainly wouldn't want to try to improve everything. Some areas just aren't as important as others and don't need improvement," Hank replied.

"The great thing about this is you could reference your IEE Business Management System as the methodology for improving your organization per ISO 9001 requirements. With this approach, you can leverage your improvement activities to the needs of the business," Jorge added.

"What about the people who say Six Sigma, and I would assume IEE, too, is just TQM repackaged?" Hank wondered.

"TQM is different. Typically, TQM was to be a separate entity within an organization to solve quality problems. Lean Six Sigma's focus has been to execute projects, where most projects were to have validated financial benefits. The IEE system is more than a project executing methodology. IEE is an enterprise system for orchestrating business activities, including measurements and improvements, which truly impact the bottom-line." Jorge explained.

"I've this twenty-foot putt for a birdie to win today's round. I believe you'll be buying lunch, or would you rather put the leadership of the free world on this?" Hank commented as he stroked the downhill putt through two breaks and into the cup.

Hank turned with a satisfied grin and headed to the clubhouse. As he walked off, he heard Jorge call after him, "That's another premise of IEE: if you putt enough times, you're bound to make one sooner or later. Even a blind squirrel finds an acorn once in a while."

7

IT'S IN THE DETAILS

THAT SAME DAY OVER LUNCH

Hank thought about the comment Jorge made about his putting. After the initial irritation, he thought he saw the point. We remember our once-in-a-lifetime shots. Sometimes they just happen, but that doesn't mean we should plan on hitting a career shot every time.

Jorge's discussion about the IEE business management system started the wheels turning in his head. He wondered why he had not heard of IEE before. He had always discounted Six Sigma as just another quality-improvement program, mostly because of the 3.4 DPMO discussions, and Lean was to reduce waste. Whether he was right or wrong did not matter. This afternoon's IEE discussion got him thinking otherwise.

Hank was frustrated that he had not tried earlier to understand IEE better when Jorge first mentioned it. The opportunities seemed endless. The idea of improving the enterprise measurement system and the way people do their jobs excited him. As he waited at the table for Jorge, he was anxious to learn more. Jorge certainly seemed to be doing well with the methodology so far. He'd find out more details over lunch.

Jorge found Hank at a table by a window with a beautiful view of the golf course.

"What took you so long? Did you three-putt?" Hank teased him from across the room. "Tell me the details about how IEE works and setting up the infrastructure. What did that entail?"

Jorge responded, "It's too bad that Wayne and Zack aren't here. I'm confident they could also gain much from what I'll be sharing."

Hank responded, "That's their loss. I'm all ears!"

Jorge continued, "Well, Hank, here goes. There'll be an overlap with some concepts that we discussed during our golf-round conversation. Still, I believe a little repetition can be beneficial for putting everything together for you.

"In my initial conversation with Ron, he provided some excellent advice.

"Four highpoints from this initial discussion were:

1. Why have past organizational improvement deployments such as TQM, Lean, and Six Sigma typically not been long-lasting and genuinely ingrained in an organization's DNA culture? One of Ron's theories for this lack of sustainability occurrence made perfect sense to me. Ron stated that his observation has been that the organizational scorecard and performance metric group are figuratively in the north wing of the building, while the process documentation and improvement folks are on the south side – and the two functions don't talk to each other. Ron stated that for organizational process improvement deployments to be productive, this lack-of-connection problem between corporate performance metric reporting and process improvement efforts needs resolution. The IEE system fulfills this need by first providing the IEE value chain vehicle for structurally linking business metrics with the processes that created them. Secondly, IEE offers a methodology for establishing an overall business-system, process-improvement methodology. The IEE approach for accomplishing this undertaking is to give focus to the business measurements that most need enhancement from a high-level process-response-output point of view. IEE 30,000-foot-level

reporting provides fulfillment of this second need, which I'll elaborate more on later.

2. An organization's CEO, president, or general manager needs to be the IEE implementation sponsor. Why is this very top-leader sponsorship important? This executive needs to agree to view his or her organization from a *systems thinking* perspective. Peter Senge popularized the term systems thinking in his 1990's book *The Fifth Discipline* (Senge 1990); however, Ron stated that he hadn't seen organizations truly embrace the concepts in the management of their business. IEE provides the organizational structure and Enterprise Performance Reporting System (EPRS) software for the establishment of systems thinking and a learning organization environment like that described by Senge. EPRS software also provides a vehicle to document *tribal knowledge* methodologies so that these procedures are readily viewable by everyone and can be improved.

3. The CEO, president, or general manager needs to require that metrics and their reporting be from a predictive, process-output perspective. Why is this important? Traditional metrics reporting such as red-yellow-green (RYG) scorecards and table of numbers are common-place practices. However, these conventional forms of reporting have issues relative to systems thinking. A RYG scorecard compares individual measurements to a goal. A table of numbers may compare a current month's performance to a previous month or similar month last year. Neither of these two forms of reporting provides process output statements that include the variation between time intervals. The IEE system provides 30,000-foot-level reports that not only include process variation but also can offer a predictive-statement for those processes statistically-concluded to be stable, where if the futuristic statement is undesirable, process improvement is needed."

Hank interrupted, "Wow! These aspects of the IEE system makes so much sense. The business management issues that you've described sound so familiar."

Jorge continued, "Yes, Hank, neither your organization nor mine has a monopoly on these issues. The final highpoint was:

4. The CEO, president, or general manager needs to be intimately involved in an IEE implementation since, among other things, sometimes organizational policies need to be changed. Ron shared a real example to illustrate this point. The president of a technology company asked Ron for assistance in establishing an IEE system in one of his facilities. The president said the site had undertaken Lean efforts and other process improvement programs over the years that were not effective. From his meeting with the president and his team, it became clear to Ron that the organization had a strict meet-the-monthly-numbers-or-else culture. Ron explained to the president that, for the IEE implementation to be successful, he would need to personally view and ask for performance measure reporting different from current practices, including the establishment of goals. The president agreed to make this change in his behavior, which would lead others to a similar way of thinking. The president of this corporate division resided outside the United States and periodically traveled to the US manufacturing location that was undertaking this IEE implementation. Ron and his team then worked with the company's team to create an IEE infrastructure. Ron stated that significant progress occurred in only a few months. Among other things, IEE's Enterprise Performance Reporting System, that is, EPRS software was providing the company's IEE value chain with automatically-updated predictive performance measures. The team was beginning to work on executing improvements so that crucial business IEE value chain metrics would be enhanced through IEE improvement projects, and the company's mean monthly profit would transition to an improved level of performance. Unfortunately, the president became ill and could not travel to the US; hence, the company's president, who was the sponsor for IEE's deployment, *fell out of the picture*. In this same time frame, the com-

68

pany had hired a new CEO who was not technically inclined. This CEO continued the old-company culture of meeting next month's arbitrarily-set goals, or else. This company-culture policy led to very harmful behaviors, where there was a pull of future orders into a current month to meet a monthly goal, at great expense to the organization as a whole. Everybody in the company seemed to realize that this monthly-goal-setting-and-achievement cultural policy was terrible; however, nobody dared to highlight the issue to the new CEO. Hence, the IEE implementation encountered a sustainability problem simply because the company wouldn't change its policy from focusing on the achievement of an arbitrary monthly financial objective to undertaking an enhancement of an IEE financial-metric such as mean monthly profit.

"From my initial conversation with Ron, we agreed that a conference call conversation was needed involving our CEO, Ron, and me. No one else should participate in this discussion since a candid conversation was needed, and the more people involved in any discussion, the less candid the conversation would be. Individuals from other departments can be defensive. The goal of the conference call would be to introduce IEE techniques and how the methodology could resolve the significant issues that we have. Because of this, it would be more productive for this initial meeting that just the three of us meet. I had to do some organizational navigation so that nobody would later feel undermined by this conference call. Still, I was able to pull off creating a conference call with our CEO and Ron."

Author Note

It is important to have a one-on-one IEE conversation with the person who has responsibility for an organization's financials and its "health." This person could be a CEO, president, general manager, or chair of the board of directors. In a government agency, this person could be a director. In a school district, this person could be a superintendent. However, many who are examining this book might consider it impossible to set up such a meeting.

The audio version of this book could be used to address this valid observation and need. For those who believe that their organization could benefit from IEE, they could suggest that their manager or others listen to this book when commuting to-and-from work or while exercising. If the book described concepts make sense to this manager, he or she could suggest this audio book to others.

One initial casual book-listening suggestion could lead to an audio-book organizational dissemination of IEE concept and the benefits. In time, the CEO, or another organization leader, could receive the suggestion that he or she listen to the audio book. Those leaders who then want to investigate IEE further for their organization, after listening to the book, should then be asking for the book described IEE one-on-one meeting.

For additional thoughts on how to present the IEE business management system to others see Appendix A, Web page 18.

Lunch arrived, and, as always, Jorge was amazed at how much food Hank could consume. "Where do you put all that food?" he asked incredulously. "If I ate as much as you do, I'd be over 300 pounds in no time!"

"The key, my friend, is exercise," Hank replied, "I run for an hour four mornings a week and lift weights the three other mornings. If you think about it, with 15 useful hours in a day, that's only about 6.7% of my week. For so little effort, I receive a lot of benefits. I can still beat the boys in basketball, and I seem to have more energy. Sharon and I have even been swing dancing on Saturday nights, which keeps the romance alive."

Jorge thought for a moment about Sharon. She was the first woman whom Hank had dated more than a few times after his divorce. They were right for each other, and Jorge figured that their romance was pretty healthy, even without the dancing.

"You know, I've tried to stick with a daily exercise regimen, but I just can't seem to stay committed," lamented Jorge.

"Consistency is the key; you have to keep at it," urged Hank.

"That's funny," Jorge laughed. "Our IEE system has the same basic ideas: reduce variation and stick to the roadmap."

"So, speaking of consistency, do you think I should create a 30,000-foot-level reporting for both distance and direction for all my clubs?" asked Hank, thinking about the consistency and reduced variation arguments.

"Actually," Jorge said, "you probably already have. For example, I would estimate that from a 7 iron you get a distance between 130 and 150 yards 80% of the time. With these estimates, you should plan accordingly. Don't depend upon hitting your personal best shot, or even your average shot, when picking your club."

After Hank had devoured his large lunch, the conversation turned back to business.

Jorge started the conversation, saying, "My wife and I were at a charity benefit last night. Someone at our table mentioned Lean Six Sigma, and it turned out that many of those we talked to were from companies that are implementing Lean Six Sigma. As you might expect, it became apparent during our discussions that companies were experiencing different degrees of success with Lean Six Sigma. Some companies haven't had the kind of executive support from their CEO that we're experiencing, and it seems that they've been less successful. For these situations, I cannot help but think that they could benefit from an IEE structure. I would suspect that in these organizations, the focus is towards meeting the month's numbers instead of creating a no-nonsense measurement and improvement system that orchestrates everyone's activities. I'm glad we were able to get Janice Davis, our CEO, not only to support the implementation but to ask people for information that was consistent with the IEE methodology.

"Also, it's evident that some of these companies weren't asking the right questions or using the best metrics, and their results suffered. For example, some companies were spending a lot of resources counting defects. They were trying to create a defect metric they could use for their entire company. Some of them had even been trying to calculate an overall sigma level in every area of their business. With a sigma level measurement approach, a six-sigma level for operations occurs when a defect rate of 3.4 defects per million opportunities occurs. A three-sigma level is about 66,800 DPMO. A four-sigma level is about 6210 DPMO, while a five-sigma level is about 233 DPMO.

"Some companies try to use this metric as a primary driver for their Lean Six Sigma implementation, and, while it sounds like a perfect metric, it has major problems. To use it, you have to define opportunities for failure for all activities within your company. This undertaking would not only be huge but also there can be large counting discrepancies. Take your business, for example. What would you consider to be an opportunity for a defect on one of your printed circuit boards?"

Hank thought for a minute and answered, "When manufacturing circuit boards, we could have material problems, assembly problems, handling damage…"

Jorge interrupted, "Yeah, but what are the specific opportunities for defects? For example, what type of material problems?"

"Unfortunately, there are many. You could have components that are out of tolerance or broken. You could also have a cracked board. And then there're the assembly problems such as solder bridging, unsoldered joints, reversed parts, missing parts, even wrong parts."

Jorge replied, "From what I've learned, there's a standard approach for this situation. You don't count every way a component can have a problem. Instead, each component is considered an opportunity count, which has multiple defect types. With this method, the addition of the number of components and solder joints results in a total number of opportunities."

Jorge continued, "Let's approximate the sigma level of your printed circuit board manufacturing lines. How many components would there be per board?"

Hank chewed his fingernail, took a minute to count silently, and responded, "I'd say 300 to 400 for the Mach II line."

"About how many solder connections would you have?"

"About 600 to 800," Hank responded.

"Okay, let's say the total number of solder joints and components is 1000. How many boards would you make in a typical week? And also, how many defects would you expect?" Jorge asked as he jotted the numbers down on the napkin under the list of project parameters.

"We've been running about 5000 a week, and our yield is around 98%," Hank responded immediately.

"Your yield is running about 98%, but how does this value translate to the number of created defects? There could be more than one defect on a printed circuit board. Also, there could be defects repaired but not counted against the yield. What would you guess defects would be if they were all counted?"

Hank wavered and finally responded, "Well, I'm not certain, but we once did an engineering study on that line, indicating 1250 defects per week. I believe that included all the uncounted touchups and reworks."

"Okay," Jorge said, working the numbers on a new napkin. "For one week, you have 5000 boards, and each board has 1000 opportunities for defects. That's 5,000,000 opportunities for defects per week. If you divide 1250 defects by 5,000,000, you would have a 250 DPMO rate, which is about a five-sigma level."

Hank responded, "That's pretty good. With just a little effort, I could be at a six-sigma level!"

"Not so fast, sigma boy. For one thing, you're operating at a 250 DPMO rate or a five-sigma level. The sigma quality-level metric is not linear. Each incremental improvement is harder than the one before.

You would have to make significant process changes to operate at a 3.4 DPMO rate.

"Secondly, consider the average number of defects you have per board. You have 1250 defects for the 5000 boards you make per week. That translates to an average rework rate of 25%. That doesn't sound so good to me. It looks like you've what I have learned is a *hidden factory*. You're doing a lot of rework that's hidden and isn't showing up in your yield numbers. So, you can see how the sigma-level metric and even the final yield number are sometimes deceiving.

"Hank, also, it's important to keep in mind that DPMO is a ratio of the number of defects or flaws in one million opportunities, where a manufactured part or transaction could contain more than one defect. If we were to examine the entire part or transaction as a whole relative to compliance, we would be making a statement of whether the unit is defective or not. In Six Sigma, per million (PPM) units can express a non-conformance rate. That is, a PPM rate quantifies the number of defective units in one million units evaluated," Jorge elaborated and paused to let Hank take it all in. His wheels were spinning.

"Let's step back a second and ask yourself why you have these measures," Jorge spoke, breaking Hank's thought stream.

Hank responded, "We use them as part of our cost of operations. We want to see if we're improving or not. We also want to keep customers happy by delivering good products."

Jorge then replied, "Okay, let's talk costs. Shouldn't you be counting all reworks in your cost calculations? If you're only focusing on final yield numbers, you're missing the cost impact of all those reworks. With a Six Sigma approach, one might determine an associated cost of poor quality (COPQ) value. In IEE, the cost of doing nothing differently (CODND) calculation is preferred. Unlike COPQ, a CODND number can provide a financial, monetary value for what's happening in both operations and transactional processes, whether there's a specification or not.

"Rather than patting yourself on the back for having a 98% yield or quoting a five sigma level, in IEE, you would track the overall DPMO rate over time and could convert that rate to a CODND monetary value. By doing calculations this way, you have an accurate cost estimate. Besides, there can be a determination for hidden factory defects, which could offer focus improvement details that subsequently reduce costs.

"Some might say that CODND is simply a *possible cost savings amount*; however, to me, CODND is different than a potential amount of savings. To illustrate this point, I'll use a CODND calculation for work in progress or WIP. For many situations, WIP cannot be zero but instead have a reasonable minimal non-zero amount, which is situation dependent. Because of this non-zero lower boundary, the phrase *possible cost savings amount* isn't accurate.

In IEE, a process improvement effort might have reduced the amount WIP. An estimated financial benefit from the project could then be simply determined as the difference between a CODND calculation before any process change and then after the improvement project's completion."

Hank sat silently with a perplexed frown. He folded the two napkins carefully and placed them in his worn billfold. After a few minutes, Jorge grew uneasy with the silence, asking his friend if he had rambled too much.

"No, everything makes perfect sense. I'm just wondering how much 98% yield is costing the business. First thing on Monday, I'm going to have someone get me the numbers," Hank resolved.

Jorge added, "Well, you've got the idea, but there are a few more areas in which the sigma level can be deceiving. I'll give your brain a rest and explain those another time."

Hank beat Jorge to the bill when it arrived. Jorge protested that Hank had won on the last hole, but Hank just smiled and said that this was the most cost-effective business lunch he had ever had. It not only had helped him fix his golf game but had given him a new perspective on his attempts to improve his business. Jorge settled for a chance to buy Hank a beer in the bar.

Hank was hungry for more details, relentless in his search for ways to work more efficiently, and asked, "Jorge, I understand that you're not a fan of the sigma-level metric. What do you suggest as a replacement?"

"One main takeaway I've had from our IEE implementation is the value and creation of 30,000-foot-level metrics, which I spoke of earlier.

Satellite-level measures are similar to 30,000-foot-level measurements, the difference being that satellite-level metrics track financial measurements. An example: monthly is the typical satellite-level-report-period for profit margins, where there's no calendar-year bounding for these measurements.

"This 30,000-foot-level charting approach applies not only to tracking a performance metric that's to be enhanced through a process-improvement project but also to the reporting of IEE value chain performance metrics. Unlike red-yellow-green scorecards and table-of-numbers reporting, this form of performance metric reporting can get companies out of the firefighting mode."

"You know, Jorge, I don't see any high-level type metrics in our Lean rollout. Don't get me wrong; Lean techniques are helping us make some gains, but we're not getting any high-level view of our operation from the methodology. Now that I think of it, much confusion and debates are occurring over where to focus our efforts."

"Hank, you really should look into using 30,000-foot-level metrics for helping the focus of your Lean efforts. The other day, the woman next to me on my flight home was a Lean champion, similar to a Lean Six Sigma Black Belt. She told me that one of the first projects their Lean consultant had them do was reduce finished goods inventory to almost nothing. As you might guess, as soon as the stock went down, a big order came in. A lot of money needed to be then spent on overtime payments, among other things, to fulfill the shipment need.

"I then told her about how we're learning to start with a satellite-level metric response that was to be enhanced, which led to 30,000-foot-level metrics that were to be improved through our process improvement efforts so that the big-picture benefits. She told me that they would never have chosen some of their projects if they had initially considered this type of high-level view of their operations.

"Then, we talked about how the project might have gone if they'd followed the IEE Define, Measure, Analyze, Improve, and Control (DMAIC) process improvement project roadmap. We sketched a rough plan out for her, which considered the demand pattern and cycle time of the system and then determined what the finished goods inventory level should have been. Hank, I need to walk you through the IEE DMAIC roadmap. That'll take some time. I'll do that later."

After shoveling a handful of pretzels into his mouth and washing it down with ice water, Hank made the statement, "You mentioned earlier the *Fifth Discipline* by Peter Senge (Senge 1990). I've read this book and our conversation got me thinking."

Hank explained, "Senge talks about a learning organization. If implemented wisely, I would think that we could use these metrics and other IEE tools to help our organization become a learning organization. We would become curious about our processes, embrace change, and gain confidence with each successful improvement. This thought and action progression could transform our organization and increase growth, which is tangible to our shareholders."

Jorge stole the pretzel bowl away from Hank before Hank devoured them all. Now he was starving. Jorge looked down at his watch, surprised to find that it was already time for dinner. Time just flew whenever he started talking about IEE and its benefits. Maybe he should consider becoming a full-time IEE consultant.

As the sun began to set on the golf course, Jorge and Hank decided to stay and have dinner on the patio of the clubhouse, enjoying the sunset and finishing their discussion.

Once they had ordered, Jorge continued, "Ron stressed that organizations achieving success learn to apply the most appropriate tool or measure for each process. There's no one-size-fits-all metric or tool appropriate for all processes."

"Hmmm…. Sort of like learning that changing to a 3 iron off the tee isn't the answer for everyone. You're saying that IEE offers some useful metrics that could be beneficial to a particular process but not necessarily to all processes," Hank reiterated.

"As I mentioned earlier, DPMO is a metric that some organizations try to force onto every process, but it's not always easy to describe what an opportunity is for every process." Jorge fished around for something to sketch on, but the napkins were cloth, causing them both to chuckle.

Improvising, Jorge pulled a receipt from his billfold and illustrated an example for defects on a piece of sheet metal. A natural teacher, as he drew, he lectured, "You could describe a defect opportunity as one square inch, one square foot, or one square millimeter. You can see the confusion that could arise with multiple definitions for opportunities. In transactional processes, this practice gets even crazier. However, as we talked about before, DPMO does have its uses."

Hank eagerly picked up the receipt, folded it carefully, and placed it in his billfold next to the napkins from lunch, as Jorge continued, "Another Six Sigma metric, which may, or may not, be useful, is rolled-throughput-yield (RTY). This metric can be useful to describe the hidden factory we talked about earlier. RTY is the multiplication of yields for each step of the process. RTY can highlight the amount of rework within a process and where it's occurring. However, this metric can require a lot of work to generate and isn't appropriate for all situations."

The waiter brought their dinners, and they each ordered a beer, which was inspired by Jorge's recent trip to Ireland with Sandra. They took a break from their informal class and devoured the battered, deep-fried fish and salty fries. Jorge shared the highlights of their week-long bicycling tour, mostly detailing the pubs and the people of Ireland.

After dinner, the waiter delivered the coffee Hank had requested. Jorge continued his lecture but warned Hank that he would have to wrap things up soon and get home.

"So, after deciding a primary 30,000-foot-level metric that's important to the business as a whole, organizations then assess whether the process is stable and can deliver a desirable output. If the process isn't capable of meeting customer requirements and it's important to the business, one of the first things to do is to tap into the wisdom of the organization through structured conversations with the people who know the process intimately. The end goal is to solicit improvement ideas using brainstorming tools such as cause-and-effect diagrams."

Hank, intrigued but confused, asked, "Can you give me an actual example?"

Jorge then stopped himself and said, "Hank, before we get into all the details of process improvement, we need to step back to the big picture."

"Earlier, I stated that there was a conference call with our CEO, Ron, and me. You must note that to get on our CEO's radar-screen, there was no attempt to sell IEE. I called Janice, our CEO, and said, "We've rah-rah posters that say *work smarter, not harder*, but I want to discuss a way to give our people the tools to work smarter, not just a slogan. It was a bold thing to do, but she appreciated the initiative and allocated 60 minutes. Per my request, she agreed to a first-thing-in-the-morning conference call in two days."

"For the conference call, I was in Janice's office. We called Ron on his mobile phone. After I made a simple introduction, Ron told us to access SmarterSolutions.com on our computer. During our short CEO-conference-call conversation, the focus was given to a one-minute IEE benefits video and the article "Positive Metric Performance Poor Business Performance: How does this happen?"

"I want you to see the one-minute video that I showed Janice, which you can access through the link I just texted to you (SmarterSolutions.com/iee-one-minute-video). Take a look while I hit the head" (See Figures 7.1 and 7.2).

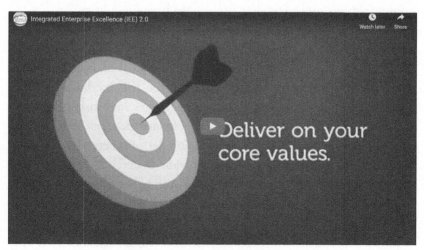

Figure 7.1: One-minute IEE Introduction Video
(SmarterSolutions.com/iee-one-minute-video)

Inconclusive performance metrics are a disaster waiting to happen. When it does, how can you know what caused it and if it will happen again?

Problems look different at 30,000 feet than they do on the ground.

What if there was a performance reporting system that illuminated the underlying root cause of underperformance and helped you avoid it in the future by providing metrics that tell everyone what to expect?

IEE is that system. Its performance reporting system software uses your existing data that distinguishes between expected trends and unusual events that deviate from desired results.

IEE provides the insights you and your team need to make step change improvements for better performance and better outcomes.

IEE can stop reaction-based management and get you back to the work that matters.

Figure 7.2: Text in IEE One Minute Video

When Jorge returned to the table, Hank commented, "IEE looks great. The video described how performance metrics, not unlike our scorecards, are often inconclusive, which can lead to disaster. The video stated that what's needed are metrics that provide information on future expectations. I presume that if you don't like the anticipated results, something different needs to occur at the process level so that the future process-output performance response is improved."

Jorge responded, "Hank, exactly! You described perfectly the benefits of IEE 30,000-foot-level reporting, which we discussed previously!"

Hank then said, "I liked the reference at the end of the video to a stopfirefighting.com web page. Boy, do we have firefighting!"

"Jorge, the video mentioned application software. Please tell me more about the IEE software. We've not talked much about that yet."

Jorge then responded, "Yes, Hank, it's essential to install software that'll provide a vehicle for implementing the IEE methodology. For organizations, there are many software packages for storing data and conducting exploratory analyses. These software packages often address *what-if* statements such as 'Does one region perform better in sales than another?' These packages can also provide scorecards; however, this reporting might only contain a table of numbers or red-yellow-green scorecards, where RYG scorecard reports assess current output responses relative to goals. Zack is probably using red-yellow-green scorecards in his balanced scorecard deployment, where, if a metric color is red, action needs to occur since there was no achievement of the measurement goal. I suspect if we were to ask him, he would tell us management likes this scorecard reporting; however, often, what happens is there can be a transition between colors where nothing has changed."

Hank then interjected, "We have RYG scorecards at Hi-Tech Computers. In our company, when we look for a reason for a green to red color transition, typically, nothing can be found. Often we do not know what to do to change a red color back to green. We've noted, though, that if we wait long enough, the color often changes back to green even though we did nothing. It's apparent to me that many in our company now ignore the triggers from these color changes and create stories that they might use when talking about a metric in a meeting."

Jorge then replied, "What you're describing happens all the time with red-yellow-green scorecard reports. Frequently what occurs with these scorecards is that the setting of red and yellow trigger points is within the process's common-cause range of variation—this form of reporting can result in much firefighting.

"EPRS software that we used in our IEE implementation, among other things, replaces red-yellow-green scorecards with 30,000-foot-level performance-metric reports. Where, this high-level reporting-metric format had daily automatic updates and a structured IEE value chain linkage to the processes that created the measurement performance response. For an IEE deployment to be successful, there needs to be software that facilitates its implementation. This software must provide the functions offered by the EPRS software that we used.

"I think that we've graduated from napkins and sketches on sheets of paper. I've an article in my car that provides a high-level IEE explanation. Give me a couple of minutes to get the article."

As Jorge was leaving, the wheels in Hank's head started turning on how his organization could benefit from the techniques that Jorge was using.

Upon his return, Jorge opened a document and said, "Let's walk through this 'Positive Metrics Poor Business Performance' article. Here's your copy."

Jorge continued, "In our initial conversation, Ron had me use my computer to access the SmarterSolution.com website. I listened to the one-minute video just as you did through the same website link (Reference Appendix A, Web page 1). I was then instructed by Ron to link to the website's 'Positive Metric Performance Poor Business

Performance: How does this happen?' article (Reference Appendix A, Web page 2), which I just gave you as a hardcopy. He then walked me through the high points of the article, as I'll do in the next few minutes with you.

"To reiterate, the first conversation I had with Ron was just between him and me. In a follow-up conversation, Ron walked Janice through this same article after we viewed the video in Janice's office. Because I began seeing how Harris Hospital could specifically benefit from IEE, I interjected a few comments during Ron's article walkthrough.

"You experienced how the video described the benefits of IEE, while the article provides a high-level description of the overall IEE system. I could see Janice starting to get engaged after the video. She could relate to the described issues.

"In our conversations, Ron first had us scroll to page 2 of the article (See Figure 7.3). He then asked Janice whether she believed that her organization had an issue with any of the listed management attributes."

Effective Management Attributes

Executive Performance Management Reviews
- Require minimal preparation resources.
- Provide productive dialog that results in whole-enterprise benefits.

Decision-making Process
- Incorporates a blend of analytics and innovative team-thinking.
- Avoids *gut-based* decisions.

Strategies
- Are achieved in a timely fashion.
- Don't *fall off people's plates* because of day-to-day crises.

Scorecard Reporting
- Is consistent across the organization.
- Has clear actions or non-actions to be undertaken from these reports.
- Encourages *fire prevention*, and risk management.

Organizational Improvement Efforts
- Give focus to analytically-determined, targeted business areas so that there will be big-picture benefits.

Figure 7.3: Effective Management Attributes
from Page 2 of the Article

Jorge then stated, "Hank, I would like you first to read each of the five highlighted items on page 2 of the article. After you've completed the reading, I would like next to hear whether any one of the listed items is an issue in your organization. If so, which one? Next, I would like your thoughts about any challenges that your organization has for each listed item."

Hank's response, after completing Jorge's reading assignment was, "Jorge, wrong! We don't have issues with any one of these five highlighted statements. **All** of the five listed items in the article are significant problems in our company! Let me elaborate.

"The fifth listed item, ***Organizational Improvement Efforts***, really strikes home with me. The additional statement, 'Gives focus to analytically determined, targeted business areas so there'll be *big picture benefits*' provided some good food-for-thought to me.

"I'm not sure if other Lean deployments have this issue or not, but our organization spends a lot of time and effort in conducting kaizen events that are to reduce organizational waste. It's not apparent to me how this massive amount of spent energy has improved our process output responses so that there's a business-as-a-whole financial benefit.

"We also have a few Lean Six Sigma zealots who have pushed for using this methodology in our organization. What I've noted is that a mini-Lean Six Sigma deployment, of sorts, has also emerged. As part of this Lean Six Sigma effort, it seems to me that their process improvement projects often don't have a timely completion, if projects get completed at all. It appears that this mini-Lean Six Sigma deployment has become a training exercise for individuals to enhance their resume by obtaining Black Belt or Green Belt certification upon completing a project. Also, those projects that do get completed may be reporting huge savings; however, it's difficult to see how these amounts of reported savings are genuinely impacting the big-picture reported financials.

"Let me now elaborate on item number three, ***Strategies***, in the listing of five items. Like Zack, with his balanced scorecard deployment, our organization is also giving focus to creating some alignment of metric scorecard reporting with the execution of our strategies. The strategies inquiry in the article asks 'Are strategies achieved in a timely fashion' and 'don't fall off people's plates because of day-to-day crisis.' Boy, these two points precisely describe what's happening in our organization!

"Okay, now for the article's fourth item, *Scorecard Reporting*. It's not pleasant to say this, but our organization probably gets a grade of *D*, if not an *F* for all three of this category's follow-up statements, which were: 'Is consistent across the organization;' 'Has clear action or non-actions to be undertaken from these reports;' 'Encourage fire prevention and risk management.'

"Let me next describe what happens in our organization relative to item one in the article's listing, *Executive Performance Management Reviews*. One function in our organization creates monthly executive reports. I spoke with the person who has a full-time job working with others to create these reports. She told me that it takes her three weeks to develop a 60+ page presentation report. She then said that, in all honesty, she did not believe that the reporting had any real value helping the organization identify specific actions on what the organization should or should not do. From this statement, you can see that we've issues with both of these subgroup bullets for this listing, which are 'Require minimal preparation resources' and 'Provide productive dialog that results in whole-enterprise benefits.'

"Our organization also has issues with the article's second listed item, *Decision-making Process*. Our organization does not do well with all this item's sub-inquiries, which are 'Incorporates a blend of analytics and innovative team thinking' and 'Avoids gut-based decisions.'

"Jorge, my conclusion is that our organization is batting 1000 with having all these management issues."

In response, Jorge said, "Hank, you summarized what Janice stated in our conference call. Ron then stated that IEE provides the structure to address all these issues – at the same time!

"Ron then proceeded through the article discussing each figure, noting that the material can later be leisurely read for more details. Hank, I'll now point out the article's high points, as Ron did in Janice's conference-call discussion.

"Turn now to pages five and six of the article. These pages contain actual company scorecard examples that the article's author was permitted to use. IEE gives focus not only to what's measured but to the methodology used to report the metrics, as described later in this article."

Hank then said, "This red-yellow-green scorecard (See Figure 7.4) looks just like a scorecard report that was sent to me yesterday! If I counted correctly, there're 30 rows and 12 columns of response numbers that have a red, yellow, or green color in this scorecard. For the 30 tracked measurements, some have a red color, while others transition back and forth between colors.

Site ABC KPI Metrics Scorecard

Perspective	Key Messages	No.	Key KPIs	Jan-13 Perf. %	Feb-13 Perf. %	Mar-13 Perf. %	Apr-13 Perf. %	May-13 Perf. %	Jun-13 Perf. %	Jul-13 Perf. %	Aug-13 Perf. %	Sep-13 Perf. %	Oct-13 Perf. %	Nov-13 Perf. %	Dec-13 Perf. %
Operational Excellence	Satisfied customers through Innovation, Quality and Cost Leadership	1	Productivity factor company	112	106	89	91	83	99	108	96	88	102	80	100
		2	Stock turnover	100	61	67	80	79	84	80	84	76	75	75	80
		3	Productivity of Production ($/unit)	107	105	109	106	109	118	103	93	100	106	100	103
		4	ABC Scrap Costs of Production	23	55	137	50	103	67	94	99	82	104	91	79
		5	KAIZEN CIs completed	37	39	122	63	100	41	98	33	61	255	46	207
		6	Kaizen Continous Improvements per employee	37	36	120	72	130	50	100	32	60	250	50	220
		7	Local Manufacturing (%)	93	93	88	87	91	84	87	97	83	87	91	102
		8	Environment Cost savings - $/Unit	#DIV/0!	106	119	173	80	90	87	97	92	68	83	138
		9	Local Purchase (%)	91	69	76	72	73	85	86	60	75	76	81	51
Employees	We employ and develop responsible, cost-conscious, loyal and innovative employees	10	Invest in Education (hours per employee)	99	99	99	100	100	100	99	100	60	120	135	90
		11	Employee Safety & Health - %	70	127	127	100	66	46	43	90	40	30	73	29
		12	Skill Matrix -%	100	100	100	100	100	100	100	100	100	100	100	100
Quality	The premium brand when it comes to quality and quality culture	13	ABC Quality Cost Production ($/unit)	23	390	128	47	126	113	87	92	83	199	85	91
		14	On time Delivery Performance - Line items %	93	97	101	97	93	94	83	96	84	95	95	88
		15	Final inspection (ppm)	31	174	4775	69	36	38	32	0	64	15	17	15
		15.1	Customer Defects (ppm)	631	135	260	0	1028	74	31	193	494	84	55	148
		16	Lead time order confirmation within 24 hours (%)	96	92	97	97	99.9	104	100	100	98	99	97	97
		16.1	Lead time order confirmation within 48 hours (%)		Introduced May 2013			99	102	99	101	99	99	99	97
		17	Total Unclean sales orders%	228	290	199	146		204	124	249	135	135	190	164
		17.1	Avoidable Unclean Sales Orders -%	210	395	194	166	0	240	104	264	188	188	236	184
		18	FPY%	101	101	101	100	101	101	101	101	100	101	100	101
		19	Complaints %; contained in 48 hours	105	105	105	105	105	105	105	105	105	105	105	105
		19.1	Complaints % solved in <20 days	100	100	100	100	100	100	100	100	100	1400	100	100
		20	Incoming Inspection (Local supplier and XYZ) %	104	104	104	104	104	104	103	104	104	104	104	100
Financial	Gaining sustainable market share through profitable growth	21.1	ABC Growth Orders ($US Millions)	97	96	73	35	87	74	105	95	92	127	98	85
		21.2	ABC Growth Net Sales ($US Millions)	97	91	78	88	84	79	92	97	97	105	105	110
		22.1	ABC+ XYZ Growth Orders ($US Millions)	122	84	72	88	90	90	166	48	105	114	84	75
		22.2	ABC+ XYZ Growth Sales ($US Millions)	93	86	80	56	83	95	98	104	108	111	95	96
		23	Return on total assets (ROA) %	163	95	55	65	51	59	102	75	52	101	66	79
		24	Return on net sales (ROS) %	136	119	84	87	70	87	123	87	72	111	84	86
					100+%		99-95%		<95%						
					100+%		99-95%		<95%						

Figure 7.4: Red-yellow-green Scorecard Example
Color shading for black and white printouts of this figure:
Red is *dark gray*, yellow is *white*, and green is *light gray*.

"I can hardly read the numbers since they're so small, just like our reports at Hi-Tech Computers. I almost need a magnifying glass to read the numbers.

"But, if I squint and look closely at line 15.1, I see a key performance indicator (KPI) title 'Customer Defects PPM.' I assume that the values in this row are monthly PPM rates, where, PPM is a rate of non-compliance, as we discussed earlier. In this row, there're eight red-colored measurements and four green for these PPM numbers. The first colored metric in the time series is red, and the last digit is also red, and the metric colors are sometimes green in the progression of time intervals. I notice one metric value is zero and colored red. It seems to me that a zero PPM would be excellent. Why is there a red color for this zero time-frame metric value? I'm wondering how many people actually read the details of this actual company scorecard and also make the best decisions so that KPI responses have long-lasting improvements. My thought is that this type of scorecard does not lead to the best action or non-action decisions.

"At Hi-Tech Computers, we have the same issues with the red-yellow-green scorecards. Initially, I thought RYG scorecards would be good. Now I don't have the same positive feeling. There must be a better way to report metrics and assess how the organization is performing relative to its measurements and making improvements that'll help the business as a whole."

Jorge responded, "Yes, Hank, I too have seen stoplight scorecards over the years and have had the same questions. It seems to me that most folks mentally question the value of their organization's measurement reports, like this RYG scorecard, but are hesitant to say anything. I think that organizational scorecard reporting, including table-of-numbers monthly reporting, often could be considered the *elephant in the room* that's not being candidly addressed for its value relative to leading to the most appropriate actions in an organization. One comment that Ron made was that this type of reporting leads to an attempt to manage the Ys of an organization. What occurs, if you remember from your school days, is that Y is a response output to a function of its inputs or Xs. Mathematically, if you recall, this statement for the magnitude of

Y could then be expressed as Y=f(X). For a process, we could then say that the output of a process is a function of its inputs. I believe that you understand where I'm coming from, but we need to have everyone in the organization thoroughly understand this relationship, with its related implications. The main point that everyone throughout the chain of command needs to appreciate is that if a Y response needs long-lasting enhancement, one or more of the Xs in the process needs improvement."

Hank responded, "Yes, I do understand the implications, but it can be helpful if you share a couple of examples."

Jorge replied, "Okay, here are a couple of illustrations.

"Example inputs, or Xs, to a manufacturing process are the process's execution steps, supplier product quality, operator performance, time-of-day, day-of-the-week, machine operating temperature, and cavity of a mold. Each of these Xs could impact quality and/or on-time delivery Y metrics for a manufactured product.

"A Y-response example is the number of products shipped in a month, which can be dependent on the effectiveness of the organization's functional Xs such as marketing, sales personnel, supply chain management, and manufacturing workflow. Additional inputs that can affect product shipment volume in any month are the health of the world's economy, product competition, product pricing, product demand, capability to produce desired product volume, month-of-year, and sales force compensation policies.

"I hope that these examples are helpful to illustrate how the output of a process can be dependent upon many inputs. Some of these processes inputs, such as the health of the world's economy, cannot be controlled while others such as marketing and sales are outside the operations function but can have a major impact."

Hank responded, "Jorge, I like your illustrative examples. I want to comment on one X input that you listed, which was sales force compensation policies. I like your inclusion of the word policies. We have a sales force compensation policy that gives bonuses if there's an achievement of quarterly sales targets. Data analysis showed that near the end of each quarter, there was a spike in production volume demands. This quarterly spike leads to additional manufacturing expenses because of over-time pay and other expedited needs. Also, there's probably an increase in defects because of additional operation personnel's expediting demands. I'm not sure what the people in the sales organization are doing to meet their targets. Perhaps they're giving customers special deals to get sales completed before the end of the quarter. I don't know for sure, but these spikes are negatively impacting manufacturing expenses and the company's overall profit. Oh yes, the sales force is also receiving their financial kicker from the top line of the company's financials, not from the bottom-line."

Jorge commented, "Agree with your point. The more I get involved in this IEE effort, the more I see that some of an organization's sacred cow policies need changing to make long-lasting beneficial enhancements to the business. Bad policies can stymie practical process improvement work virtually every time. That's why it's so important to have the CEO or president asking for IEE upfront because policy changes may provide the most enhancement potential for overall business performance.

"Again, everyone throughout the chain of command needs to appreciate that the output management of process at its Y level can result in firefighting and incur very bad, if not destructive, behaviors. Leadership and others need to appreciate that people can feel compelled to play games with the numbers to avoid consequences that may occur if the achievement of numerical goals is not occurring."

Hank then stated, "Agreed. The next table of numbers figure in the article (See Figure 7.5) also looks very familiar. In our last executive leadership review meeting, one person presented a similar chart. He must have provided a fifteen-minute story of why one of the metrics had not done well this month when compared to last month. In all honesty, my eyes were glazing over by the massive numbers in the table.

Product A

New Sales	% Change vs prev week	Total Sales	% Change vs prev week	Market Share New	Share Change vs prev week	Market Share Total	Share Change vs prev week
13,766	26.6%	47,831	23.3%	16.3%	0.4%	16.3%	-0.1%
16,543	20.2%	50,525	5.6%	15.8%	-0.6%	16.0%	-0.2%
14,944	-9.7%	46,176	-8.6%	15.4%	-0.3%	16.0%	0.0%
14,180	-5.1%	44,156	-4.4%	15.4%	0.0%	16.1%	0.0%
14,590	2.9%	44,962	1.8%	16.0%	0.5%	16.0%	0.0%
15,672	7.4%	49,380	9.8%	15.6%	-0.4%	15.9%	-0.1%
15,629	-0.3%	48,811	-5.2%	16.2%	0.6%	16.3%	0.4%
15,252	-2.4%	45,623	-2.5%	16.3%	0.1%	16.3%	0.0%
15,659	2.7%	47,178	3.4%	16.4%	0.1%	16.4%	0.1%
16,655	6.4%	50,764	7.6%	16.6%	0.5%	16.2%	-0.2%
16,399	-1.5%	47,655	-6.1%	17.1%	0.4%	16.5%	0.3%
16,098	-1.8%	47,039	-1.3%	16.6%	0.1%	16.6%	0.1%
15,294	-5.0%	46,242	-1.7%	16.6%	-0.6%	16.5%	-0.1%
16,565	8.3%	50,045	8.2%	17.0%	0.4%	16.6%	0.0%
15,305	-7.6%	47,943	-4.2%	16.3%	-0.7%	16.8%	0.3%
15,764	3.0%	46,619	-2.8%	16.9%	0.6%	16.8%	0.2%
16,139	2.4%	47,265	1.4%	17.3%	0.3%	16.6%	0.3%
16,195	0.3%	48,898	3.5%	17.3%	0.0%	16.6%	0.0%
16,790	3.7%	50,040	2.3%	17.1%	-0.2%	16.6%	0.1%
16,018	-4.6%	48,037	-4.0%	17.2%	0.1%	17.0%	0.3%
16,706	4.3%	49,400	2.8%	17.2%	0.0%	17.0%	0.0%
16,381	-14.0%	46,153	-6.6%	16.9%	-0.3%	16.9%	-0.1%
17,090	19.0%	52,563	13.9%	17.2%	0.3%	16.8%	0.0%
16,571	-3.0%	49,576	-5.7%	17.6%	0.4%	17.2%	0.4%
16,064	-1.0%	49,084	-1.0%	17.3%	-0.4%	17.2%	0.0%
16,292	1.4%	49,335	0.5%	17.7%	0.4%	17.3%	0.1%
16,607	1.9%	53,662	8.8%	17.3%	-0.2%	17.2%	-0.1%
16,807	1.9%	51,201	-4.6%	17.8%	0.5%	17.8%	0.1%
16,401	-3.1%	49,970	-2.4%	17.2%	-0.4%	17.1%	-0.2%

Product B

New Sales	% Change vs prev week	Total Sales	% Change vs prev week	Market Share New	Share Change vs prev week	Market Share Total	Share Change vs prev week
16,474	22.9%	66,900	21.7%	15.0%	0.3%	16.6%	0.1%
20,676	25.5%	71,833	7.4%	15.8%	0.7%	16.9%	0.3%
18,043	-12.7%	64,307	-10.5%	15.1%	-0.6%	16.5%	-0.3%
17,035	-5.6%	61,152	-4.9%	14.8%	-0.3%	16.3%	-0.2%
17,037	0.0%	61,974	1.3%	14.9%	0.1%	16.3%	0.0%
18,802	10.4%	69,285	11.8%	15.3%	0.4%	16.6%	0.3%
17,677	-6.0%	64,067	-7.5%	15.0%	-0.3%	16.5%	-0.1%
17,040	-3.6%	61,264	-4.4%	14.9%	-0.1%	16.3%	-0.2%
17,772	4.3%	63,058	2.9%	15.0%	0.1%	16.2%	-0.1%
19,700	10.8%	70,595	12.0%	15.7%	0.7%	16.6%	0.4%
18,139	-7.9%	64,781	-8.2%	15.3%	-0.4%	16.6%	0.0%
18,442	1.7%	63,487	-2.0%	15.8%	0.5%	16.5%	0.0%
17,982	-2.5%	62,445	-1.6%	15.6%	-0.2%	16.4%	-0.1%
18,602	3.4%	67,219	7.6%	15.3%	-0.3%	16.4%	0.0%
17,458	-6.1%	64,249	-4.4%	15.2%	-0.1%	16.4%	0.0%
17,443	-0.1%	63,398	-1.3%	15.3%	0.1%	16.4%	0.0%
17,818	2.1%	62,423	-1.5%	15.7%	0.4%	16.5%	0.0%
17,426	-2.2%	65,171	4.4%	15.2%	-0.5%	16.5%	-0.5%
18,609	6.8%	66,981	2.8%	15.7%	0.5%	16.6%	0.2%
17,440	-6.3%	62,864	-6.1%	15.2%	-0.4%	16.4%	-0.2%
17,355	-0.5%	63,588	1.2%	15.2%	0.0%	16.4%	0.0%
18,028	-7.7%	60,815	-4.4%	15.2%	-0.1%	16.4%	-0.1%
18,385	14.8%	68,453	12.6%	15.3%	0.1%	16.5%	0.1%
17,506	-4.8%	64,245	-6.1%	15.4%	0.1%	16.5%	0.1%
17,465	-0.3%	63,120	-1.7%	15.4%	0.0%	16.5%	0.1%
17,466	0.1%	63,170	0.1%	15.5%	0.1%	16.5%	0.0%
18,501	5.9%	70,202	11.1%	15.8%	0.3%	16.6%	0.1%
18,454	-0.3%	67,052	-4.5%	15.5%	-0.3%	16.8%	0.2%
18,398	-0.3%	65,442	-2.4%	15.5%	0.0%	16.8%	-0.3%

Product C

New Sales	% Change vs prev week	Total Sales	% Change vs prev week	Market Share New	Share Change vs prev week	Market Share Total	Share Change vs prev week
11,103	18.1%	41,041	19.6%	1.6%	-0.1%	1.6%	0.0%
12,314	10.9%	41,157	0.3%	1.5%	-0.1%	1.6%	0.0%
11,551	-6.2%	37,770	-8.2%	1.5%	0.0%	1.5%	0.0%
10,720	-7.2%	35,852	-5.6%	1.3%	-0.1%	1.5%	0.0%
10,833	1.1%	36,645	1.4%	1.3%	0.0%	1.5%	0.0%
12,405	14.5%	41,159	13.9%	1.4%	0.1%	1.5%	0.1%
11,346	-8.5%	37,360	-9.2%	1.3%	-0.1%	1.5%	-0.1%
10,761	-5.0%	35,725	-4.4%	1.3%	0.0%	1.5%	0.0%
11,292	4.7%	37,441	4.8%	1.3%	0.0%	1.5%	0.0%
12,351	9.4%	42,090	12.4%	1.4%	0.1%	1.6%	0.1%
11,388	-7.8%	37,568	-9.8%	1.4%	0.0%	1.5%	-0.1%
11,202	-1.6%	36,747	-3.2%	1.4%	0.0%	1.5%	0.0%
10,721	-4.3%	36,585	-0.4%	1.4%	0.0%	1.5%	0.0%
11,788	10.0%	40,105	9.6%	1.5%	0.1%	1.5%	0.1%
10,758	-8.7%	36,332	-9.4%	1.4%	-0.1%	1.5%	-0.1%
10,578	-1.7%	35,341	-2.7%	1.4%	0.0%	1.5%	0.0%
10,487	-0.9%	34,756	-1.7%	1.4%	0.0%	1.5%	0.0%
10,866	3.6%	37,136	6.8%	1.4%	0.0%	1.5%	0.1%
10,967	0.9%	37,423	0.8%	1.4%	0.0%	1.5%	0.0%
10,461	-8.5%	34,199	-8.6%	1.4%	-0.1%	1.4%	-0.1%
10,432	-0.3%	35,730	4.5%	1.4%	0.0%	1.5%	0.0%
9,321	-10.8%	32,690	-8.5%	1.4%	0.0%	1.4%	0.0%
11,439	22.7%	39,125	19.7%	1.4%	0.1%	1.4%	0.1%
10,206	-2.9%	33,963	-1.1%	1.4%	-0.1%	1.4%	0.0%
9,552	-6.4%	33,591	1.1%	1.4%	0.1%	1.4%	0.0%
10,831	13.4%	38,905	15.8%	1.5%	0.1%	1.5%	0.1%
10,252	-5.3%	34,457	-11.4%	1.4%	0.1%	1.4%	-0.1%
10,415	1.6%	34,774	0.9%	1.5%	0.1%	1.4%	0.0%

Product D

New Sales	% Change vs prev week	Total Sales	% Change vs prev week	Market Share New	Share Change vs prev week	Market Share Total	Share Change vs prev week
20,666	22.3%	71,409	22.2%	13.5%	-0.2%	12.7%	0.1%
24,581	23.8%	75,818	6.2%	14.0%	0.5%	12.9%	0.2%
24,457	-0.5%	72,104	-4.9%	14.1%	0.1%	13.0%	0.1%
23,584	-3.6%	69,904	-3.1%	13.9%	-0.2%	13.1%	-0.2%
24,185	2.5%	69,990	0.1%	13.9%	0.1%	12.9%	-0.2%
26,335	8.9%	75,735	8.2%	14.1%	0.2%	12.8%	0.2%
25,389	-3.6%	73,045	-3.6%	14.0%	0.0%	13.1%	0.3%
25,441	0.2%	71,843	-1.6%	14.3%	0.3%	13.1%	0.0%
26,342	3.5%	73,728	2.6%	14.3%	0.0%	13.1%	0.0%
27,865	5.8%	80,373	9.0%	14.5%	0.2%	13.1%	0.0%
27,408	-1.6%	75,339	-6.3%	14.9%	0.4%	13.2%	0.2%
26,575	-3.0%	74,892	-0.6%	14.9%	0.0%	13.2%	0.0%
26,955	1.4%	74,064	-1.1%	15.2%	0.3%	13.4%	0.3%
27,043	0.3%	78,818	6.4%	14.7%	-0.5%	13.2%	-0.2%
25,434	-5.9%	74,021	-6.1%	15.1%	0.4%	13.4%	0.2%
24,951	-1.9%	73,496	-0.7%	14.3%	-0.4%	13.1%	-0.2%
25,869	3.7%	73,614	0.2%	14.3%	-0.2%	13.2%	0.1%
26,217	1.3%	77,765	5.6%	14.7%	-0.1%	13.3%	0.1%
25,817	-1.5%	77,014	-1.0%	14.5%	-0.2%	13.3%	-0.1%
25,661	-0.6%	74,165	-3.7%	15.0%	0.5%	13.3%	-0.1%
25,955	1.1%	76,249	2.8%	14.6%	-0.4%	13.3%	0.0%
22,997	-11.4%	70,038	-8.2%	14.6%	-0.1%	13.3%	0.0%
26,443	15.0%	60,977	5.5%	14.7%	0.6%	13.5%	0.1%
26,069	-1.4%	76,465	-0.5%	14.6%	-0.2%	13.5%	0.0%
25,480	-2.3%	76,062	-0.3%	14.6%	-0.3%	13.5%	0.0%
24,916	-2.2%	76,084	-0.3%	14.2%	0.2%	13.5%	0.2%
26,143	4.9%	82,605	8.6%	14.5%	0.2%	13.2%	-0.3%
26,005	-0.5%	77,745	-5.9%	14.3%	-0.1%	13.3%	0.3%
26,797	3.0%	79,598	2.4%	14.7%	0.4%	13.6%	0.2%

Figure 7.5: Table of Numbers

"For this particular table, I see, when using my magnifying vision, the metrics from four products listed across the top of the table. For each product, there are eight columns of reported measurements. The rows in this table are a time-series sequence of week ending dates, where the earliest date appears at the top of the table.

"This table provides numbers for revenue for new sales, total sales, and market share with a comparison to previous weeks. Why make comparisons to previous weeks? Wouldn't we simply like to do something, perhaps differently, to increase sales? I do not get why making these between-week comparisons provides any real value for accomplishing increased revenue in the future. What insight does this form of reporting provide to stimulate the most appropriate actions for one or more of these four products that this company produces?"

Jorge said, "I agree! Remember, this report was not fabricated and is an actual company reporting."

Hank then continued, saying, "Let's now look at the next organizational scorecard report example in this article. This article's following figure shows a time-series plot chart with some reported data displayed in a table (See Figure 7.6). This graphic is a better chart than the two previous organizational reports since the graphic provides information on how measurements are changing over time.

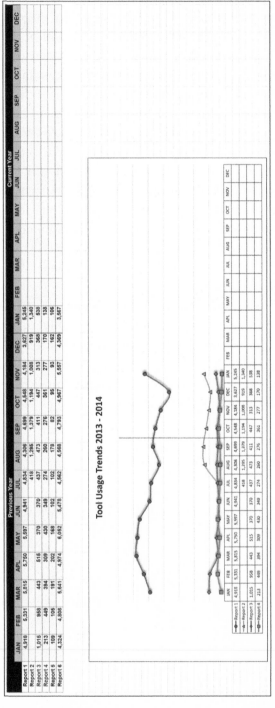

Figure 7.6: Time-series Plot

"However, I'm not sure what Report 1 through Report 6 means. For the months shown, it looks like there're differences in response amplitudes, but what does this mean? It seems like readers of this graphic would have difficulty in determining what, if any, actions need to be undertaken or not?

"Jorge, I think the last chart shown is also thought-provoking in that it shows twelve monthly values with a YTD or year-to-date response (See Figure 7.7).

Yield												
	Jan	Feb	Mar	Apr	May	Jun	Jul	Aug	Sep	Oct	Nov	Dec
Wastage	4.92	5.08	5.18	5.34	5.41	5.35	5.66	5.09	5.48	5.23	5.26	5.63

Figure 7.7: Percentages in a Table

"One question I've about this measurement reporting approach is: What happens the first month of a new year? Typically the magnitude of a process-output response does not magically have a different amount of change from the last month of a fiscal year to the first month of the next fiscal year when being compared to other between-month-changes that occur throughout the year.

"With this form of reporting, it would seem that the report would display only January results at the beginning of a new calendar year. If so, why would this be done? To answer my question, I suspect that at the beginning of each calendar year, there's a redirection of focus to a new yearly goal. Our organization has this type of annual goal-setting management practice too, which I'm thinking has difficulties relative to encouraging the best behaviors.

"The general question that I have, Jorge, is whether there is a better way to set and manage the achievement of goals."

Jorge then said, "Exactly, Hank. All the traditional management metric reports that we discussed are attempting to manage the Ys in an organization, which can lead to very harmful organizational behaviors, as we previously discussed! Also, all of these performance-metric reports are not predictive. Using these non-predictive forms of reporting is not unlike trying to drive a car by only looking at the rearview mirror. Let's now talk about a better way to report metrics that can lead to the most appropriate actions for a given situation.

"Hank, if you recall from our earlier conversation, we talked about common- and special-cause variation.

"To re-iterate, IEE offers a robust, unique approach to present time-series, process-output data. 30,000-foot-level is the reference used for this method of high-level reporting. As we have discussed previously, this form of metric reporting separates common cause variation from special cause events.

"To reiterate, common causes of variation are those sources that are part of the process as currently designed and deployed. Special causes are those reasons that are outside the process as it is currently defined or something changed within the process's execution. A response level beyond a statistically calculated upper control limit (UCL) or lower control limit (LCL) boundary is an identified special-cause event. But special-cause conditions can also cause patterns, such as trends or shifts, in the variation shown on a control chart. If a process 30,000-level output response exhibits a special-cause condition, this occurrence is justification for an investigation into why the special-cause event occurred and what to do to resolve any issue.

"If a 30,000-foot-level performance metric is stable, that's an indication that the process, from a high-level perspective, is only experiencing common-cause variation. For stable processes, one should *not react* to all the up-and-down response gyrations that occur in a 30,000-foot-level's control-chart plot of the data. These changes in response levels aren't special-cause events but only the outcome of input-noise within the overall system.

"When a process is considered stable, the creation of a 30,000-foot-level chart utilizes all the raw data from its recent region of stability to provide a prediction statement in the report. If this predictive statement is undesirable, the metric's associated process needs improvement. When there has been a successful process enhancement that impacts its 30,000-foot-level performance metric, this high-level reporting chart will demonstrate a statistical response enhancement. Also, if the new process-output-response is considered stable, a new prediction statement is provided in the reporting.

"The figure on page eight of the article is an attribute 30,000-foot-level chart. This graphic provides a wastage, non-conformance percentage rate. Like the four previous scorecards, this metric performance report originated from a company's provided data, not fabricated values" (See Figure 7.8).

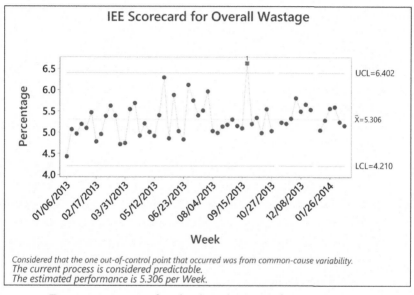

Figure 7.8: 30,000-foot-level Predictive Performance Report

"With this attribute 30,000-foot-level charting format, a monthly PPM rate could be tracked over time. Or, this monthly parts per million rate could be converted and tracked as a percentage non-conformance rate or a proportion non-conformance rate."

Hank then said, "This graphic looks similar to a statistical control chart, which we've used in manufacturing to determine if a process has special-cause conditions that need investigation for timely resolution.

"Let me expound on how we've been using some control charts in operations to control manufacturing processes so that, if there's an out-of-control signal, we can take timely action to resolve the issue. In your chart, one point is above the upper control limit of 6.460, which is an out-of-control signal and should trigger the considerations for investigation according to statistical process control (SPC) application guidelines. Corrective action may be needed to resolve this out-of-control condition. Or, after investigation of the data from a particular time frame, no root-cause may be uncovered, resulting in a probable conclusion that this out-of-control occurrence happened by chance."

Jorge responded, "Hank, I understand that this report can initially appear to be simply a control chart since the mathematics behind this chart is the same as an individuals statistical control chart. However, the creation and usage of 30,000-foot-level performance metric reports are different from process control charts used in manufacturing operations, as we touched on earlier.

"Consider the following differences for this article's 30,000-foot-level performance metric report figure:

1. The charting time interval for this article's chart is a week. In manufacturing, the control chart time interval between successive data plot points for actively controlling processes would be much shorter. The reason for a shortened time frame in traditional control charts is so that timely corrective action can be taken for any special-cause conditions that occurred, as you mentioned earlier.

2. There's also a predictive performance metric statement included in the report, which does not appear in traditional SPC charts."

Hank responded, "I hear what you're saying, Jorge, but this will take some time to soak into the gray matter between my ears. I agree that this high-level or 30,000-foot-level form of reporting and its objective seems to be quite different from traditional control charts."

Jorge replied, "Yes, Hank, 30,000-foot-level reports have several significant differences when compared to traditional control charts. This high-level form of metric reporting is also very useful in tracking the outputs of transactional processes. For example, Zack could benefit from using these techniques to monitor the responses from his Z-Credit

Financial operations and take appropriate action when needed. This IEE performance metric reporting technique has application to monitoring the output of processes in your company's support functions such as Human Resources (HR) and Information Technology (IT).

"The 30,000-foot-level format is useful to monitor virtually every type of process-output response. However, the graphs' appearances can be quite different from traditional reporting and are much easier to understand and interpret than conventional scorecard-reporting approaches. It's beneficial when explaining this charting approach to highlight the statement below the chart's graphics.

"One characteristic of 30,000-foot-level reporting is that there's always an easy-to-understand statement below the report's charting. Again, this statement is much easier to understand than a traditional scorecard statement or presentation. Whenever a process is considered statistically stable, this statement provides an expectation for future performance if nothing were to change.

"It's essential to keep in mind that this metric performance report is not a variance-to-an-organizational-set goal statement but instead is how the process is performing. This statement can be considered a process-output response from an external or internal customer point of view.

"To illustrate this point, let's consider two illustrations. For the first example, let's suppose that a process-output-response is stable, and there is a customer specification requirement. For this situation, the 30,000-foot-level report would include an estimated non-conformance rate statement. For the second example, consider that an organization is tracking monthly work in progress (WIP) expenses. For this situation, there are no specifications. If the WIP individuals chart response is considered stable, there's an included estimation statement for mean and an 80% frequency of monthly occurrence amounts. In IEE, this 80% statement frequency of occurrence statement when no specification exists provides the chart-reader a quantification of expected process variation; that is, an expectation that four out of five reporting occurrences will be in the 80% frequency of occurrence range.

"In both of these 30,000-foot-level reports, it's essential to remember that, if a futuristic performance metric statement is undesirable, the associated process or processes that impact the magnitude or variation of the metric's response need enhancement. If this process enhancement effort is undertaken and proves to be beneficial, the 30,000-foot-level individuals chart will indicate that an improved level of performance has occurred. If this new enhanced-state is stable, a new performance-metric-predictive statement will appear in the report.

"The additional process insight gained from a 30,000-foot-level performance-metric charting approach provides many benefits over traditional singular process-metric traditional statements, such as sigma level, DPMO, PPM, process capability/performance indices, variance-to-budget, and variance-to-goals.

"There are two steps to create a 30,000-foot-level performance metric chart:

1. Determine if the processes are stable.
2. Provide a process stability assessment statement below the report's charts. If the process is considered stable, this statement provides a prediction of future expectations, whether a specification exists or not."

Jorge then stated, "Hank, I think that it'll be best for me to go *a little technical* to describe the mathematical differences between the time-series tracking of traditional control charting and 30,000-foot-level reporting. You need to gain this basic understanding."

Hank responded, "That sounds good to me. I need to appreciate the differences."

Jorge continued, "For the assessment of process stability with 30,000-foot-level reports, the same mathematics for the creation of an individuals control chart is used, even for attribute-pass/fail rate-tracking situations. The chart's upper control limit (UCL) and lower control limit (LCL) calculations for the creation of an SPC individuals chart are simply:

$$UCL = \bar{x} + 2.66 \times \overline{MR}$$

$$LCL = \bar{x} - 2.66 \times \overline{MR}$$

"These relationships, as you know, have nothing to do with any specification that may exist for the process. These equations have two factors. One factor is the overall mean of the plotted values, $\bar{x}$ in the equation. The second factor is the overall mean of adjacent time-series time values, $\overline{MR}$ in the equation."

Hank then interrupted, "Jorge, I've been looking at some control charts but haven't examined their equations in years. I understand that the mean value in your equation is simply the average of all time-series data points. However, to determine the mean moving range for the equation, I suspect one would need first to determine the absolute value for the magnitude of the difference between all time-series adjacent values. When performing this moving range calculation, there would then be one less value than the number of data points. Next, to get an overall mean for moving range for this equation, one would simply average all these moving-range values. Jorge, is this correct?"

Jorge responded, "Exactly, Hank.

"Determination of the upper control limit or UCL is by the addition of an amount to the overall mean of reported values while the determination of the lower control limit or LCL is the subtraction of this same value. For these relationships, the amount to add or subtract is the product of 2.66 and the mean of the moving range values."

Hank then asked, "Why the 2.66 value, Jorge?"

Jorge responded, "In statistics for a normal distribution, the expectation is that about 99.7 percent of reported values occur within a three standard deviation variation calculation of the mean. In statistics, when a data point occurs beyond a three-standard-deviation of a calculated mean value, this data-point-value can be considered an unusual event, which may warrant an investigation.

"Calculation of upper and lower control chart limits follows a similar determination; however, the standard deviation used for control chart upper and lower control charting limits is the sampling standard deviation, not population standard deviation. The mean moving range value multiplication by 2.66 is simply a sampling plan estimate for this charting methodology's three-sampling-plan standard deviation value."

Hank then commented, "Jorge, got it! On a separate point, I've often seen individuals control charts accompanied by a control chart of the moving range response as two-chart-paired reporting. XmR is a common reference for this pair of charts. Why does a 30,000-foot-level report not include this moving range addition with an individuals control chart plot?"

Jorge's response was, "Hank, I'm glad you asked that question. A moving range chart, whether accompanied by a related individuals chart or shown individually, is redundant to the information contained in an individuals chart. The moving range control chart simply assesses between-time-interval-swings for originating from common-cause or special-cause variation. For simplicity in reporting, an IEE 30,000-foot-level report does not include the tracking of moving range in its report.

"While we're at it, Hank, statistical process control (SPC) $\overline{X}$ and R chart, p-chart, and c-chart techniques aren't used in 30,000-foot-level reporting for assessing process stability. I'll now give you a brief reason; however, additional mathematical details are available at SmarterSolutions.com (Reference Appendix A, Web page 11).

"The basic mathematical reason for the exclusion of these non-individuals control charts involves the calculation of both the upper (UCL) and lower (LCL) values. As discussed previously, the sampling 3 standard deviation for an individuals process control chart is the product of 2.66 and the mean of moving range. It is essential to note the calculation of the mean moving range for an individuals chart is from the variation between adjacent time-series values. A close examination of the mathematics for $\overline{X}$ and R chart (pronounced X-bar and R chart), p-chart, and c-chart UCL and LCL calculations will show that the variation between adjacent time series values has no impact on calculated control limit values! This between-subgroup-variability not being considered a source for common-cause variability mathematical truism is a big deal that I've not seen highlighted in traditional control chart 101 training."

Hank responded, "Traditional control charting has been around since the 1920s. I'll need to look at these equations. But why is this important?"

Jorge continued, "Traditional control charts can be satisfactory when used for controlling the Xs of a process. However, when one evaluates the Y of a process from a high-level perspective using these traditional charting methodologies, unexpected signals can occur.

"Hank, do you believe that calculated upper and lower control limit calculations should be consistent with our beliefs of what are common and special cause occurrences? When responding to this question, you need to keep in mind that UCL and LCL values identify when special-cause events occur, or the process has changed for some reason."

Hank then said, "Makes sense to me that UCL and LCL calculated values are consistent with our beliefs of what a common- or special-cause event is."

Jorge then stated, "Okay. Let's consider that a quality response for a product that your company produces is dependent upon the output value of a supplier's product, which is an input to your product response level. For illustration purposes, consider that for some reason, unknown to you, that the lot-to-lot supplier input component's viscosity differences impact an essential response for your product's performance. It's necessary to highlight that I did not say that the component's viscosity adversely affected the quality of your product's performance relative to any specification requirement, but that the component's input does affect the magnitude of an overall response-measurement for your product.

"Let's also consider that your organization receives and uses a new daily lot from your supplier in its manufacturing process. The question is: should the variation between days, which reflects basic lot-to-lot differences, be considered a source from special-cause or special-cause variation?"

After thinking about it for a while, Hank responded, "I'd say that the lot-to-lot variation from this supplier would be a common-cause process input. The reason for this conclusion is that the process for manufacturing this product would regularly experience this component variation, whether this input is good or bad to a critical response for our product."

Jorge followed-up by saying, "Agreed! Because of this 30,000-foot-level process-stability-assessment-requirement need, the mathematics for calculation UCL and LCL must include between adjacent reading values in the calculations. An individuals chart fulfills these calculation needs for upper and lower control limits, which the other control charting techniques that we discussed do not do.

"In the past, I've observed many control charts that had out-of-control signals, where we could find no root cause reason for the special-cause incident identified by the control chart. The articles and books at SmarterSolutions.com provide the mathematical details why many traditional out-of-control special-cause signals could be from a between-time-interval, common-cause-variation condition.

"Ron walked me through the mathematics for various control charting methodologies and the importance of using individuals charts as part of 30,000-foot-level reporting, which made perfect sense to me. It's alarming to me that SPC Control Charting 101 training does not typically cover these issues."

Hank then stated, "Wow, Jorge! What you describe is what we've seen! We often experience processes that have out-of-control special-cause signals that do not seem real. There are often so many occurrences that it would be doubtful that these instances could be occurring by chance. This situation occurs very frequently with p-charts."

Jorge then responded, "Hank, yes, p-charts are very prone to having false out-of-control signals because the fundamental assumptions for the p-chart aren't appropriate for many, if not most, real-world Y-process-output tracking. Hank, I suggest that you read information about issues with the traditional use of p-charts on the SmarterSolutions.com website (Reference Appendix A, Web page 11). I want to stress that it's imperative that, when you read this documentation, you keep an open mind, since the documents describe a fundamental paradigm shift to traditional-control-chart usage and thinking."

Hank then said, "Will do. I'm looking forward to learning about the mathematical aspects of SPC control charting to assess how our usage of the methodology can be inconsistent with the chart's underlying assumptions. Jorge, on another point, the statement below the report's charting is a type of process capability reporting. We've been using process capability/performance indices to report how a process is performing relative to specifications, but these Cp, Cpk, Pp, and Ppk reports are so confusing."

Jorge then said, "I'm impressed! Hank, you're doing a great job grasping 30,000-foot-level concepts. Yes, the statement below the report's charting is a form of process capability reporting using words that are easy to understand, and again you don't even need a specification for this reporting statement.

"It's essential to highlight that with 30,000-foot-level reporting, one chart provides both process stability and an overall process performance or capability assessment! The statement below the report's charting provides, for stable processes, a common-cause predictive assessment. With this form of reporting, one or more data points above or below UCL or LCL individuals chart values result in a statement below the report's charting that the process is not predictable. However, when there are no identified values beyond UCL and LCL values, the process is considered stable, from a 30,000-foot-level reporting perspective. For this situation, this report provides a best-estimate predictive statement below the report's charting. As discussed previously, if this futuristic Y-process-output statement is not desirable, process enhancement activities can provide improvements to the process Xs that positively impact the Y response. I need to point out that when there's a lot of data, it's probable that one or more plotted points will be beyond the individuals chart's UCL and LCL lines, even when only common-cause variation exists. Because of this frequently encountered situation, an EPRS-metrics software option is available to override a *not predictable* statement to provide a best-estimate prediction statement.

"Hank, not sure you know this or not, but the process sampling approach that provides data for a process capability determination can have a substantial impact on reported values. What this means is that, for a given process, one person can declare a set of process capability indices numbers. In contrast, another person could report, for the same process, a very different set of numbers. This difference in reported process capability indices isn't from the *luck of the draw* that will occur when sampling. Cp and Cpk process capability results from multiple sampling subgroupings can be quite different when compared to a single-sample time interval selection alternative. The reason for this difference is that the standard deviation calculated for these two situations is different. The articles and books on the SmarterSolutions.com website provide the details and advantages of 30,000-foot-level process capability over traditional process capability indices." (Reference Appendix A, Web page 11)."

Hank then said, "The 30,000-foot-level reporting format looks to be very powerful and beneficial over traditional reporting formats such as red-yellow-green scorecards and a table of numbers. However, in all honesty, I think that it would be challenging to get my leadership team to want to change to a 30,000-foot-level reporting format."

Jorge responded, "That's the same point that I made to Ron. He agreed there would probably be a lack of willingness by mid-level management for transitioning to 30,000-foot-level reporting. Ron then stated that's why it's vital to work upfront with the CEO, president, general manager when initiating an IEE implementation. The CEO needs to say, 'Here are the tools to work smarter. If you are smart, you'll use them.'"

"Ron elaborated that the CEO or president is responsible for the entire organization. If this person wants to continue managing by applying pressure to hit high-level goals, it'll be tough to initiate the IEE systems thinking methodology. But if this leader wants to encourage the right behaviors that are consistent with the five-effective-management attributes describe earlier in this article, he or she must be willing to do things differently. The best way for individuals to describe the benefits and encourage the use of IEE in an organization he/she needs to work with the top-management person on the basics of how to read and interpret 30,000-foot-level performance metric reporting.

"Are you familiar with Dr. Edwards Deming's Red Bead Experiment?"

Hank responded, "Didn't Deming help Japan turn around the manufacturing quality problems that were occurring in their country in the 1950s?"

Jorge then said, "Yes, Hank, Deming is credited for Japan's transformation in the management of their businesses, which resulted in improved quality of their products.

"Deming coined the terms common- and special-cause variation that we've been previously discussing. However, it's essential to highlight that Deming used these terms to address traditional control charting methodologies, which are to identify unusual events and stimulate their resolution promptly. From an IEE perspective, traditional control charts could be beneficial for controlling the Xs in a process.

"In IEE, the reference to the common-cause and special-cause variation terminology is different from the use of these words when referencing traditional control charts. This difference is that with 30,000-foot-level charting, one is examining the process output from a high-level, Y-output, perspective. With this alternative charting approach, one isn't attempting to use information from this high-level process response charting perspective to make timely adjustments to a process. If you recall, we discussed earlier an IEE high-level perspective for common-cause variation in a supplier lot-to-lot viscosity variation illustration."

Hank then responded, "Jorge, I'm glad that you described these two differing perspectives for the use of the terms common-cause and special-cause variation. This contrasting-perspectives discussion is helping me understand and is making a lot of sense to me."

Jorge continued, "Good to hear, Hank. Deming also had seminars in the 1980s about his management philosophy. One of Deming's renowned exercises in these sessions was his *red bead experiment*. An internet search on the 'red bead experiment' will provide many videos that illustrate the execution of this experiment."

Jorge continued, "I'll now summarize Deming's Red Bead Experiment and its teachings, which he conducted in his management training sessions. For this exercise, Deming had a container of red and white beads in the front of the room. In the box, twenty percent of the beads were red. The white represented acceptable products, while a red-colored-bead represented defective products. Overall there was an actual 0.20 non-conformance, common-cause variation rate, i.e., the proportion of red beads in the container.

"For this classroom training exercise, Deming had a few volunteers from the audience go to the front of the class and assume various roles in his fictitious company. *Willing workers* for this company filled a 50-hole paddle with beads by placing and then removing the paddle from the container. Quality Inspectors then counted and recorded the number of red-paddle-beads.

"In this exercise, management tracked the performance of individual workers against the company's leadership-provided goal of three red beads or fewer in a paddle draw. As noted earlier, twenty percent of the container-beads were red, which translates to a 0.20 common-cause non-conformance rate. Because of this proportion of red beads in the container, an average 50-hole-paddle-draw would contain ten red-colored-beads. The achievement of management's three-red-bead goal for an individual 50-hole paddle draw was an improbable event. The occurrence of any individual willing worker having fewer red beads in a single paddle-draw than another worker was only by chance.

"In this fictitious company red-bead goal exercise, Deming terminated employment for those workers who had more red beads than other *willing workers*. The company's leadership believed that those employees, who at one point in time, did not perform as well in the company's product-quality metric as the other employees were not as good at producing a quality product. Because of this leadership belief, there was the termination of these lesser-quality-performing workers from the company. We understand that any differences between the numbers of red beads in a paddle draw were simply common-cause variation occurrences. Through the red bead experiment, Deming demonstrated how attempts to manage arbitrary goals without improving the underlying process that produced the metric results are not proper management practices.

"Using IEE terminology, a major takeaway from Deming's red-bead experiment is that this fictitious company had a measurement reporting system that reacted to the results from each paddle draw as though these events were special-cause. However, they were reacting to each up-and-down variation movement that one can expect from common-cause variation."

Hank then interjected with the comment, "Jorge, what you're describing is how we're working with metrics in my company."

Jorge then said, "Your company doesn't have a monopoly on this practice. I've seen this form of managing to the Ys in the relationship Y as a function of X everywhere! Organizations need to do something differently relative to this commonly-used management style (Reference Appendix A, Web page 10).

"Ron then made an interesting reference to a quote from Deming's 1986 book *Out of the Crisis* (Deming 1986). This quote by Dr. Lloyd S. Nelson was: 'If you can improve productivity, or sales, or quality, or anything else, by (e.g.,) five percent next year without a rational plan for improvement, then why were you not doing it last year?'"

Hank then said, "That quote is so accurate! If the organization needs long-lasting improvement to a metric's performance, one should be giving thought to how to accomplish the metric's improvement objective through enhancing processes that are associated with that measurement."

Jorge then followed up on Hank's comment, saying, "What I find interesting is that Deming in the 1980s talked about business management issues and the need for policy changes in the management of organizations. Deming used the red-bead experiment to dramatize the need for metric-reporting changes. However, it's now decades later, but I'm still not seeing organizations embrace the fundamental metric reporting concepts that Deming said were needed."

Hank then stated, "Jorge, I'll ditto that. We've metric reports that aren't consistent across our organization, where each report can take a very long time to create. I've often wondered how many people use these reports to take actions that will lead to the best organizational behaviors."

Jorge responded, "Yes, Harris Hospital has had those reporting issues, too. The ignoring of typical organizational performance reporting seems to be a portion of that infamous elephant in the room.

"I've had many one-on-one conversations that our metric reporting is only not useful but can lead to very destructive behaviors. In these discussions, there's general agreement that our scorecard-reporting methodology has issues. The question I've been asking myself is why organizations aren't addressing this Deming-described issue. My conclusion is that a metric reporting methodology has not been readily available to address this fundamental issue head-on. The 30,000-foot-level reporting methodology resolves this traditional metric reporting shortcoming.

"To explain the fallacies and what could be done differently from a red-yellow-green scorecard reporting format, Ron suggested reading an article that's available on the SmarterSolutions.com website (Reference Appendix A, Web page 4). The title of this article is 'The Improvement of Scorecard Management: Comparing Deming's Red Bead Experiment to red-yellow-green scorecards.' This article uses a randomly-generated dataset to show how 30,000-foot-level reporting is a better alternative than red-yellow-green scorecards, which is no different than the red bead experiment style of management that Deming highlighted had issues many years ago."

Hank then interjected, "With our company scorecards, executives, including me, have created so many metrics goals. I'll bet that, if we examined these metrics from a 30,000-foot-level perspective over several years, we would see that for most of these performance metrics, there has been little, if any, response enhancements. I'll also wager that the people involved in improving these metrics aren't looking at what should be done differently from a process enhancement point of view to have a long-lasting improvement for the resulting metric response. In all honesty, many of these performance measurement improvement goals are arbitrarily set.

"First, again, I'm confident that most functions aren't focusing on what should be done differently at the process level so that a metric enhancement objective will occur in future time frames. It seems to me that functions more often than not are giving focus on what to do to meet a specific time-frame number, even though the activity to enhance a particular metric may not be healthy to the organization's big picture.

"Secondly, the question of whether a specific functional metric goal was met or not has often been based only on the examination of an individual value at some point in time and not from an overall process-output perspective.

"Thirdly, I'm questioning the value of the many metrics appearing in reports and those measurements that are to be improved; it also seems as if some essential measures aren't reported and receive no attention. We've had a somewhat helter-skelter approach for metric selection. One area of our organization simply asked every functional group what should be measured.

"Fourthly, when there're so many metric goals throughout an organization, the amount of effort to address all these objectives from a business process improvement perspective would probably be overwhelming and not realistic!

"Finally, I mentioned this previously, but more needs to be said about the situation. We do have some folks in our company that are Six Sigma zealots. Having these evangelists is not bad, but just another approach beyond our company-sponsored Lean deployment.

"These individuals focus on the execution of Six Sigma projects. For this effort, execution focus and project reports emphasize reporting cost savings. This process-output-benefit statement initially sounds good, but it has been my observation that these declarations are often questionable, even though the number was to have come from Finance. Also, the Six Sigma project reports that I've seen do not show, in one chart, any metric enhancement from the process-improvement effort and how this metric enrichment was important to the business financials as a whole."

Jorge then excitedly responded, "Wow! The comments that you've made, Hank, are excellent and a perfect lead-in to the next sections of the 'Positive Metric Performance Poor Business Performance' article! I'll attempt to address your points when walking through the remainder of this article.

"After demonstrating the benefits of 30,000-foot-level reporting to an organization's CEO or equivalent for obtaining his or her buy-in for this form of reporting, it's next necessary to describe how to incorporate this form of metric reports throughout an organization.

"As I mentioned earlier, an organization's scorecard and metric performance group can be figuratively in the north wing of the building, while the process documentation and improvement functions reside in the south side, where these two services don't formally communicate with each other. This isolating structure can lead to an organizational management through-the-Ys style, which isn't right. An IEE value chain provides a vehicle to overcome this corporate separation of performance measurement reporting from process documentation and improvement.

"The next Figure in the article provides an example IEE hospital value chain at its enterprise-level (See Figure 7.9).

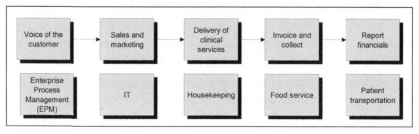

Figure 7.9: Hospital Value Chain

"In this Figure, the main functions of a hospital are connected by arrows across the top of the image. Each organizational function is shown in a primary sequence with other functional areas but can have interconnections with the other functions. The main hospital functions are Voice of the Customer; Sales and marketing; Delivery of clinical services; Invoice and collect; Report financials. Support functions listed in the Figure for this hospital IEE value chain are IT, Housekeeping, Foodservice, Patient Transportation, and Enterprise Process Management (EPM). I'll discuss EPM later.

"The hospital's support functions are shown at the bottom of the figure and not connected with an arrow. For example, Housekeeping is a support hospital function. I think it's safe to say that nobody goes to a hospital for its housekeeping; hence, this activity is a necessary hospital function but resides as a supporting function in the organization's IEE value chain.

"Some might say that hospitals don't have a *sales function*. Indeed, hospitals don't typically have a Sales Department like many other industries, who may use *cold calls* and other sales activities to increase revenue. But, whether hospitals view it that way or not, they're engaged in traditional selling – attracting the right patients, doctors, and other practitioners. So it's helpful to view these activities as 'sales' in the more general sense.

"Both for-profit and non-profit hospitals benefit from the documentation of their sales process and a structured evaluation of what to do differently, when appropriate, from a process improvement perspective to increase sales. In a hospital, the most important driver for growing sales revenue might be the establishment and improvement of relationships between physicians and the hospital. If this relationship is essential to hospital sales, a description of the nurturing of these associations should be included in a 'Sales and Marketing' function drill-down.

"What organizations need is an IEE value chain that contains up-to-date information and is available to everyone in the organization who has authorization access through a so-called simple *click of a mouse*. At Harris Hospital, we fulfilled this need using Enterprise Performance Reporting System (EPRS) software, which I mentioned previously.

"A representation of what an organization might be experiencing when *clicking on* the shaded box titled 'Delivery of clinical services' is shown in the next article figure (See Figure 7.10)."

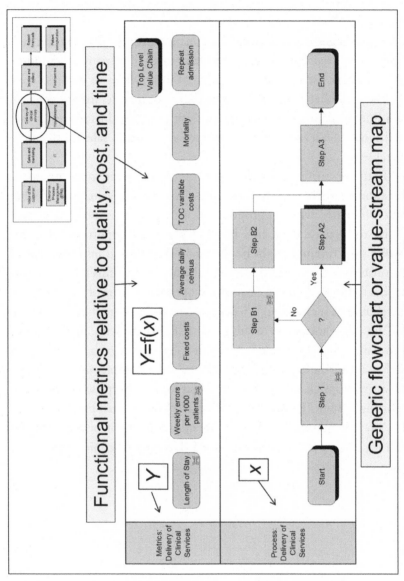

Figure 7.10: IEE Hospital Value Chain Drill Down

Hank interjected, "Wow! Can the IEE value chain be tweaked for our organization? Would everyone, including our CEO, have access to this information that shows the procedures we follow and the resulting organizational predictive metrics?"

Jorge responded, "Yes, exactly, Hank – to both questions! If you were to implement IEE, your value chain would be tailored to your specific organizational functions by your implementation team and management. Everyone authorized would also have access to the IEE value chain, 24/7.

"Often, in organizations, information is filtered for executive reviews because of fear of so-called *shooting the messenger* consequences. A unique benefit of the IEE value chain is the transparency of its reporting structure. EPRS software offers a vehicle for no filtering of information up the chain-of-command for executive reviews.

"Leadership reports that filter information can lead to severe consequences, even fatalities when risks and product issues are hidden and not addressed head-on by leadership and others. With this approach for information availability, periodic executive reports can now reference and highlight various aspects of the IEE value chain, which all interested parties can follow, if they wish, at a later point in time. Relative to those in the workplace trenches and information collection systems, it's only essential to ensure accurate data are presented in the IEE value chain and let the chips fall where they may.

"With this change in reporting, many people in an organization could be fearful of this *open kimono* approach to information flow throughout the enterprise. Initially, this fear may be justified, since often in the past messengers of bad news have encountered a not-so-pleasant resulting experience.

"It's essential to address this organizational culture issue if it's present. Instead of blaming individuals or functions for the occurrence of problems, organizations benefit when they transition from a finger-pointing approach for blame identification to what could be done as a team to resolve any undesirable situation. With this approach, the effort would give focus on addressing both short-term fixes and long-term desires where there's less chance of the problem or a similar problem reoccurring.

"For such an organizational culture change to occur, the CEO or President needs to be the driving force for the IEE effort. Hence, this person must lead the charge for an IEE implementation."

Jorge continued, "This article figure shows the previous hospital enterprise level in the upper right corner of the picture where the 'Delivery of clinical services' function has been graphically *clicked to* create the functional drill shown. Notice how there are two process-flow-charting swim lanes, where the top swim lane contains selected metrics associated with this function, and the bottom swim lane includes the function's processes. Through this IEE value chain drill-down, the north wing of the building, which we had figuratively indicated addressed scorecards, is structurally brought together with the south side of the building that metaphorically addresses processes associated with the measurements.

"Notice how the top swim lane of this functional drill-down states that measurements should give focus to metrics that address quality, cost, and time, where these three categories are to encompass process efficiency, productivity, and customer satisfaction. Hank, you questioned the value of reporting many measures in your organization, where there's an exclusion of some crucial measurements. You also state that the Lean Six Sigma projects pursued in your company aren't typically showing a baseline for a specific metric that's to be improved, and then how a process improvement effort enhanced the performance of this metric.

"I'll now address both of these issues. First, consider the two truisms, 'what gets measured gets done' and 'tell me how you measure me, and I'll tell you how I will behave.' I heard about a supermarket that incentivized faster check-outs. When check-out clerks scanned an item that did not register, they often just let the check-out-item pass for free, since typing the barcode numbers slowed them up. The IEE system and 30,000-foot-level metric reporting can address both of these business needs head-on so that the most beneficial behaviors occur.

"Next, let's discuss the how-to to make this happen.

"Ron facilitated this effort with Harris Hospital's leadership and other teams to create the framework for our IEE value chain functions and metrics. This IEE value chain included a hierarchical numbering for both functional-areas and their performance-metrics. This systematic numbering approach was necessary so that both specific functional-areas and functional-metrics would have a location identification for EPRS software database access.

"This work also addressed how to track and collect data from our existing databases and to put the information in a format that the EPRS software could use to create up-to-date daily performance measurement information behind Harris's firewall.

"Ron taught our executives and my core team all the ins and outs of implementing IEE. In only a couple of months, Harris Hospital had its basic IEE structure created and, with Ron's periodic assistance, was working an over-time refinement of our IEE value chain. The amount accomplished in a short time was incredible! Ron taught Harris to fish, as opposed to giving us fish.

"Hank, you previously questioned the value of the many metrics that your organization was reporting and how some critical measurements were not getting visibility. Do you now see how with the IEE system, an organization can structurally determine metrics that have organizational-functional alignment and give measurement focus on what should matter to each function?"

Hank responded, "Yes, Jorge, I do! As I noted earlier, we often are asking people what should be measured. There's no real structural alignment of these measurements to the processes that created the metrics. Often what results are metrics that are easy to obtain but aren't necessarily very informative on leading to the most appropriate actions. I see the value of this IEE approach for metric selection; however, if we create metrics using the IEE approach, I suspect that often we'll have no data for many of these selected measurements."

Jorge responded, "Hank, it's good to hear that you appreciate the value of the IEE value-chain approach that Harris used for selecting metrics. Relative to your comment about not having historical data for the measurement, a famous Chinese proverb states: 'The best time to plant a tree was 20 years ago. The second best time is now.' Similarly, from a lack-of-historical-data point of view, there should be an investment of time as soon as possible to determine how to capture data that provide useful information for assessing and improving how well these functional areas with a shortage of data perform.

"There's one other point that I do not want to forget to mention. All IEE value-chain metrics need to have an owner. This person is to have first-hand responsibility for the metric's performance, and completion of any determined process improvement work that's to enhance his or her metric."

Hank then commented, "I'm confident that at Hi-Tech Computers, there'll be a *lot of tree planting opportunities* relative to creating both comprehensive and useful 30,000-foot-level metrics for an IEE value chain. It could take much time and effort to accomplish this objective, but in the long run, this investment of our organization's energy could have many benefits. Also, we need to think about how to address the metrics that need improvement through Lean Six Sigma projects."

Jorge then said, "Hank, great to hear that you appreciate the importance of asking for functional performance metrics that are good to monitor, whether data are currently available or not. Let's now give some thought to Lean and Lean Six Sigma project metrics.

"Ron has emphasized, over and over again, the importance of determining the best metric or metrics to enhance from any project's improvement effort. Another thing Ron said that stuck with me was when he asked, 'If you were the CEO, wouldn't you like to see, in an easy graphical format, that the output of a process showed actual statistical improvement through a project process-enhancement effort?' This self-assessment question made sense to me and led to a resounding *yes*. Even though Janice might not be asking for this particular graphic, I'm confident that this pictorial demonstration would be appreciated and asked for in the future – which is a good thing.

"A 30,000-foot-level chart provides the vehicle for demonstrating process enhancement. It has been my experience that often, people have difficulty determining a process-output response to track as part of an effort to improve a process defined in a Lean Six Sigma problem statement. If no metric is apparent for a Lean Six Sigma Project improvement effort, one could question the value of the project. This project-metric-need statement does not mean that every project must have a specific metric to enhance, but most projects should. A just-do-it project may be necessary to the business financials where it may not be possible to determine a particular 30,000-foot-level metric to track from a baseline and process improvement point of view, but this should be an exceptional situation.

"In addition to Lean Six Sigma projects having an IEE value-chain metric to improve, each project metric needs an owner. For strategic defined process improvement projects, this value-chain metric owner should be periodically reporting to his or her management the status of the 30,000-foot-level performance-metric enhancement work and associated process improvement efforts.

"In IEE, functional processes with their enhancements should be documented in the IEE value chain. This document can take the form of flowcharts or a value-stream map with *clickable drill-downs*, PDF documents, and/or web page links.

Again, the IEE value chain with appropriate software can provide a convenient vehicle for addressing the Ys as a function of Xs throughout an organization so that all information is current and readily available through the *click of a mouse.*"

Hank then said, "Jorge, this is making sense to me."

Jorge responded, "Great to hear, Hank. Let's now progress to the determination of strategic defined process improvement projects that'll help the business as a whole.

"In the next figure of the 'Positive Metrics Poor Business Performance' article, the upper right corner of the graphic shows a representation of a *mouse click* on the Enterprise Process Management (EPM) functional in the Hospital Enterprise IEE value chain" (See Figure 7.11).

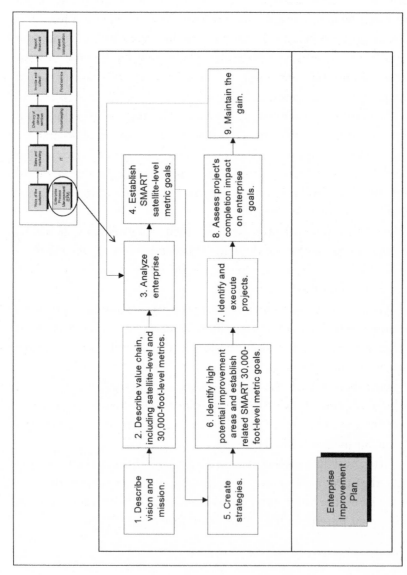

Figure 7.11: Enterprise Process Management Functional Drill Down

Jorge continued, "In this figure, the top swim lane shows the 9-step IEE business management system. An enterprise improvement plan (EIP) is in the bottom swim lane. I'll again discuss the 9-step IEE system first and EIP later.

"If you recall, we previously discussed these 9-steps using my IEE cheat sheet during our golfing round when making a comparison of IEE to Zack's balanced scorecard. I'll now speak to these 9-steps again. There'll be some redundancies in my description; however, understanding these steps is critical to benefiting from the IEE system. Explanation redundancy can be a good thing.

"**Step 1** of the IEE system in the top swim lane is the vision and mission of the organization, which should be relatively consistent over time. The remaining IEE 8 steps shown are to be in alignment with step 1.

"In **step 2,** an IEE value chain describes what an organization does and how it measures what's done, providing the ability for predictive performance metrics KPI statements. I hope that you now feel comfortable from our past conversation with what the IEE value chain fundamentally does."

Hank responded, "Yes, Jorge, I'm catching onto the basics. Now I'm looking forward to increasing my understanding of the details. Redundancy is a good thing for the grey matter between my ears. I'll share with you this time around some of the thoughts that are going through my head."

Jorge continued, "Great to hear, Hank. I'll now continue my walk through the 9-steps. Yes, jump in when you would like to discuss any topic in more depth."

Hank responded, "I sure will. I want to get all the details about IEE that I can. It's too bad that Wayne and Zack are missing this learning experience that I'm having. That's just their loss."

Jorge then said, "Yes, too bad Wayne and Zack aren't here. I know that they would benefit a lot from applying what we're discussing in both of their organizations. But ...moving on.

"The enterprise analytics used in **step 3** of the IEE governance system includes, among other things, a structured approach for collective assessing *Voice of the Customer (VOC), business competition, the theory of* *constraints (TOC), and business innovation thoughts.* This step considers all critical aspects of evaluating the enterprise as a whole, in addition to the current performance of 30,000-foot-level metrics throughout the organization, as reported in step 2's IEE value chain.

"This analysis can then lead to the creation of reasonable SMART financial improvement objectives in **step 4**, where an IEE definition for the SMART acronym is specific, measurable, actionable, relevant, and time-based. Step 5 creates from these financial objectives organizational-targeted strategies."

Hank interrupted, saying, "You just said that there should be an alignment of targeted strategies with the financial goals, after a structured IEE value chain metrics and enterprise analysis. The creation of our strategic directional statements originates from an annual two-day executive retreat. I'm not sure how much-structured data analyses went into creating these statements.

"Results from our high-level meetings have often led to hard-to-get-your-arms-around statements that can result in many differences in opinion on the specifics of how-to-interpret-and-implement details. I would think that, in Zack's organization, there would be a focus on the use of the balanced scorecard to implement these strategies, which incidentally can also change from year to year because of leadership changes and other reasons."

Jorge responded, "Yes, Hank. I understand and agree with your points. In the IEE 9-step system, **step 5** gives focus to targeted strategic statements rather than statements like 'expanding production capacity.' An IEE strategic statement may focus on reducing costs to improve profits, which results in specific action to decrease non-conformance rates or reworks. This particular reduction in defective rates would be an example of the identification of performance metric improvement efforts in **step 6** with an associated SMART objective."

Hank interjected, "Jorge, this makes so much more sense than what we're now doing in our organization. I like the IEE 9-step system more and more.

"As part of our Lean deployment, we're using hoshin kanri. The hoshin kanri method is to ensure that the strategic goals of a company drive progress and action at every level within the company. The X-Matrix that we created as part of hoshin kanri took much effort and is so complicated. I'm not sure what value our X-Matrix provides relative to positively impacting the bottom-line.

"I like how in step 2 of the 9-step system, an IEE value chain provides a detailed description of what's done and the measurement of functions throughout the enterprise. This fundamental basic structure won't change over time, unlike what leadership may have been stating each year as our strategic goals, which are often different from those of the previous year. I also like how targeted strategies in step 5 are in alignment with the financial needs in step 4, and there's structured high-level analytics occurring before the determination of business-financial goals, targeted strategies, and performance metrics that are to be improved.

Jorge then said, "Great to hear, Hank! We're on the same page! Glad that you see the benefits of the overall IEE system. I previously mentioned this but want to reiterate that the metric identified in Step 6 to improve through a project needs to have an owner.

"From a strategic improvement need, which is in alignment with the overall organization's financials, the measurement's owner will be asking for the timely completion of his or her improvement projects that positively impact the performance of one or more metrics. Why? Owners of these strategic metric improvement needs will be regularly reporting in the IEE system to their management on the status of the performance-measurement that they're to be improving and on associated process improvement efforts. With IEE, owners are creating and using IEE performance metric reports and methodologies as tools to do their job. These same charts also double as reports to management as a bonus. There was no *wasted time* creating a special presentation."

Hank then commented, "Jorge, this IEE point is priceless! With the group that's working Six Sigma projects, the amount of saving is the focus of their projects, which should be relevant to leadership. However, what I've noted to occur is that when there's training scheduled for next week, people scurry around trying to identify projects for participants to work on during their Six Sigma training.

"Also, after people complete their training, it typically takes a very long time for project completion, if that happens at all. The main driver for project completion seems to come from the participant. Someone from the class may simply have a strong desire to complete his or her project so that there is a symbolic Lean Six Sigma Green Belt or Black Belt stamp placed on their forehead for a resume's benefit.

"This driving force for completing a process improvement project is in stark contrast with the desire to enhance a performance metric response that's important to the business as a whole, where the metric owner is seeking to complete the process improvement effort in a timely fashion."

Jorge responded, "Hank, this is a significant point! Ron stated that he believes that the reason past process improvement deployments of all sorts haven't been, in general, long-lasting is that there was not a structured integration of these deployments with how the business is managed and run. IEE fulfills this formal integration need; however, to accomplish this assimilation, some traditional business management methodologies need to be undertaken differently.

"Hank, you mentioned earlier that when there're many metric goals throughout an organization, the amount of effort to address all these objectives, from a business process improvement perspective, is overwhelming!"

Hank responded, "I sure did. The IEE approach is looking great, but this problem is still on my mind."

Jorge then said, "I'll next describe how the IEE system addresses your *which metrics to improve dilemma*. However, in addition to giving focus on which metrics to improve, leadership should provide attention to several concepts described in a couple of books.

"Simon Sinek discusses in his book, *The Infinite Game*, (Sinek 2019) the importance of creating organizational actions that are consistent with its *just cause* for being in business and also the identification of a worthy rival.

"Jim Collins, in his book *Good to Great*, (Collins 2001) applies an ancient Greek parable's Hedgehog Concept, which stated, 'The fox knows many things, but the hedgehog knows one big thing.' Jim Collins used this concept as a metaphor for business to identify the intersection of three circles that are important for business:

1. What are you deeply passionate about?
2. At what can you be the best in the world?
3. What best drives your economic or resource engine?

"An enterprise improvement plan (EIP) gives focus to addressing process-output metrics that'll be beneficial to the organization's overall finances. However, we must not lose sight to give emphasis, at the same time, to other directional considerations such as those described in these two books.

"Because of this, before creating an EIP, leadership should obtain a consensus response for the questions:

- What is the *just cause* that our business addresses?
- Who is a worthy business rival?
- What is our organization deeply passionate about?
- At what can our business be the best in the world?
- What best drives our business economic or resource engine?

"The answer to these questions can provide important directional insight when creating an EIP."

Hank responded, "This makes sense. Our direction needs to be more than just numbers."

Jorge replied, "I need to point out that Harris created the EPM function that's shown in the figure, as Ron suggested. I'm leading this Harris EPM IEE function. EPM is much more than a Process Improvement Department. The EPM function is to provide assistance and guidance to the overall management of our business as a whole.

"Moving on. With the IEE system, the establishment of overall organizational business goals is from a big picture perspective. The next figure in the 'Positive Metrics Poor Business Performance' article explains how to address this big-picture objective (See Figure 7.12).

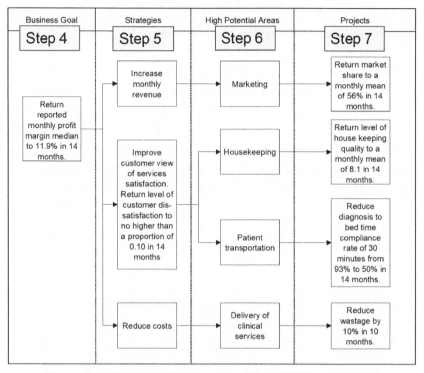

Figure 7.12: Enterprise Improvement Plan (EIP) for a Hospital

"If you recall from the 9-step IEE system, the first step is vision and mission; the second step is the organization's IEE value chain, which describes what the organization does and how it measures what's done. The third step involves analyzing the enterprise. The fourth step uses a total-system-of-processes perspective in the creation of realistic financial goals. This figure's four-column graphic summarizes actions for steps 4 through 7 for an organization's big-picture improvement effort. In IEE, the reference to this collective description of 30,000-foot-level performance metric and process improvement work is the organization's enterprise improvement plan (EIP).

"I'll now provide more information about each EIP column from left to right. The furthest column on the left offers an agreed-to mean or median monthly-reported financial target objective, with an associated achievement time frame.

"Before beginning, I need to provide some background information for this illustrative example. Consider that this hospital had a decline in revenue since a competing facility opened its doors. Because of this occurrence and the associated financial impact, the set monetary goal was a profit level enhancement to a level consistent with what existed before the competitor moved into town. Because of this hospital's underlying situation, the created EIP's specific, measurable, actionable, relavant, and time-based (SMART) business goal in the left-most column was determined to be 'Return reported monthly profit margin median to 11.9% in 14 months.'

"It's important to note that this financial target is stated as a median or mean monthly monetary value, not a particular value next month, quarter, or year. A mean or median goal for the financials should lead to an overall process improvement mindset, where many processes may need to be targeted for improvement to achieve this enterprise objective. This goal-setting-approach is in contrast to the common goal-setting practice of meeting a specific financial number for next month or next quarter, which can result in behaviors that don't have a long-lasting positive impact on the financials and organization as a whole. The associated time frame for the mean or median financial target achievement should be aggressive but not unrealistic. SmarterSolutions.com has an article that highlights the importance of setting a median or mean monthly financial goal, as opposed to the common-place goal-setting practice of meeting a particular financial number at the end of a quarter or month (Reference Appendix A, Web page 5).

"The second from the left column is strategies, while the third column from the left is high potential areas, where, again, each area for these strategically identified business improvement metrics is to have an owner. The final column, which is on the right, is a metric description of the expectations from the identified improvement projects to undertake.

"Note how each of these improvement project statements in the right-most column is specified relative to a futuristic process output response for a 30,000-foot-level metric. To elaborate more on this point, look at the comment to describe the last project listed in this right-most column. The statement for this project is 'Reduce wastage by 10% in 10 months.' Keep this project and its goal in mind, since this article will elaborate more on this particular process-output performance.

"It's essential to highlight how there's an alignment of process improvement projects on the right side of the figure with business metrics that are to be enhanced, as shown in the left column. Monitoring through 30,000-foot-level reporting in the organization's IEE value chain provides an assessment of how improvement projects are progressing against their stated output measurement objectives.

"For process-improvement projects, it's desired that an output response transitions to an enhanced performance level that's consistent with the desired target, both from a magnitude of process-output-response enhancement and a time-line perspective.

"Another point worth highlighting is that focus often rests with enhancing operational processes when organizations undertake a process-improvement deployment. However, if an organization has excess available production capacity, focus on marketing and sales might be the areas that would provide the most bang for the buck relative to the execution of improvement efforts that provide the most financial benefits to the big picture.

"Still another point to highlight is that IEE EPRS software can provide the status of improvement projects to anyone who has authorization, at any point in time."

Hank then anxiously responded, "Jorge, think I'm getting it! The IEE value chain can provide up-to-date metrics from a process-output point of view. You used EPRS software so that these metrics would be automatically updated and would take minimal resources for their maintenance.

"An organization can then basically examine the big picture through steps 4-7 to determine what metrics should be improved so that the enterprise as a whole may benefit through execution of improvement projects, as noted in **step 7**. The IEE system's EIP methodology addresses the goal-setting and number of metrics that are to be enhanced issue that I had. The way I see this is that not every function and its metrics will need improvement from a strategic perspective. I assume that it would still be okay for a manager to improve a particular 30,000-foot-level metric in the area that he or she is responsible for, where this high-level's measurement-reporting improvement need isn't strategic. This effort would not fall under the spotlight like EIP projects, but this process improvement effort could still be an excellent thing to undertake for the business as a whole."

Jorge responded, "Right on, Hank. Truly improving a 30,000-foot-level metric can take much-concentrated effort by teams. When there are so many metric goals throughout an organization, there is not, in all honesty, typically enough bandwidth to provide adequate process improvement efforts to all these measurements. With the IEE approach, there's much upfront investigation when selecting the measurements to undertake so that the big picture benefits. Then, the required resources and right people are assigned the task of enhancing the metric. Your second point is also important: Not all undertaken improvement projects need to be strategic. An owner of a 30,000-foot-level metric may want to enhance performance in his or her area. This improvement effort is great as long as the enhancement of this metric does not negatively impact another important 30,000-foot-level response at the same time. An example of potential metric conflict is improving on-time delivery at the expense of reducing the level of product quality. In IEE, this type of non-strategic process improvement effort is called a business process improvement event (BPIE)."

Hank then responded, "This is good to hear. I like how IEE-system step 2 describes what an organization does and how it measures what's done. I also like Step 5, where created strategies lead to enhancing specific metrics that have whole-enterprise benefit through execution of steps 6 and 7. This system addresses my issue of the number of measurements that are to be improved as well!"

Hank then interjected, "With Six Sigma, the focus is to undertake projects that have hard savings. Six Sigma process improvement efforts typically do not count organizational benefits for improving top-line revenues as part of the program. If someone in a Six Sigma deployment were to increase business revenue, he or she would probably not get any so-called Six Sigma project credit for the effort, since there was no reduction in either headcount or other expenses."

Jorge responded, "Yes, Hank, this is an excellent point. I did not mention this earlier, but I did have a brief conversation with Wayne over the phone the other day when he called about our next golf outing.

"Wayne started venting about his Lean Six Sigma deployment issues. One thing he talked about was the emergence of all sorts of financial benefits quandaries. For example, Wonder-Chem has a specialty chemical division. Wayne was coaching someone who said that there was only a $3,000 credit for her project's value. He then stated that this was not much savings for a Lean Six Sigma project.

"She said, 'Well, the project is worth a lot more than that to the whole site.' Her manufacturing site produces many different specialty-chemical products. She's working on improving the process to enhance the capacity for creating more of a particular chemical that's a component of all the final-products that the facility produces. She then explained that the other products aren't meeting their customer demands because of the lack of availability of the chemical component that she's working to increase. Wayne said that this is crazy.

"We then discussed the situation. I said that the project's value should consider the theory of constraints (TOC) concepts. This project is undertaking a bottleneck for the entire facility's production! Making a minor enhancement to the capacity of the product component she's working on could end up worth millions to the bottom-line of the organization because of an increase in the total volume of products shipped from the facility!"

Hank responded, "We've situations precisely like what you described was impacting Wayne's project selection and process improvement efforts. Also, what often happens with both Lean and Lean Six Sigma deployments is on the other side of the spectrum in that process improvement efforts may have local benefits but aren't benefiting the big picture.

"I like how IEE gives a strategic focus to improving 30,000-foot-level metrics that benefit the business as a whole and also does not get involved in the hard versus soft savings discussions and other related project cost-benefit issues and politics."

Jorge responded, "Hank, it's great to hear that you see how the IEE system could benefit your organization!"

Jorge continued, "Let's next discuss Step 7. The focus in IEE is to improve 30,000-foot-level reported metrics, not the use of specific tools. Hence, one should note that step 7 has the objective of identification and execution of projects and does not prescribe the use of any particular tools or methodologies to achieve a metric's enhancement.

"An improvement project execution could follow a Lean Six Sigma IEE Define, Measure, Analyze, Improve, and Control (DMAIC) improvement process roadmap. For this approach, a detailed IEE project execution roadmap can be a guide for the utilization of the most appropriate tools and methods at the right time so that there's an enhancement in the project's high-level performance-metric response. The critical result is that the targeted 30,000-foot-level reported metric shows a demonstrated improvement so that the business enterprise, as a whole, benefits. Because of this overall metric-enhancement desire, a kaizen event, plan-do-check-act (PDCA) cycle, or another methodology is an alternative to executing an IEE DMAIC roadmap.

"Before I forget it, Ron also talked about the objectives and key results (OKR) methodology that some organizations are using. OKR is a framework for defining and tracking objectives and their outcomes (Grove 1983). An EIP can be used to determine what OKRs for an organization to undertake so that the big-picture benefits. Also, IEE provides the means to track and report the success of OKR undertakings at the 30,000-foot-level."

Hank responded, "Makes sense to me. I heard about OKRs, but we've not used the methodology."

Jorge continued, "However, one thing that should be consistent among the various improvement methodologies is providing a place for the location of new process documentation so that this information can be easily found by all who have authorization. EPRS software provides this function in the IEE value chain, where, again, process procedures are in alignment with their 30,000-foot-level process-output responses."

Hank responded, "Jorge, it makes so much sense to give focus to improving 30,000-foot-level metrics that benefit the business as a whole.

"As noted earlier, in our company, there're both Lean zealots and Six Sigma evangelists. Each process-improvement-philosophy group pushes for the usage of tools in its particular toolbox.

"What I'm noting is that the IEE approach is very different from what I've seen emerging from our Lean Six Sigma group. In our organization, Lean Six Sigma presentations give focus to the demonstration of tool usage, as an integral part of someone's Green or Black Belt certification process. I have also noted that those who do complete a Lean Six Sigma project often do not complete another project and either forget or never use the tools again. It seems that our Lean Six Sigma deployment has evolved into the simple teaching of a bunch of tools to people. Besides, the taught structured-process-improvement methodologies are often never used again outside of the training or project work for a certification project."

Jorge then said, "Hank, again, it's great to hear that you appreciate the benefits of the IEE methodology. It seems that we agree that past organizational process improvement deployments are often giving focus to functional silos without a structural alignment to benefit the organization's big picture.

"To illustrate this point from another angle, Ron used a refinishing-furniture analogy. In this illustration, Ron said to consider someone who wants to undertake a cabinet refurbishing task. The person making this effort could expend a lot of effort sanding a leg of the furniture, which, after completion, looks excellent. Next, a drawer handle could be polished to look beautiful. Sanding of the right side of the furniture could result in an exceptional finish. After all this effort, one might then step back to look at the refurbished cabinet as a whole and conclude that the furniture's overall appearance does not look good.

"In an analogous situation, the described furniture refinishing task might equate to process-improvement-efforts for an organization. The sanding of a leg might be an analogy to a kaizen event. A business parallel event to the polishing of a drawer handle could be executing a Lean Six Sigma project. At the same time, the sanding of the furniture's right side could equate to the execution of a PDCA cycle. Similar to the refinishing illustration, in business, much effort executing silo improvement efforts can result in little or no improvement to the organization's big picture financials.

"Let's rethink the furniture refinishing illustration so that the results from work are better. A superior approach for enhancing the look of a piece of furniture would be to gradually improve the overall appearance of the furniture in a step-by-step fashion.

"To use this strategy, one could start with sanding the entire piece of furniture with rough, 80 grit sandpaper. After this effort, the furniture surface would be coarse but consistent. With this refinishing process, one would then repeat the sanding of the furniture with finer grit 120 sandpaper, followed by even finer 180, then 240, and then 320 grit sandpaper until achieving the desired sanding finish. In this process, there would also be the execution of other tasks, such as polishing the handle, staining, and then varnishing the surface at the appropriate times. With this process for enhancing the appearance of the furniture, the cabinet will gradually look better and better over time.

"The IEE system offers a system analogous to refinishing furniture. In this analogy, IEE offers a step-by-step process improvement methodology aligned to an over-time big picture benefit."

Jorge could see the expression of approval on Hank's face.

Hank then spoke, saying, "Jorge, I'll use an idiom that I'm not sure younger folks will understand: I sound like a broken record when I state again that this IEE approach looks excellent!

"In the Lean Six Sigma efforts elsewhere in our company, I've noted a couple of other fundamental shortcomings of this process improvement deployment methodology.

"One issue is that often end-of-project statements are anecdotal and do not show any 30,000-foot-level type chart that describes how a vital process output response was enhanced.

"Another issue is the final step in the DMAIC project execution roadmap, which is *C* or 'Control.' Some projects have made processes mistake-proof, which is excellent; however, this is not always possible. Many DMAIC projects suggest, to establish control, that someone later returns to the process-enhancement area to make sure that people are continuing to follow the new process steps. In all honesty, this manual check to make sure everybody is pursuing a new process is expensive and not practical. How does IEE address these issues?"

Jorge responded, "Hank, you made two good points. I'll address one at a time.

"Your first inquiry provides a great lead-in to step 8 of the IEE 9-step system, which is 'Assess project's completion impact on enterprise goals.' From the article's enterprise improvement plan (EIP), which we discussed earlier, I highlighted the last-listed project in the column on the right, which was 'Reduce wastage by 10% in 10 months.'

"The next figure in this article (See Figure 7.13) illustrates a 30,000-foot-level metric transitioning to an enhanced level of performance. In this chart, the last three data points after the process-staged values are from the new process, which indicates a staged, demonstrated improvement in the metric's performance. The 4.3% statement below the report's charting provides an estimate for how the new process is performing.

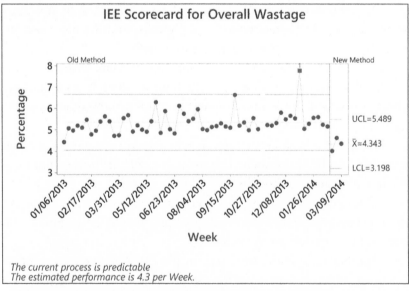

Figure 7.13: Demonstrating percentage of wastage reduction from process improvement efforts

"The earlier 30,000-foot-level introductory chart in this article was a baseline report for this process before the process change occurred. An estimation statement of process performance at this initial point in time was 5.305%. The current after process change response of 4.3%, when compared to the before-change baseline value of 5.305%, indicates achievement of the EIP 10% reduction objective.

"Ron also told me that the data for this 30,000-foot-level chart illustration is from an actual process response and improvement situation in a company. Besides, Ron said that, from an analysis of raw data from before and after the process change, a statistical hypothesis test indicated that a significant reduction in the process's waste percentage occurred between these two-time intervals.

"Upon project completion, a financial benefit can also be stated, if appropriate. When creating this financial summary, Ron suggests recording all potential economic impacts in a spreadsheet, with the inclusion of specific details for each number entered into the spreadsheet. Ron likes to include in this project-benefit-financial-summary spreadsheet estimates for not only hard and soft savings but also any indirect revenue benefits. An example of this situation would be the chemical bottle-neck illustration discussed earlier, which could more accurately reflect the true organizational benefit from eliminating or reducing the bottle-neck impact from a manufactured component, which was in short supply. Travel costs to vendors or elsewhere for the issue should also be included, along with the cost associated with any employee time dedicated to addressing the problem. It's important to keep in mind that one can use sampling techniques to make these estimations. This spreadsheet can be used to discuss the benefits of an improvement project from various angles."

Hank responded, "I'm liking this IEE approach for project selection and demonstrating process improvement. Don't forget my second question relative to the control aspect of the DMAIC roadmap."

Jorge then said, "I'd not forgotten, but your reminder is an excellent lead-in to Step 9 of the IEE system, which is 'Maintain the gain.'

"Keeping a process functioning using a different methodology than what the operational folks are accustomed to using can be very difficult.

There's a tendency for employees to return to using old practices when the process-improvement spotlight is no longer in their area. Also, how are agreed-to process execution methods, in general, to be explained to new employees? Simple word-of-mouth descriptions from current employees to new hires is not adequate and typically leads to inconsistencies in process execution. This challenge isn't unique to a Lean Six Sigma program."

Hank interjected, "I'm in 100% agreement with your point, Jorge! I'm anxious to hear how IEE addresses this challenge."

Jorge continued, "Good to see we're on the same page with the prevalence of this general process management and control issue.

"With IEE, there's another powerful benefit of including EPRS software functions in an IEE implementation.

"As mentioned earlier, the documentation details for future work is to reside in an organization's IEE value chain. The onboard training for new employees could reference a particular area of the IEE value chain that describes what they're to do using current processes, which they can later reference. Similarly, the training for employees transferred to a new role could refer to the section of the IEE value chain appropriate for their new position's process execution. The inclusion of video and website links in this overall documentation methodology can be very beneficial.

"This referencing could also be a reminder, not unlike an airline pilot's departure checklist. Besides, there could be linkage in the IEE value chain to procedural information for general process-execution training, either formal or informal.

"I want to reiterate a significant point. With EPRS software, anyone who has authorization can drill-down for all documented process details and current 30,000-foot-level metrics. This assessment can occur 24/7 by anyone who has secure behind-the-firewall access to an organization's IEE value chain, including the CEO and other organizational leaders.

"Let's now return to addressing the question of how-to-maintain the gain from procedural enhancements that were a result of process-improvement efforts. With an EPRS-type software inclusion in an IEE implementation, the gain and control challenge previously discussed can be addressed from two aspects.

"First, all process improvements need to be documented in the organization's IEE value chain, where process executions are easily found and understood. The process owner and users of the process need to agree to the necessary procedures and continually reference the documentation, where there're agreed-to refinements over time.

"The second area of control is the frequent, perhaps daily, monitoring of the process's output 30,000-foot-level metric, which was improved. This process-output-response viewing should be made with appropriate frequency by the process owner and others involved in the process. The 30,000-foot-level metric is a Y-type process-output response, not an X-type input to the process; hence, a more timely identification than daily assessment may not be possible to detect any small transition toward an undesirable response. However, this metric reporting can still provide, from a high-level perspective, the monitoring and controlling of a process, which involves no additional *checking the process* resources and associated expense."

Jorge then asked, "Hank, did this answer your question?"

Hank responded, "Jorge, you hit the nail on the head!"

Jorge then said, "I want to make one final point relative to the 9-step IEE system. Notice how Step 9 loops back to Step 3. This looping back is very important in that the executing of the IEE system should be a dynamic event and provide a plan-do-check-act (PDCA) type implementation *for the enterprise as a whole.*

"The IEE system can also provide the framework for Senge's learning organization creation, Malcolm Baldrige's criteria achievement, ISO 9001 certification, on-site customer audits, and government-mandated business disclosure practices, which can change over time."

Hank then said, "Jorge, wow! I like this overall IEE learning-organization description. Also, I'd not thought about this before you mentioned it, but our customers require ISO 9001 certification. When ISO 9001 audits occur, it seems to me that a lot of special preparation work occurs in advance of the auditors' arrival. It sure would be great if we could just walk auditors through an IEE system when they arrive. I would think that we could also do something similar to that for on-site audits by our customers. I'll need to talk to our Quality department to get their thoughts about this."

Hank then commented, "Jorge, it just occurred to me that our company looked into the Malcolm Baldrige Award criteria a few years ago. We decided to pass. It seemed that the effort for this undertaking would involve much work, and we would have to install many systems that we did not have in place."

Jorge replied, "I consider that the Baldrige criteria are not unlike an essay college test question. There's no one correct response to an essay question. That is, there is no correct prescriptive response. The college test evaluator needs to assess a student's question response relative to what the instructor considers an ideal answer. Similarly, Baldrige Award achievement and ISO 9001 certification, for that matter, are not prescriptive; hence, there's no one approach for award achievement and ISO 9001 certification.

"It seems to me that after implementing an IEE system, an organization could refer to aspects of its IEE system to address each aspect that's addressed by both the Baldrige and ISO 9001 criteria."

Hank then said, "Jorge, that's an excellent thought and a benefit of IEE. Still, another advantage of an IEE system occurred to me. Your comment relative to government-mandated business disclosure practices caught my attention. Hi-Tech Computers and other companies are continually confronting both old and new accounting and different rules that our organizations must conform to. Let's step back and consider the reasons for instituting these government mandates. I think that one reason is that one or more companies in the past tried to do whatever it took to make things appear better than they were to consumers and/or investors.

"To me, it seems that an IEE implementation is in alignment with the underlying desired objectives of these governmental requirements. The IEE system could lead, in time, to the avoidance of organizations' playing games with the numbers to make things appear better than they are. Companies will still need to address all the required governmental forms, but, in spirit, if a company follows the IEE methodology, it should be in basic alignment with the government body's desires."

Jorge then responded, "Wow, I'm impressed! Excellent observations and comments!

"There's one more figure in the 'Positive Metrics Poor Business Performance' article that I would now like to discuss (See Figure 7.14).

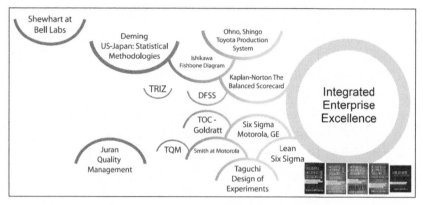

Figure 7.14: Evolution to the IEE Business Management System

"The purpose of this figure is to show a conceptual evolution of the IEE system with a set of how-to descriptive books shown on the right side of the image. The left side of the image portrays a few of the concepts from which IEE evolved.

"This portion of the graphic includes some techniques that we've discussed previously, such as Deming's statistical techniques, TQM, the balanced scorecard, Lean Six Sigma, and TOC. However, included and structurally used in IEE, among other tools, are also tools such as fishbone diagram, design of experiments (DOE), and TRIZ innovation techniques.

"Note also how there's even an inclusion of the Toyota Production System (TPS) in this graphic. The IEE system includes TPS methodologies within its architecture. TPS is a methodology often considered a benchmark for organizations, which many companies have attempted to emulate. Ron explained that he believes that TPS provides some great organizational benefits, but he thinks that even TPS has some improvement opportunities offered by IEE."

Hank then said, "This article and your comments have described how IEE is a very encompassing methodology. My next question is, what type of buy-in issues did your IEE implementation encounter?"

Jorge responded, "Hank, great question. I noticed that you did not ask if there were any implementation buy-in issues with our IEE implementation. You've been around long enough to realize that, with any change deployment effort, there'll be challenges getting everyone on board.

"What we did that minimized buy-in resistance was getting Janice on-board at the front end of IEE's initiation. This initial CEO involvement was essential. Perhaps we were lucky, but Janice was open-minded and understood that the IEE methodology was not something that could be delegated to someone else to *lead the charge* for an organization-wide IEE implementation. She realized that she would need not only to lead the effort but to view data and metrics differently.

"She also understood that merely setting monthly or quarterly financial goals as we've been doing in the past does lead to the execution of good practices and the formulation of processes that provide good long-lasting enhanced financial and customer-satisfaction results.

"I've been working with Ron on coaching Janice to ask the right questions of her subordinates that encourage the application of concepts in the IEE 9-step system. In casual conversations with Janice, I discovered she'd been suppressing much frustration; she felt that she did not know what was occurring in the organization and did not know what to do about this knowledge gap. Before IEE, she believed much waste was prevalent in her organization but did not know how to quantify and address the problem. Now Janice believes she has a much better handle on things.

"Janice liked the one-minute video that she'd viewed earlier and described issues with all five *Effective Management Attributes* listed on Page 2 of the 'Positive Metrics Poor Business Performance' Article. She was very open to implementing IEE, which was a no-nonsense approach, as she put it, that addressed all the article-listed management desired characteristics.

"Well, we've now completed skimming all the high points of the 'Positive Metrics Poor Business Performance' article. I hope that you'll read the entire article in detail and take some notes for future discussions. Make sense? Agreed?"

"Will do," Hank responded.

Hank was excited. He saw the possibilities for the IEE methodology in his company. The IEE system would allow him to restructure the implementation of his Lean program to focus on bottom-line issues. He could use this approach to attack the loss of market share! After all, that was a Y performance metric output that would surely be important as part of an organizational enterprise improvement plan (EIP). It would be interesting to view data that we had for metrics using a 30,000-foot-level format. Surely we would be able to identify some Xs that we could tackle to improve market share.

Jorge then said, "I just thought of something. The web page SmarterSolutions.com/iee-scorecard-provides illustrations of converting eight actual scorecard reports to 30,000-foot-level reporting, including the four scorecards discussed in this article. From this write-up, one can readily see how 30,000-foot-level reporting provides more useful process insight than a traditional performance reporting format."

The waiter interrupted Jorge's class and placed the bill on the table. Hank quickly grabbed it again. "I'll get this one, Jorge; it's the least I can do for the time you've spent with me today. I know you have a lot of other things going on right now; plus, I need room in my wallet for the rest of the class," Hank stated gratefully.

"Thank you, Hank, but it has been my pleasure. Let's wrap this class up, and we'll talk more on another day, probably our next golf outing. Since you're now an advanced student, you can help me explain IEE and its benefits to our friends," Jorge said jokingly.

8 TURNING POINT

SEPTEMBER

A few days before their September golf date, Jorge called Hank. "I realized that I'd not talked much about the Voice of the Customer or VOC. VOC is critical to everything else you do with IEE. Unless you understand what the customers want or need, you can't tell how they think you're doing. Haven't you been frustrated at times about poor service? Could it be that the provider doesn't know what you want?"

Hank responded, "I sure have. For example, they keep putting these surveys on the golf carts asking for our evaluation of the golf course. It sure seems like they ask the wrong questions. At the bottom of the page, I sometimes write my comments, but nothing changes. I think that it's not too much to ask that they offer a decaffeinated soft drink on the refreshment golf cart. I've mentioned it several times on the form as well as to the person driving the cart."

"Exactly," Jorge responded. "What good are customer surveys if nobody reads them or ever takes action? Important feedback often goes to some front-line employees and never gets to someone who can make a difference. Within IEE, we want to create processes that give us actionable VOC input at the IEE value chain level and use it to help drive our internal improvements."

Hank was excited to be on his way to the golf course to meet the guys. The Monday following his last golf outing with Jorge, he had a conversation with Jorge's IEE consultant, and things were progressing well. His CEO bought into the overall IEE system upfront that same week, following Jorge's buy-in model! Within the next week, there was an EPRS software installation. It's incredible what can be done moving priorities around with IT when the CEO states that something has the highest priority.

Also, his IEE implementation team was now working on building the organization's IEE value chain with the identification of appropriate 30,000-foot-level metrics. There was also an effort to revisit our current strategic plan statements.

Hank was so grateful that Jorge had insisted that his CEO be approached first in a one-on-one discussion. It was imperative to get his CEO's up-front buy-in and agreement that he, as the organization's leader, would also look at and utilize IEE metrics and process improvement methodologies. Hank's CEO immediately saw the benefits of how he could better manage the organization using these techniques and wanted to get started quickly.

Hank reminisced how fortunate it was that his company's leadership weekly team meeting was the day after his CEO meeting and conference call with Ron. Hank's CEO had changed this meeting's agenda to be a high-level description of IEE with the inclusion of a statement that Hi-Tech Computers would be starting the implementation of the IEE system immediately, with a highest-priority level.

Since that initial IEE proclamation kickoff, weekly status and coaching meetings with the CEO had been great! Hank had noticed that already his CEO was asking for performance metrics to be shown differently. Now he was asking for the transition of tables of numbers and red-yellow-green scorecards reports to a 30,000-foot-level format.

After some IEE metric report creation training, the implementation team at Hi-Tech Computers was starting to feel comfortable developing

30,000-foot-level charts on their own, including the automatic reporting, for these high-level process-response metrics.

The IEE metric training that the leadership and management teams received gives focus to the reading and interpretation of these high-level performance-metric reports, not to the details of the report's creation. The biggest issue was getting everyone up to speed relative to having a solid understanding that one should not be reacting to all the ups and downs that will occur from common-cause variation in these reportings. Everyone needed to understand, from a heartfelt perspective, that to improve a common-cause predictive response involves an enhancement of process execution methodologies.

Hank was excited to see how a first-rough-pass creation of the company's IEE value chain occurred so quickly. EPRS software was now providing information for the up-to-date *click of the mouse* leadership reports. It was great to see that Hi-Tech Computers was automatically updating more and more operational 30,000-foot-level metrics every day using EPRS software.

The IEE implementation team had success assigning the job of understanding customer needs to the marketing department. Also, an enterprise improvement plan (EIP) first-pass identified projects in new product development, warehousing, and shipping.

Also, Hank was excited about the specific project of which he was the 30,000-foot-level metric owner. The objective of this project was the reduction of manufacturing cycle time for the company's Mach II product line. As the person who was accountable for this high-level metric in the company's IEE value chain, Hank practically had the entire project's outline completed in a short time because of Jorge's discussion last month. He was also pleased that this model not only tied in nicely with his company's current Lean activities but added a new dimension.

The management team now was beginning to see how the company's Lean philosophy and both Lean and Six Sigma tools fit nicely into the IEE system, not only for improvement projects but for the total enterprise as well.

In his almost ten years with Hi-Tech, this was the first time Hank had seen the connection between the overall business goals, strategies, and planned improvement projects. He felt more confident now than when the company was implementing Lean without the IEE structure. The estimated hard savings from the IEE implementation were expected to be in the millions the first year, which would more than pay for any training, consulting, and software investments. Hank viewed the intangible value from transforming Hi-Tech Computers to an IEE culture as beyond any numbers or words.

As Hank pulled into the parking lot, he saw the others assembled around Jorge's SUV. Jorge was sitting on the back bumper with the hatch open, changing shoes.

"Good morning," Hank called out to the group as he lifted his bag from the trunk of his red convertible.

Jorge and Wayne replied, but Zack seemed preoccupied. Zack had shown up to play golf, but he was having a tough time concentrating. The CEO at Z-Credit Financial had reorganized the company and moved him to VP of operations for a smaller firm they had recently purchased. Zack was especially upset that the CEO had brought in his latest whiz kid to turn things around within Zack's former group. It had all happened over the past two weeks, but Zack was still upset and couldn't make sense of how things had gotten so bad.

"What's wrong, Zack?" Hank asked, not quite expecting the answer he received.

"We had a reorganization. My leadership reassigned me to VP of operations for some little company we just bought. Technically, it was a lateral move, but it sure feels like a demotion. I think our CEO wasn't happy with my performance, so he put me in this company that can't be screwed up any more than it already is. My replacement is a whiz kid from Harvard who used to report to me and is my son's age. I start my new job as soon as *wonder boy* gets back from vacation in two weeks."

"I'm sorry to hear that, Zack," Jorge sympathized.

"This offers you a great opportunity to take a nothing company and turn it around," Wayne offered, in an attempt to lift Zack's spirits.

Zack responded, "How can I turn around a company that's in the dumps when I couldn't run a company that had a solid performance history? I tried to improve things through the balanced scorecard deployment but was not successful. We spent a lot of time working to align and translate strategies into specific actions through the scorecards; however, I'm not sure that our strategies are that great. Our strategy wording is often hard to get our minds around."

Hank was about to jump in to say that he agreed with the point he was making about strategies and tell him all the news about IEE, but before he could get started, Jorge said, "Hey, let's play. We can talk about this later. Right now, I'm going to teach you guys a thing or two about golf."

Sensing Zack's distress, Jorge decided to change the game in an attempt to avoid a total meltdown. At the first tee, Jorge said, "Let's change things today. Let's play a two-person scramble. Each player will hit his shot, and then each team selects the better of their two shots, and both partners play their next stroke from there. We can keep the same teams so that each side has a long-ball hitter and a short-game player. It should be fun for a change. The team with the lowest total score wins. Same bet?"

Everyone agreed, although no one's heart seemed to be in it. The two-paired teams played four holes before anyone mentioned work, a course record. By that time, Zack needed to vent and said, "I don't understand what happened. I was working hard, putting together the balanced scorecard system. However, I had difficulty seeing improvements from the created projects. It seemed like everyone was going in a different direction."

Wayne commiserated, attempting to ease Zack's nerves. "You know, we've been having some success as well, but our Lean Six Sigma deployment hasn't been what I expected. We now have a whole Lean Six Sigma group that's working with some of our management team in a steering committee role. It seems that there're always disagreements and misunderstandings. The Lean Six Sigma group doesn't seem to understand the pressure on the production managers to meet their schedules and quotas. In turn, the production managers are always complaining that the

Lean Six Sigma projects shut their lines down to fix problems that don't affect production. It seems that the only projects we're having success with are the cross-functional ones in which the process owner is truly championing the project."

"That's it!" cried Hank as he missed his tee shot, which went about 60 yards. But he didn't seem to mind the distraction or the lousy shot. "That's one of the key differences between IEE and Lean Six Sigma. With IEE, the people responsible for the process are responsible for improving it. You can't achieve success with a separate group to fix problems. With a simple fix-the-problems approach, there'll be no-long-lasting buy-in. A 30,000-foot-level metric system is a no-nonsense approach for the setting of goals and monitoring to see if these goals are achieved and maintained from an overall process-output perspective."

"When did you become an expert on IEE?" probed Wayne.

"I wasn't, until last month," Hank said sarcastically while pointing his driver at Wayne and Zack. "When you two were too busy working to join us, Jorge explained IEE to me, and a light went on. You boys missed an interesting discussion."

Wayne asked, "Jorge must have said something outstanding to get you off the Lean bandwagon. What did he say?"

"I'll lay it out for you at lunch," Hank responded. "I still have all my notes, and I printed some copies of the other information that we talked about."

Out on the fairway, Hank and Jorge made the easy decision to play Jorge's drive. It was a typical Jorge shot of modest length and a slight fade. But it was on the fairway, and the green was reachable. It was far better than Hank's distracted effort. Hank commented, "I guess that was an outlier on my driver's 30,000-foot-level chart."

Jorge agreed that there probably was a real, special-cause occurrence this time: the distraction during his swing. From their position on the fairway, Jorge hit a decent fairway wood to the front edge of the green, and then Hank hit a magnificent 4 iron to the center of the green. This team stuff has its benefits in a scramble; both thought as they moved on.

Meanwhile, Wayne hit another typical drive, long and straight in the middle of the fairway, making Zack's wild hook of no consequence.

Hank thought briefly, "My maximum distance is better than Wayne's, but his distance and directional variation are less than half of mine. I should benchmark his driving process."

Wayne and Zack both hit their second shots, with short irons, from where Wayne's drive had landed. When they reached the green, they were farther away and putted first. Zack looked over the 18-footer and putted. Zack saw the break, and his read was perfect, but his stroke was a bit strong. His ball rimmed out of the cup and spun about two feet past it.

"Good read, partner—good putt," said Wayne. He had been standing directly behind Zack on line with the hole during his putt. He had not seen the subtle break at the end of the putt, but, armed with knowledge, he stepped up and sweetly stroked the 18-footer into the back of the cup.

"Great putt," exclaimed Zack. "Way to go, partner."

"It was easy once you showed me the line," said Wayne. "How did you know it would break at the end like that?"

Zack was confused, "What do you mean? I just looked at it and could see the break at the end. Also, I could see the grain was against us, so it would be a little slower and break a bit more. All I did was look at it. That's all I ever do."

"Me too," said Wayne, "But I certainly didn't see that little break or the grain." Suddenly it struck him. "You know, I've been having some trouble finding my ball when it's not on the fairway, too. Ellen is right! Maybe I do need to get my eyes checked."

Hank chimed in, "You know, they say that Tiger some time ago was seeing the breaks in the green better after he got that laser eye surgery. It was right before he started that incredible run of victories. I think they can even make corrections for you guys with bifocals."

"Of course," Wayne nodded. "My problem wasn't a bad putter at all. It was a bad read because I couldn't see the subtle changes in the green. Zack, you've made my day. Thanks, partner."

Zack began to feel better and appreciated any affirmation from a golfer of Wayne's caliber. Besides, with Zack's reading and Wayne's putting, they easily won the scramble!

During lunch, Hank elaborated, with help from Jorge and his typed last-golf-outing notes, on the insights he had recently gained from IEE. He explained how Jorge had analyzed some of his data and showed that there was a common-cause problem that should be addressed head-on with an IEE project. Still, more importantly, Jorge showed him how to initiate deployment of the entire IEE 9-step system – quickly. After Hank and Jorge split the bill, they all walked together toward their cars.

Zack asked, "OK, I think I get it, but how does this affect my business?"

Ignoring Zack's question, Wayne interrupted, "Hank, you were making a point about IEE. Could you finish that?"

Jorge was glad to see that his friends were interested. He knew how exciting it could be to understand the power of the IEE system.

"As I was saying," Hank stated proudly, "The success of Lean Six Sigma tends to be through projects selected by a steering committee. This type of project selection sounds good. However, often in deployments, these projects don't have the real backing of the process owner and management. The thing is, these projects often are not only out of alignment with *what* but also *how* they're measured."

Wayne interrupted, "I'll co-sign that. What you're describing is what I've been experiencing!"

Hank continued, "This is not the case in an IEE implementation. Since it's a business management system, it focuses on building upon your IEE value chain with a no-nonsense measurement system that addresses not only *what* but also *how* you report measurements. Also, there's a structured approach with detailed roadmaps that guide you through both an enterprise business system and an improvement project execution. Process owners and management will now give more support to improvement projects since they understand that the completion of these projects is necessary for them to achieve their goals. With IEE, there's an orchestration of projects across functions.

"Our IEE system with EPRS software and appropriate training for management and employees is going to change how they do their jobs. For the first time, I feel that we've control over our business. Well, *business control* may be too strong a phrase, but perhaps not with our EPRS software installation.

"Besides, with the IEE system, we understand where our problems are and have a roadmap to eliminate them. The IEE business management system techniques apply to all areas of the business, from marketing to manufacturing to customer service.

"So, Zack, when you said you inherited a loser, that just makes your opportunities that much greater. You'll be able to make big improvements quickly, and you'll be the hero."

Hank continued, "There are people who do great things with their organizations. The problem is that the gains can't be maintained when the person leaves. Results are dependent on the person. That's why I used to reorganize so often. I was looking for those special supermen or superwomen people. With IEE, getting results becomes ingrained in the system and not in the person. The key is to find executives and managers who'll execute the IEE business strategy. They don't have to be superheroes; after all, there are only so many of those."

As they reached his SUV, Jorge said, "Well, here we are again. We can now put another good day on the golf course in the record book. Tell you what. Now that you're all up to speed on what I've been doing up until last month, I'll treat you to breakfast tomorrow and elaborate on my more recent events."

"Wow, we can hardly wait," Wayne, Zack, and Hank echoed.

9 IMPROVEMENT

BREAKFAST THE NEXT DAY

They all knew what they wanted to order for breakfast the next morning, so Jorge jumped right in.

"As Hank and I described earlier, IEE uses a 9-step methodology to analyze the business as a *system*. When the IEE value chain 30,000-foot-level metric improvement needs *pull* for project creation, it only makes sense that the process owner and management will be interested in project completion."

Jorge then had Wayne and Zack pull out their cell phones, access the SmarterSolutions.com website, and listen to the one-minute video individually, which he had shared with Hank in their previous golf outing.

Jorge then gave each of his friends a copy of the "Positive Metrics Poor Business Performance" article. He then walked Wayne and Zack through the article's figures as he had done previously with Hank. In this discussion, Hank periodically interjected his IEE implementation experiences.

After completing his summary of the article, Jorge said, "Let's now concentrate on enhancing an IEE value chain 30,000-foot-level metric highlighted in an organizational enterprise improvement plan (EIP)." Jorge handed two sheets of paper to each of his friends.

He then told them to look at the first sheet of paper, which describes how an improvement effort could involve either Lean or Six Sigma tools, or both, depending upon the situation (See Figure 9.1).

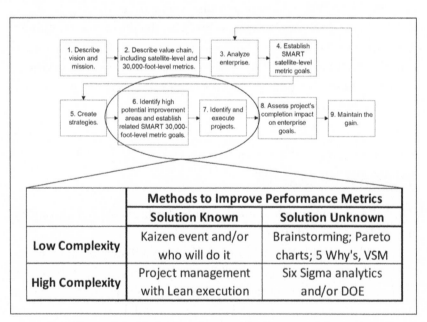

Figure 9.1: Methods to Improve Performance Metrics

Jorge then said, "The graphic on this page presents a basic thought methodology for selecting a process improvement approach for situations that depend upon the condition's complexity and whether a solution is known or not.

"A significant takeaway from this graphic should be that there's not one specific process improvement methodology that's always better than another. What this figure conveys is that one should utilize a method that efficiently and effectively leads to process improvements so that its project 30,000-foot-level metric is enhanced.

"This graphic highlights steps 6 and 7 of the 9-step IEE system with linkage to process improvement methodologies and tools for improving a 30,000-foot-level measurement process-output response.

"The four-quadrant options table shown in this graphic provides process improvement approaches and tools for when a solution is known or not, and whether the expected answer is complex or not.

"From this table, when a solution is known, and its complexity is low, a short-duration team kaizen event may be appropriate, or perhaps someone might just undertake a *just do it* process change. When a basic solution is known, and its implementation is more complex, project management with a Lean execution may be more appropriate.

"If a solution is not known, this table describes a couple of process-improvement methodology alternatives. For a low-complex situation, an approach to enhance a 30,000-foot-level metric may involve brainstorming, Pareto charts, 5 why's, and/or value stream mapping (VSM). If a solution is more complex, Six Sigma analytics and/or design of experiments (DOE) techniques may be beneficial.

"The second sheet of paper that I gave you provides another visual for the utilization of process improvement tools (See Figure 9.2).

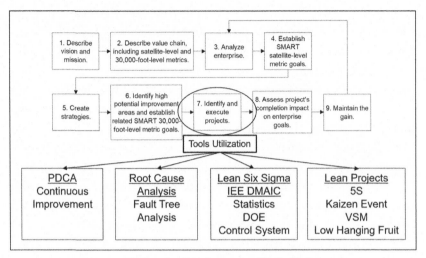

Figure 9.2: Process Improvement Tools Utilization

"The graphic on this second sheet of paper provides a tools-to-use approach for undertaking the execution of step 7 in the 9-step IEE system. These listed implementation alternatives are:

- Plan-do-check-act (PDCA) cycle usage for continuous improvement
- Root-cause investigation using a fault tree analysis approach for the determination of a specific problem cause
- Lean Six Sigma IEE Define, Measure, Analyze, Improve, and Control (DMAIC) roadmap using tools such as statistics, design of experiments (DOE), and a control system.
- Lean projects using tools such as 5S workplace organization, kaizen event, value stream mapping (VSM), or implementation of low-hanging fruit opportunities

"One needs to keep in mind that the thought processes described on these two sheets of the paper apply to both enhancing EIP identified 30,000-foot-level metrics and functional-local metrics which need improvement but are not strategic.

"Reiterating, a primary focus of IEE is to enhance satellite-level and 30,000-foot-level metrics. In IEE, there's no prescribed specific process-improvement methodology to accomplish this objective. The desire is that IEE improvement efforts demonstrate enhancements to 30,000-foot-level metrics in both operational and transactional processes so that the organization's customers and financials benefit. This basic thought process can address both common- and special-cause 30,000-foot-level response situations."

Jorge then asked, "Are you with me?"

Jorge was happy to see three smiling faces and three thumbs-up signs from his friends.

Jorge then said, "Let's move on to the details of using the IEE DMAIC roadmap for process improvement. Hank and I did not get into the how-to aspects of executing an IEE Lean Six Sigma DMAIC project in our previous discussion. I'll do that now.

"The IEE Lean Six Sigma project-execution roadmap has some differences from the DMAIC that you may have seen taught in traditional Lean Six Sigma training.

"Let's again use our phones to access the Internet. In your browser, access SmarterSolutions.com/roadmap. This web page provides *clickable* access to an IEE enhanced DMAIC roadmap (See Figure 9.3).

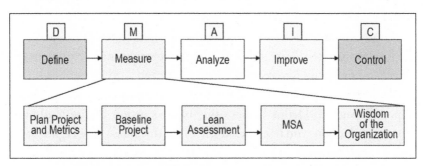

Figure 9.3: IEE DMAIC Project Execution Roadmap
(www.SmarterSolutions.com/roadmap)

"Several books provide execution details for this IEE DMAIC road-map with its high-level and drill-down steps (Reference Appendix A, Web page 16). The sequence of topics in two IEE books follows this roadmap, which structurally integrates Lean and Six Sigma tools, so the most appropriate tool is used at the right time to enhance a process output metric's response. Today we'll only discuss a high-level view of these IEE DMAIC roadmap steps.

"The first thing you'll note from your phone's image is that the 'Measure phase' has five additional drill-down steps. The author of these books initially presented this 'Measure phase' refinement to the DMAIC roadmap in 1999 with the first edition of his book, *Implementing Six Sigma* (Breyfogle 2003). The reason for this 'Measure phase' drill-down addition was to clarify the DMAIC phase where some tools were to be used, according to a GE deployment of Six Sigma.

"For example, the GE model that the author, Breyfogle, experienced in the late 1990s included the tools cause-and-effect diagram, flowchart-ing, and some other brainstorming-type tools in the 'Measure phase.' To Breyfogle, it wouldn't be evident to users of the DMAIC roadmap to include these tools in the DMAIC 'Measure phase;' hence, he created a 'Wisdom of the Organization' drill-down that included these tools.

"Moving on. My thought is that I'll now walk through this IEE DMAIC roadmap and the tasks to consider for each step. Keep in mind that this roadmap lists tools that are appropriate for each phase of the roadmap. Users of the roadmap are to determine which tools are appropriate for their particular process improvement situation. Will this work for you?"

Jorge was happy to see three thumbs-up signs from his friends.

Jorge continued, "Great! Jump in anytime you want to comment on something or would like more details.

"The first IEE DMAIC phase in the SmarterSolutions.com/road-map web page is 'Define.' Select this phase portion of the roadmap. After this selection, you'll see a drill-down for this phase (See Figure 9.4).

"This drill-down and other DMAIC phase drill-downs will simi-larly show a flowchart with a sequence of steps. When following this

IEE DMAIC roadmap, the order for executing steps in a drill-down execution is flexible."

Wayne then commented, "Wow, this website IEE DMAIC road-map *click-through* tool is slick! And, you said books provide execution details for each high-level and drill-down step?"

Jorge responded, "Yep, the books provide not only the how-tos of individual tool usage but also how all the tools hook together for effective execution of an improvement project that enhances a 30,000-foot-level metric.

"In this 'Define phase' drill-down, you'll see the tasks to consider as part of this phase's execution. For example, this drill-down includes for a project its problem statement, project charter, selection of the team, Voice of the Customer (VOC), and cost of doing nothing differently (CODND). You'll also see a description of how there's to be a demonstrated linkage of the project's 30,000-foot-level metric to a satellite-level metric enhancement objective. It's important to remember that the reporting of IEE satellite-level and 30,000-foot-level metrics are similar, where a satellite-level reporting is for financial measurement such as monthly profit. In IEE, an enterprise improvement plan (EIP) graphic shows the linkage of strategic-performance-metric-improvement projects to overall business needs."

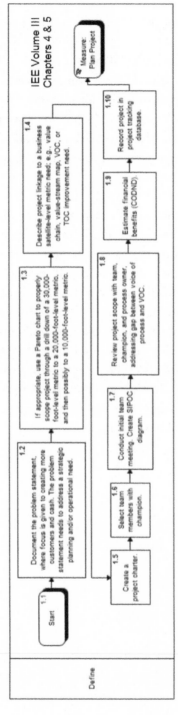

Figure 9.4: IEE DMAIC Roadmap – Define Phase

Hank then said, "Jorge, we were discussing Voice of the Customer earlier and how traditional surveys, which are typically related to VOC work, have shortcomings. Now it seems as if you're referencing VOC at the project level. Please explain."

Jorge responded, "Great observation, Hank! In IEE, there're two aspects on which VOC receives focused attention. One VOC aspect is the enterprise, while the other is improvement project execution.

"The 'Positive Metric Performance Poor Business Performance' article that we discussed earlier included VOC as a first step in the article's enterprise-level IEE value chain. An organization can gain much if there's dedicated thought and effort to the refinement of this step's process relative to the creation of productive customer and organizational communication. What IEE suggests is that a value chain VOC drill-down is much more than surveys.

"If you'll bear with me, I would like to elaborate more about enterprise VOC and then return to project VOC.

"A friend of mine, Emma, had a personal experience that highlights the need for an organization to have an effective system to solicit real-time VOC inputs and then take timely action to resolve any identified issues.

"Emma enrolled her young dog in an obedience training class at a small facility near her home. She purchased weekly training-class sessions that would occur over two months. The dog-training instructor was not the owner of the facility.

"Emma told me how this instructor used a very harsh, critical style for communicating instruction to both the dog and its owner. All participants in the class were dissatisfied with the training sessions and were not finding that the instructional techniques helped their dogs improve their behavior and execution of commands.

"The training-class size dwindled from eight to only Emma, who ended up quitting the class before the purchased training sessions were complete. Emma later saw another person who'd attended the same dog-training class. This person recommended another training facility. The next meeting of dog training that Emma attended with her dog was at this suggested facility. Emma was happy with her dog's instruction and the results, even though the class costs were higher.

"Later, Emma was curious and returned to the facility where she'd received her first dog-training sessions. Sure enough, the not-so-good instructor was still there and providing training.

"Emma told me that she wonders why the owner did not provide some means by which she and others could provide timely, confidential feedback about the training. Emma thought that everyone in her first dog-training class was scared of the instructor and, because of this fear, did not provide unsolicited feedback to the owner. Emma was confident that the owner's lack of receiving timely VOC feedback about the class's lack of quality resulted in a very negative hit to the facility's financials.

"If the owner had received timely VOC feedback, a possible resolution to the issue would have been that the owner first talk to the instructor about her instructor-class behavior. After an instructor-owner discussion, if the owner did not see an improvement in the instructor's conduct through personal observation and student discussions, then the owner should pursue conducting the training herself or have someone else provide the training.

"This is an example of the type of VOC communication that should be prevalent and encouraged not only in small dog-training classes but in organizations in general, independently of their size.

"A timely VOC organizational feedback system can provide a significant financial benefit. A drill-down of an organization's IEE enterprise VOC function can describe the process of gaining this valuable customer insight."

Hank responded, "This makes perfect sense to me, Jorge. What about VOC at the improvement project level?"

Jorge responded, "Hank, for process improvement efforts, it's essential that there's VOC feedback from all stakeholders who are involved in or impacted by the current process and its performance. When executing an improvement project, one needs to summarize all VOC gathered information in the project's documentation and reporting."

Hank then said, "Great explanation, Jorge! I like the IEE system more and more as you progress through the details of the methodology. I appreciate the value of the entire scope of this business management system!"

Jorge responded, "Great to hear, Hank!

"While I'm thinking of it, I just mentioned documentation and reporting for improvement projects. For Six Sigma or Lean Six Sigma, there is a periodic presentation of this report to management."

Wayne interjected, "Exactly. People who are attending Lean Six Sigma training create a presentation that provides the status and findings from the execution of their project. There is then an in-class presentation of this information for critique by the instructor and other participants in the training. Our company established a repository system for storing improvement-project information. Still, it seems to me that both the entry and utilization of project-execution details in this repository are ineffective."

Jorge responded, "Wayne, I understand. I don't believe that I mentioned this to you previously. Your repository-of-information comment got me thinking that you would probably be interested in incorporating an additional EPRS software function beyond its organizational IEE value chain creation capability. Organizations benefit when they also include a listing of improvement projects and linkage to up-to-date reports and status meeting summaries that every one authorized can access 24x7, including the CEO."

Hank responded, "My take is that there are two aspects to this repository discussion. First, organizations benefit if they have an IEE value chain repository for process procedures and documentation with associated 30,000-foot-level process-output metrics, where EPRS software provides automatic metric updates. Secondly, organizations gain much when this EPRS software includes repository details about the execution of improvement projects that have 24x7 access availability by everyone authorized. Using Lean terms, this overall approach in business management significantly reduces organizational waste!"

Jorge then said, "Hank, your IEE summary is excellent!

"Let now walk through the IEE DMAIC 'Measure phase' sub-phase drill-downs shown on the SmarterSolutions.com/roadmap web page.

"The 'Measure: Plan Project and Metrics' sub-phase drill-down provides guidelines for proper project planning and the need for Six Sigma in-process metrics (See Figure 9.5).

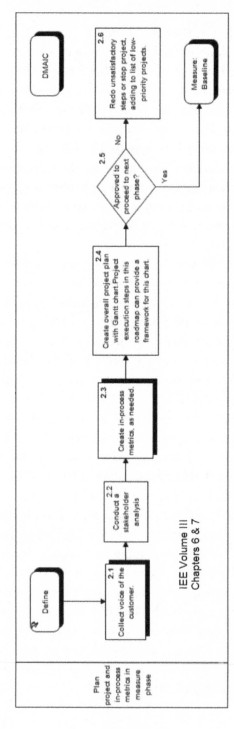

Figure 9.5: IEE DMAIC Roadmap – Measure Phase (Plan Project and Metrics)

"Also described in this link drill-down is a fundamental process for collecting VOC from stakeholders of the process, as was mentioned in our earlier 'Define phase' overview. Example stakeholders are those involved with the execution of down-stream steps of an overall value-stream process or a product's end users. Additional stakeholder examples are suppliers, unions, and government agencies for both product and services improvement projects.

"The next IEE DMAIC sub-phase SmarterSolutions.com/roadmap web page drill-down is 'Measure: Baseline Project' (See Figure 9.6). The steps in this sub-phase drill-down are crucial aspects of the IEE system. Described in Steps 3.2 and 3.3 of this SmarterSolutions.com/roadmap drill-down is the how-to methodology for creating a 30,000-foot-level metric baseline for a majority of process-output situations. This metric performance report is where process-improvement efforts give its enhancement focus.

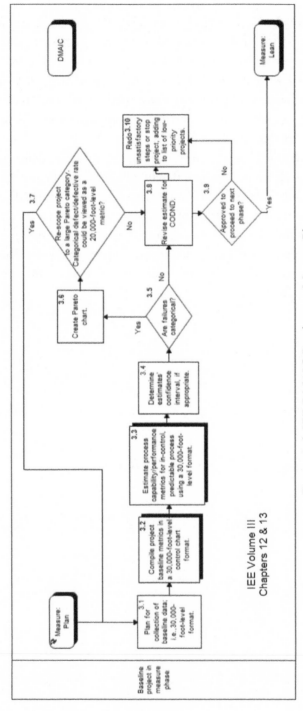

Figure 9.6: IEE DMAIC Roadmap – Measure Phase (Baseline Project)

"These two steps describe the techniques that one would use to create a 30,000-foot-level response, manually using typically provided statistical software functions; however, EPRS-metrics software provides an easy-to-create methodology for creating this high-level metrics report. The 30,000-foot-level creation methodology described in this drill-down is applicable not only for project metrics but for IEE value-chain enterprise performance metrics as well.

"I need to highlight that there's more than one version of EPRS software. EPRS-metrics software (Reference Appendix A, Web page 13) provides the means to create a 30,000-foot-level report from a dataset. While, EPRS-IEE software (Reference Appendix A, Web page 14) provides a vehicle for setting up an entire IEE organizational business management system, including automatically updated 30,000-foot-level and satellite-level metric predictive reports. EPRS-IEE software is often referenced as simply EPRS software."

Zack then asked, "Jorge, can you provide some example 30,000-foot-level reports that a process improvement project is to enhance?"

Jorge responded, "Zack, I anticipated this question and printed a few examples of 30,000-foot-level reports to share with you."

Jorge continued, "The data for creating these charts were randomly generated from a normal distribution." Jorge then handed each friend three sheets of paper.

"The 30,000-foot-level report on one of these sheets of paper is titled 'IEE Scorecard for Expense (Dollars)' (See Figure 9.7)".

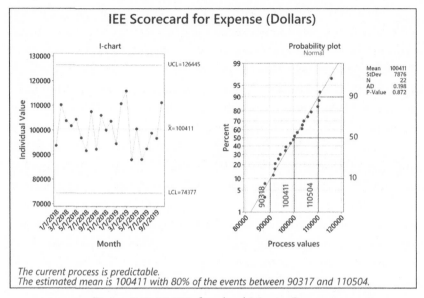

Figure 9.7: 30,000-foot-level Metric: Expense

"This 30,000-foot-level tracked expense item could be a work in progress (WIP) or another organizational cost. As an alternative to *expense*, this metric could be the revenue generated for a particular service that an organization offers. In any case, this single-response metric is continuous, as opposed to an attribute pass/fail measurement, and is updated monthly.

"The individuals chart on the left side of this report indicates that the metric response is stable; hence, the process response is predictable. Since there are no measurement specifications, a futuristic estimation statement is determined from the probability plot's best-estimate line and stated at the bottom of the report as a mean and 80% occurrence frequency rate. This 30,000-foot-level report indicates an expected $100,411 mean monthly expense. There is also an expectation that eighty percent of the time individual monthly expenses will be between $90,317 and $110,504."

Jorge continued saying, "Let's proceed to another 30,000-foot-level report, which is titled 'IEE Scorecard for Lead Time' (See Figure 9.8).

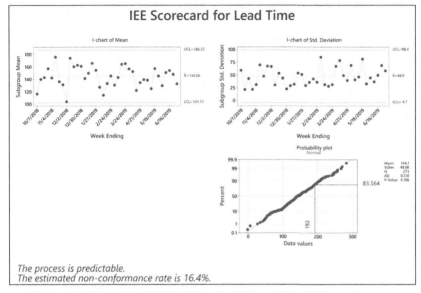

Figure 9.8: 30,000-foot-level Metric: Lead Time

"For this chart, consider that an organization delivers a service that has a customer completion requirement of eight days or 192 hours. Belief is that the completion day of the week could impact the magnitude of this lead-time response; hence, a weekly subgrouping interval was selected. For the generation of this 30,000-foot-level report, there was a random selection of one service delivery occurrence every day of a seven-day-work week.

"For this weekly subgrouping situation, two individuals charts are used to assess process stability. One of these two charts tracks a weekly mean response, while the other tracks the standard deviation of the weekly responses. Since these two individuals charts have no value beyond the charts' UCL and LCL horizontal lines, the process is considered stable.

"The probability plot in this report indicates that about 16.4% of the transactions are not expected to meet the 192-hour criterion. A simple statement at the bottom of the report conveys this non-conformance rate expectation.

"Let's now look at the third 30,000-foot-level report (See Figure 9.9).

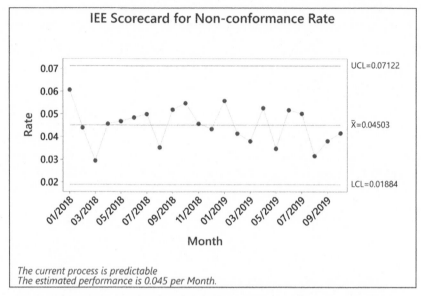

Figure 9.9: 30,000-foot-level Metric: Non-conformance Rate

"Since the response in this 30,000-foot-level report is an attribute non-conformance rate, there is no probability plot included in the reporting. If data aren't transformed when creating this report, the centerline of the individuals chart is the estimated predictive non-conformance rate statement for stable processes. The individuals chart in this report indicates that the process-response is stable; hence, there's a simple estimated 0.045 non-conformance rate statement at the bottom of the chart.

"As we've discussed previously, if a predictive statement in a 30,000-foot-level report is undesirable, there's a need for process improvement. In IEE, strategic 30,000-foot-level metrics that are to be improved, which will benefit the business as a whole, appear in an organization's enterprise improvement plan (EIP)."

Zack then said, "Wow, the reporting of performance metrics from a process-output response point of view, which includes variation, makes so much more sense than striving to achieve a particular number on a certain date."

Jorge responded, "Zack, it's good that you're seeing what we've been discussing applies to more than just manufacturing processes. Your internalization of the applicability of IEE techniques to your transactional processes is superb!

"The next IEE DMAIC sub-phase SmarterSolutions.com/roadmap web page drill-down is 'Measure: Lean Assessment' (See Figure 9.10). Breyfogle, in his IEE books, includes, as a component of the 'Measure phase,' several Lean tools in this sub-phase drill-down. The IEE DMAIC 'Analyze phase' drill-down also includes Lean tools as well. The purpose of these two Lean references in the IEE DMAIC overall roadmap is to address the applicability of Lean tools and integration with Six Sigma tools so that the right tool is used at the right time to improve a project's 30,000-foot-level metric.

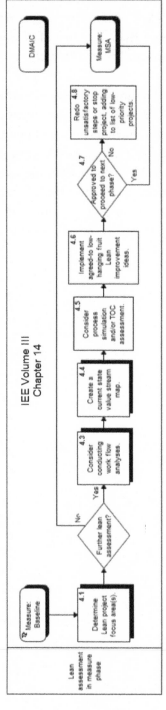

Figure 9.10: IEE DMAIC Roadmap – Measure Phase
(Lean Assessment)

"This 'Measure: Lean Assessment' sub-phase drill-down includes the consideration of workflow analysis, values stream mapping, and the determining of Lean project focus areas.

"If you'd next select on the sub-process 'Determine Lean project focus area(s),' you'll see IEE DMAIC roadmap considerations for this phase when undertaking a process improvement project. From this website link, you'll note the areas for attention are workplace, people, and system.

"In this 'Measure: Lean Assessment' sub-phase drill-down, there is a 'Further Lean assessment?' flowcharting diamond step. Before proceeding with the other steps in this roadmap drill-down, let's expound on this decision-making step.

"In IEE, no attempt is given to *push* for the application and use of Six Sigma or Lean tools in the execution of a project. Instead, there's a best-tool-at-the-right-time focus for the enhancement of a 30,000-foot-level metric through the implementation of an improvement project.

"To illustrate when a Lean and Six Sigma tool might be the best approach for a process-improvement effort, consider two 30,000-foot-level metrics that are to be improved. The first improvement project is to reduce the time for providing customer quotes. The second improvement project is to cut a product's non-conformance rate. Let's next discuss some general thoughts on which path to take relative to further the applicability of Lean tools in this drill-down for these two projects.

"Since the first described project involves the reduction of time, a *yes* response for this flowcharting decision step would seem appropriate because of the potential-beneficial application of tools in this drill-down for improving workflow, like value stream mapping.

"Since the second described response is an attribute non-conformance rate response, a *no* answer for this flowcharting decision step would initially seem most appropriate.

"Let me elaborate more on a decision flowchart, *no* selection. The tools that flow from a *yes* response could be beneficial. However, when executing an improvement project, it's most important to give focus on areas of the IEE DMAIC roadmap that should provide the most bang for the buck.

"To illustrate this point, Ron provided a story. He told us about a situation where he was using a video conferencing call to coach someone on his Lean Six Sigma project's execution. This student had a 30,000-foot-level non-conformance rate metric that was to be improved.

"Ron told us about how the student's reporting to him showed the expenditure of much effort to create a detailed value stream map. Ron then asked the student, 'What did you gain from all this work relative to reducing your project's 30,000-foot-level non-conformance rate metric?' The answer Ron received was, 'nothing.' Before this student's IEE training, he'd had much instruction in Lean, where a significant takeaway from this training was that improvement projects were to include a value stream map.

"Ron suggests giving focus to the use of tools that provide the most bang for the buck for improving a project's 30,000-foot-level metric response in the shortest time. For this person's improvement-project, the creation of a value-stream map was not the best use of his time.

"On the other side of the coin, a Six Sigma zealot may state that all projects need to include analysis as part of executing the Lean Six Sigma DMAIC roadmap, even if the team believes that it knows what to do to improve the process-output response. With an IEE approach for improving processes, there are no issues with attempting to implement a so-called *believed solution*, given that this process change can be done quickly and undone if not demonstrated to be effective. For this situation, like all IEE improvement projects, a quantifiable process-output response metric improvement needs to be shown, through the 30,000-foot-level improvement project's metric transitioning to an enhanced level of performance."

Hank then said, "Jorge, I can relate to everything that you've said. We have both Lean and Six Sigma zealots who are pushing for the application of the tools in their bag of tricks. In both cases for our organization, I primarily see anecdotal project-completion statements. Organizations gain much when there's a targeted focus on improving an identified 30,000-foot-level reported metric output response for the process that's to be improved."

Wayne then stated, "I agree 100%! At Wonder-Chem, we're having the same issues with our Lean Six Sigma deployment."

Zack then provided his thoughts. "From this conversation, I'm beginning to understand why our balanced scorecard deployment had issues, and what I might do differently in my new position."

Jorge then responded, "Again, it's great to hear that everyone sees the applicability of the IEE system and the DMAIC process-improvement roadmap in their organization.

"Am I providing the right level of details for this conversation?"

A broad smile appeared on Jorge's face when he again saw a thumbs-up sign from all his friends.

Jorge continued, "The next IEE DMAIC sub-phase SmarterSolutions. com/roadmap web page drill-down is 'Measure: MSA,' where the meaning of MSA is measurement system analysis (See Figure 9.11). In manufacturing, MSA issues can impact the pass/fail decisions of supplier parts and other testing responses in an overall manufacturing process and/or final product inspection.

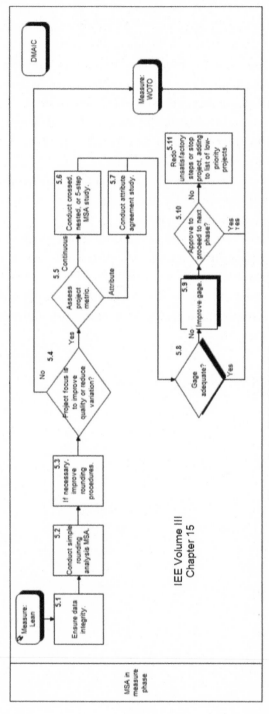

Figure 9.11: IEE DMAIC Roadmap – Measure Phase
(Measurement System Analysis)

"MSA considerations aren't only applicable to manufacturing. Measurement issues can be prevalent in many situations that we may not normally consider. Measurement difference in readings for a given circumstance can result because of many conditions, such as:

- The person who makes the measurement statement
- Equipment used when taking the measurement
- Environment condition at the time of the reading
- Error because someone transcribed a number incorrectly

"An erroneous measurement reporting can lead to an inappropriate pursuit action because of the measured value. For example, a false negative or false positive HIV or other virus test result can have severe consequences.

"Let me illustrate another potential measurement system analysis issue at a personal-testing level. Consider that during a recent annual physical examination, your physician stated that your blood pressure was a little higher than desired, and she wants to prescribe a prescription drug for you.

"This decision-based blood pressure reading might be from a left-arm measurement; however, if the blood-pressure measurement had been taken in your right arm, there could have been a lower reading. If so, which measurement reading should stimulate any decision for medication treatment? A higher left-arm value? Would this indeed be the best decision from a differences-between-arms readings occurrence?

"Besides, consider that you tend to become stressed in a physician's office. Because of this uneasiness, your blood pressure measurement could be higher than normal during a doctor-office visit. Your blood pressure under normal circumstances may be well within a desirable range of values for blood pressure. If you ended up using the prescribed drug that a physician recommends because of a slightly elevated office-visit blood pressure reading, this might not be a good decision relative to your overall health."

Hank then interrupted, "I agree, Jorge. MSA in manufacturing often may give focus to the assessment of measurement tools, but there are many more implications for this aspect of your overall IEE DMAIC roadmap. I've a question for you: Let's consider that a particular improvement project has some data integrity issues for whatever reasons. Should these issues be resolved before we create a 30,000-foot-level baseline?"

Jorge responded, "The success of an improvement project is a function of the quality of the analyzed data. The MSA IEE DMAIC drill-down provides the tools needed both to assess and improve the quality of the data used in the project.

"What's encouraged in IEE is that 30,000-foot-level baseline responses reflect, as accurately as possible, the current perceived level of a process output response. Note, I did not say how the process is performing. The difference between how a process is being viewed and is performing can be the result of data integrity or other issues. In many cases, this MSA step alone has resolved perceived business problems through the identification and resolution of measurement related problem causes.

"The importance of data integrity and having a sound data collection system cannot be overemphasized, not only for process improvement projects but in general. Also, when selecting samples, the sample must be a *random sample* of the population of interest and unbiased representation of that population. Keep in mind the saying, *garbage in, garbage o*ut, when creating a measurement system."

Hank then said, "That makes sense to me, Jorge."

Jorge continued, "Great to hear, Hank.

"The next IEE DMAIC sub-phase in our SmarterSolutions.com/ roadmap web page drill down progression is 'Measure: Wisdom of the Organization' (See Figure 9.12). The primary objective of this phase is to compile organizational wisdom for the identification of process improvement opportunities. This compilation offers two broad benefits. First, the identification of low-hanging fruit items that, when implemented in a short amount of time, could expediently improve the project's 30,000-foot-level metric. Secondarily, the creation of a list of potential Xs that could impact a project's Y response, which would have a later assessment for statistical significance through hypothesis testing in the 'Analyze phase' of the IEE DMAIC roadmap. The knowledge gained from uncovering Xs that have a statistical-significant impact on a Y response can be invaluable in determining what to do to improve a process that results in an enhanced project's Y response.

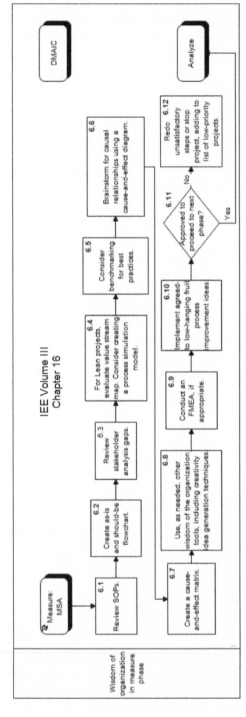

Figure 9.12: IEE DMAIC Roadmap – Measure Phase
(Wisdom of the Organization)

"The wisdom of the organization (WOTO) sub-phase of the over-all IEE DMAIC roadmap provides several idea generation tools that can be beneficial for executing this portion of an IEE DMAIC project's roadmap.

"Four tools that are often explicitly associated with this portion of the IEE DMAIC project execution roadmap are:

1. Creating an as-is and should-be flowchart.
2. Brainstorming for potential Xs that impact Y in the relationship Y=f(X) using a cause-and-effect diagram.
3. Creating a cause-and-effect matrix to prioritize brainstorming ideas.
4. Conducting a Failure Mode and Effects Analysis (FMEA), if appropriate, to document current knowledge and potential actions relative to addressing the risks of failures.

"These WOTO steps can shorten the length of a project by targeting project focus and reducing the chance of *analysis paralysis* in the 'Analyze phase' portion of the IEE DMAIC roadmap. Excessive analyses that do not provide process-improvement value can negatively impact the timely completion of a process improvement project."

Wayne commented, "I like the IEE DMAIC roadmap structure for executing process improvement projects. I'm going to get our team together on Monday to discuss how we could use this approach to enhance our Lean Six Sigma deployment."

Jorge responded, "Wayne, great to hear. Let's now discuss the 'Analyze phase.'

"As noted earlier, for a 30,000-foot-level process-output response, an organization should not react to all the up-and-down variation that may be occurring over time. When an individuals chart in a 30,000-foot-level performance metric report indicates process stability, and a predicted process-output response is undesirable, the underlying process needs improvement for the enhancement of the process's output response.

"Hypothesis tests can assess theories for statistical significance on what might be impacting a stable process-output response. This information can be precious for gaining insight for the determination of where to focus improvement efforts so that the process output response improves.

"As just noted, execution of the WOTO step in the IEE DMAIC sub-phase drill-down provides a listing of process insight thoughts for the development of improvement efforts to the process. A next step can be to conduct passive analyses hypothesis testing in a search for the statistical significance of inputs that affect the level of the 30,000-foot-level project's response.

"The phrase *passive analyses* is used here to describe analyses where inputs are not changed to assess the impact of these inputs that could affect a process-output response. In the IEE DMAIC 'Improve phase,' design of experiments (DOE) techniques can provide a proactive analysis methodology where process input variables are changed in a structured fashion to assess whether an evaluated input level has a statistically significant effect on an output response.

"An input that affects a key process output variable (KPOV) is called a key process input variable (KPIV). As we discussed earlier, we could describe this relationship through equation $Y=f(X)$. Y would be the KPOV, while the KPIV would be an X.

"An IEE DMAIC analysis does not, by itself, improve a process-output response, even when an input variable is found significant. The analysis phase in IEE DMAIC is not unlike the search for clues in *whodunnit* mysteries. Process inputs that are found significant can provide insight into process-improvement changes that could improve a process output response significantly.

"When selecting the IEE DMAIC 'Analyze phase' in the SmarterSolutions.com/roadmap (See Figure 9.13), you'll see an 'Analyze phase' drill-down in the roadmap. Let's focus on Steps 7.3 and 7.6 of this image. The drill-down of Step 7.3 provides a tree diagram for the selection of the most appropriate visualization of data techniques for a majority of process input and output dataset situations, which can provide valuable insight into processes. The drill-down of Step 7.6 also provides a tree diagram. This tree diagram provides the appropriate hypothesis test to use for a majority of process input and output dataset situations for the assessment of statistical-significance of X inputs on a Y response."

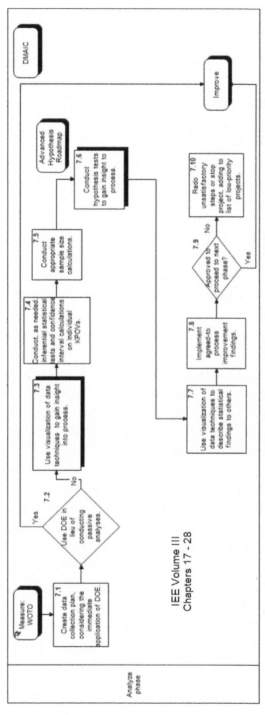

Figure 9.13: IEE DMAIC Roadmap – Analyze Phase

Jorge then said, "It's important that there be no confusion with the overall thought process for bridging from team brainstorming in the IEE DMAIC 'Measure phase' to the roadmap's 'Analyze phase' and then to the correct usage of tools in the 'Analyze phase.' How about me walking through an application example?"

Three thumbs-up signs quickly appeared from Jorge's friends as a powerful positive go-ahead signal.

Jorge's then continued his discussion. "Great, I'll use a call-center-problem-resolution-time reduction project to illustrate the application of these concepts.

"Consider that a company's enterprise improvement plan (EIP) goal is to increase monthly profit, which has declined, as shown in the company's monthly satellite-level charting of profit. An enterprise analysis in step two of the 9-step IEE system indicates that there's lost business because of the time taken to resolve customer call-in problems.

"Many past customers have moved their business to competitors since there was not a timely resolution to their identified product issues. The company and its customers were incurring much frustration and expense because of the lack of timely-call-in problem resolutions. The chosen 30,000-foot-level response for this identified EIP improvement project was the reduction of call-center-problem-resolution time.

"The company's IEE value-chain 30,000-foot-level metric for the time it took to provide a satisfactory resolution to call center inquiries had an individuals' chart weekly subgrouping. The reason for selecting a weekly subgrouping was that some problem resolutions would begin in one week with completion in another week; that is, after a weekend. For this situation, if we chose a daily 30,000-foot-level response reporting, differences between days-of-the-week for closures could appear as special-cause events in the individuals chart reporting. However, common-cause variation would be the actual source for any day-of-the-week differences in problem closure times. A weekly subgrouping of response times resolves this erroneous special-cause reporting issue."

Wayne then said, "Jorge, this makes so much sense. I wonder if our current methodology for control chart subgrouping is giving the appearance of many out-of-control, special-cause signals that are originating from common-cause variation. I need to check this out."

Jorge responded, "Good to see Wayne. Let's now consider that this high-level, continuous response-time process output has been stable for the last 33 weeks.

"The corporate director, who was responsible for all call centers, would be the owner of this overall-company-call-center-resolution time metric. Because of this EIP identified metric, the director should be working closely with her managers and the created process-improvement team so that there would be an enhancement to the call-center-problem-resolution-time measurement in a timely fashion.

"This director would be reporting out this 30,000-foot-level metric, and the status of the process improvement project work monthly to the company's leadership. This ten-minute maximum monthly presentation would link to the company IEE value chain and real-time improvement project reports through the use of the organization's EPRS software.

"A brainstorming session for this IEE DMAIC project provided the following list of Xs thought could impact the project's Y response for call-center-problem-resolution times:

- Six call-center locations
- Day of week
- Work-day shift
- Specific product or service that caused the inquiry
- Type of inquiry; e.g., set-up or product/service failure
- The difficulty of an inquiry on a scale of 1-5, where 5 is most difficult
- Inquiry not included in the call-center database that provides answers to common questions
- Individual answering an inquiry
- How long the person answering inquiries has worked in the call center
- In-charge manager when the call was initially received
- The time before and after work-shift changes: Time before is minus, and time after is a plus

"The data used for these assessments is the raw data from each call-center response occurrence during the latest stability region of the Y-response 30,000-foot-level chart. Where, the recent stability region from this reporting could be three days, three weeks, three months, or three years, as identified by the high-level report's individuals chart or charts.

"In these cause-and-effect analyses, there should be an awareness that a combination of X-input factors could affect the Y response.

"One item from this project's WOTO effort was that there could be a difference in the problem-resolution durations between the six facilities that respond to similar types of problems.

"For this example, the Y response is time, which is a continuous response, while the X response for the six call center locations is categorical.

"To determine the most appropriate visualization tools to use for this type of output and input situation, an examination of the IEE DMAIC 'Analyze phase' drill-down tree sequences in Step 7.3 of this SmarterSolutions.com/roadmap web page yields:

1. Step 7.3.5 Output: Continuous
2. Step 7.3.11 Input: Discrete
3. Step 7.3.12 Observing effect of input levels
4. Step 7.3.13 Box plot, dot plot, marginal plot

"The conclusion from progressing through this decision tree is that appropriate visualization tools for assessing a continuous response with a categorical input are a box plot, dot plot, and marginal plot.

"To determine the most appropriate hypothesis tools to use for this type of output and input situation, an examination of the decision-tree sequences in Step 7.6 of this SmarterSolutions.com/roadmap web page yields:

1. 7.6.22 Output: Continuous
2. 7.6.27 Input: Categorical
3. 7.6.32 Mean equality test

4. 7.6.34 Two or more samples: ANOVA, ANOM, multiple comparisons

"The conclusion from progressing through this decision tree is that appropriate hypothesis test tools for assessing a continuous response with a discrete input are an analysis of variance (ANOVA), analysis of means (ANOM), and multiple comparisons.

"From this analysis, one might find a significant difference between locations in the time it takes to provide a satisfactory response to a call-inquiry. This information could lead to a determination of what call-center-location provides the shortest completion time so that there could be an examination of its process and elsewhere replicated, if appropriate.

"From a similar analysis, one might observe a significant difference among individuals in the time it takes to provide a satisfactory response to a call-inquiry. This information could lead to a determination of who provides the shortest completion time. From this determination, there could be an examination of his or her process and, when appropriate, replicated elsewhere.

"Another significant uncovered difference from an IEE DMAIC analysis inquiry could be the difficulty of identified problems and how people answered the most challenging issues. A further investigation might then lead to a determination of who answered the most complicated inquiries fastest so that their process might be modeled and documented for process execution elsewhere.

"A fourth significant difference that an IEE DMAIC analysis may uncover is that the time to complete an inquiry is much longer when the call-center database does not include the type of call-in- investigation issue. If this lack of guidance-for-issue-resolution factor were significant, a more frequent update to the database might be appropriate for call-in inquiries that have occurred more than one time.

"Work in this project could evolve to team-member inquiries that might include such questions as to why we have these call-in product issues in the first place. This very-good question then might lead to the creation of a new EIP project that addresses actions to undertake for reducing the frequency of product-problem issues experienced by customers, in general."

Zack was the first to respond, "This is so cool! I haven't conducted any statistical analyses since university days. I'm assuming that the books you mentioned provide the how-to's for these analyses."

Wayne then said, "I like more and more the IEE approach that you're describing, which provides an overall thought process both at the enterprise and process execution level. I also think it's great that your illustration did not jump immediately into a problem statement but started with the big picture enterprise revenue need, which could be a burning platform issue in an organization."

Hank then interjected, "You defined the problem statement to be the length of time it takes to resolve a call-in problem. I thought it was terrific that this problem then led to another process-improvement project that was to address the issue of why the problem occurred in the first place and process improvement work to undertake so the call-in-issue is less likely to reoccur in the future. When you were walking us through this scenario, this same 'why did this problem occur?' question was in the back of my mind to ask you; however, you answered my question before I had a chance to ask it."

Jorge responded, "Three superb observations! First, Zack and Wayne, glad you appreciate the benefits of IEE techniques. Yes, Zack, execution details are provided in one or more books from the IEE series. Wayne, yep, aligning strategic projects to the big picture where there's also a process owner in an IEE value chain, who's driving the effort for improving a metric through an improvement project's execution, is vital.

"Hank, great to hear that our thinking is on the same page. We agree that there should be another effort that goes beyond the current defined Six Sigma problem statement. The focus of this new effort would be the determination of what to do to reduce the likelihood of a similar problem reoccurrence.

"Let's now consider a basic approach for undertaking this second project opportunity, which is an alternative to attempting to permanently resolve all problems so that they all do not occur again, a close to an impossible scenario for most situations. However, there're typically some natural grouping categories for the issues relative to frequency-of-occurrence and cost. The presentation of this information in a Pareto chart format can provide direction on where to start to reduce the likelihood of future similar occurrences. The process improvement team would begin with issues that impact customers and the business the most, as displayed in the Pareto chart, and work downward in the frequency of issue occurrence.

Hank responded, "Jorge, your response to my inquiry makes perfect sense to me. The learnings from one IEE improvement project can lead to the creation and thoughts about what to do in another project."

Jorge then said, "Great, Hank. I think that now I might share some thoughts about the application of analytical tools on one of my other projects. This project is to reduce the number of days-sales-outstanding or DSO for invoices. A high potential area in our organizational EIP for the reduction of corporate expenses identified this DSO reduction project. Our finance director is the owner of this IEE value-chain process and is responsible for reducing DSO through the execution of this project. This director, with the process-improvement-team, will provide a ten-minute monthly project metric and process improvement update to the leadership-team for this strategic project.

"Traditionally, DSO, as you know, is considered as a measurement for the average number of days taken to collect payment after the completion of a sale. However, for a DSO measurement from a 30,000-foot-level point of view, one needs to include in its report the variation from individual payments, in addition to a central tendency mean response. This 30,000-foot-level response format provides much more insight than a simple mean-value reporting."

Wayne interrupted, saying, "Jorge, I like how you used the EIP for linkage of this DSO reduction project to overall business needs. Also, I think it's great how the IEE value chain process owners are to provide a short monthly reporting about the status of both the current DSO metric's performance and associated process improvement efforts. Ownership of processes and their outputs are critical. A frequent improvement-project presentation would provide a spotlight that would surely expedite a project's completion.

"From your earlier comments, I suspect that, as part of this reporting, a conference room internet connection would access EPRS software to provide in real-time:

1. A project executive summary used dynamically during meetings, with appropriate links. Where, this meeting could be accessed remotely by those working from home or throughout the world.
2. Automatically-updated DSO 30,000-foot-level metric performance.
3. An IEE value chain *clickable* drill-down to the DSO process and its current metric's performance.
4. Location of additional information about the improvement project's execution details, including minutes from the project's team meetings, which anyone authorized can access 24x7."

Jorge responded, "Wayne, exactly! What you just described is the process that Harris is using for all strategic process improvement monthly reporting. Since Janice owns the overall EIP financial satellite-level goal and there're IEE improvement projects that are to improve various 30,000-foot-level performance metrics that have alignment to this financial objective, there would be a high level of interest by everyone in the meeting.

"Previously, these meetings had people talking about what occurred last month and how a number in a report compares to a previous month. There were a bunch of stories presented where there was little if any discussion about changes that would enhance future performance.

"Now, in our two-hour leadership meetings, there's much healthy discussion about the seven current EIP prioritized projects that'll improve performance metrics in our IEE value chain and benefit the business-as-a-whole upon their completion."

Wayne then said, "Your whole system for providing updates and tracking is so much better and more efficient than what occurs in our Lean Six Sigma deployment with its reporting."

Jorge then followed up, saying, "Wayne, great to hear that you're seeing IEE benefits. Perhaps your organization can take advantage of IEE techniques down the road.

"If it's okay with you, I'll continue my discussion about some of the things that we did with this DSO reduction project."

Hank, Wayne, and Zack all gave a thumbs-up sign again.

Jorge then said, "The wisdom of the organization IEE DMAIC step for this project provided many potential Xs. From this listing, some items were low-hanging fruit opportunities that could be accomplished with less effort than others; for example, having all the billing departments follow a single procedure.

"When a consistent process was agreed-to and followed by all billing departments, our 30,000-foot-level individuals chart shifted to a new, improved region of stability. We also did some statistical analyses that quantified, with a confidence interval, our expectation for long-term improvement."

"What's a confidence interval?" Zack interrupted.

"Confidence intervals are similar to the margin of error statements reported during elections. Confidence intervals are important because they quantify the uncertainties related to making statements from samples," Jorge explained.

Zack said, "You know, I think that happened to me the other day. We made a process change that we thought was an improvement. We felt good when we ran a couple of trials, and it appeared there was an improvement. However, I'm not convinced that the process response did change. Now I think that the changes that appeared may just have been from common-cause variation."

Zack elaborated, "It's unfortunate that we don't have a 30,000-foot-level metric chart reporting format as a baseline so we could see what happened over the long haul. The sad point is, we made some costly changes to our process, and we don't have a clue whether the changes were beneficial or detrimental at the enterprise level. By the time we're finally able to tell for sure, we may have spent a lot of money and wasted a lot of time."

"Zack, you're right on," Hank said. "I think this happens a lot. Without IEE, you can be answering the wrong question, perhaps to the third decimal place. Previously, we all had our own biases on what was causing defects in the printed circuit manufacturing process. When we let our prejudices about processes guide us without conducting a statistical analysis, it often led to major cost implications."

Jorge continued, "We followed the IEE DMAIC roadmap for the DSO metric for our invoicing process. Wisdom of the organization's input led us to think that there might be a difference between companies in the duration of time to receive payment. Also, we thought that the charged-amount in an invoice might make a difference. Our passive statistical analysis, using the techniques and IEE DMAIC drill-downs that we discussed earlier, showed that mean DSO was significantly different between companies. However, the relationship between the size of an invoice and DSO was not statistically significant."

"Jorge, you're beginning to sound like a statistician," Wayne joked.

Jorge responded, "I guess so—a little bit. I'm getting excited because I'm starting to see people make decisions based on information rather than on sketchy data and gut feel."

Hank then said, "Let me tell you about what happened to us on one of our projects. We used Gage Repeatability and Reproducibility or Gage R&R techniques to quantify the consistency of the measurement system in one of our projects. Gage repeatability is an assessment of how well an individual will get a similar result for a manufactured part dimension if she inspected the same item many times. At the same time, gage reproducibility makes a similar assessment but only addresses differences between inspectors.

"Gage R&R is an area we often overlook, and we were extremely surprised by the results. Almost 40% of our total process variation was due to measurement differences. With the existing gage, we were often accepting bad parts and rejecting good parts. When we included the cost of rework, lost production, and replacing customer shipments, we calculated that this gage alone was costing us five million dollars a year. We wouldn't have found this without a structured methodology like that provided by the IEE DMAIC roadmap. We just assumed that, as long as there was a timely calibration of the gage, everything was okay. We never realized that calibration of the measurement system was only one part of the equation."

Wayne interrupted, "That's sort of like my eyes. They were not capable of measuring the break or the speed of a putt, so I was missing them in all directions. All of the money I wasted on new putters pales in comparison to the money I've lost to you guys because I couldn't see the line on the putting green. You'll all be happy to know that I've got an eye appointment next week, and I should be making a lot more putts soon."

Hank and Jorge groaned, but Hank thought about resurrecting his idea of sponsoring Wayne on the senior tour as an investment opportunity.

"Do you remember a couple of months ago when I was having problems with transactional errors?" Zack asked.

Jorge laughingly responded, "Your ears must have been burning last week. Hank and I had a long discussion on how we thought your situation lends itself directly to IEE."

Zack responded, "If I could make some low-hanging fruit improvements, I might get my job back or at least leave with some scrap of dignity—if I can make some quick improvements. What *wisdom on the green* did I miss?"

For the next few minutes, Hank and Jorge filled Zack in on the particulars of the conversation they had had last month. They agreed to look at some of Zack's data and help him outline a strategy.

Jorge then added, "Before I leave this IEE DMAIC 'Analyze phase' drill-down discussion, I want to highlight that this same decision tree is applicable in enterprise analyses, which is step 3 of the IEE 9-step system."

As they stood up to leave the breakfast table, Jorge looked at Zack and offered, "Now that we've helped with Wayne's golf game, would you like a suggestion?"

Zack felt like he was on a roll here and responded, "Sure, shoot!"

"Well, Wayne's problem was not his putter, but his vision. Hank's problem was one of course management; that is, making smarter club selections based not just on his best-ever-shot, but on the expected variation with different clubs."

"OK, but what about me?" Zack asked impatiently.

Jorge replied, "Your problem is different. You don't have any particular club issue, and your problem is certainly not physical. Your eyes are great, and your physique is good, too. Your problem is more basic. Your problem is very fundamental. Your grip, your alignment, even your swing are all too much like your old baseball-playing days. As a result, you have processes with too much variation. Hooks, slices, topped shots, thin shots, a little of everything."

"I guess I should just give up the game then," Zack moaned.

"Not at all," said Jorge. "It's easy to fix these golf-swing necessities. Just get a little coaching on the fundamentals of the stance, grip, and swing, and practice with your 7 iron until your swing feels natural. An hour with a pro and a few buckets of balls on a driving range are all it'll take for you to break 90 almost every time."

"But what about all the other clubs? Don't I need a new driver?" Zack questioned.

Jorge finished, "Don't worry about that now. Your problems are so fundamental that you can fix them without much effort. The 7 iron is the easiest club to use, and it'll surely help you ingrain the fundamental changes quickly. Only then can you tell whether you need to make any adjustments in your equipment. My guess is you won't need to make any."

"Wow," said Zack, "With all the help you're giving me in my business and my golf game, I'll have enough time to salvage my family life, too!"

10 ENLIGHTENMENT

OCTOBER

With paper in hand, Jorge approached the boys on their way to the practice green. Excitedly, he called out, "Zack. We were right about your data. It appears to be a common-cause problem. A 30,000-foot-level report of your transactional errors indicates that your process is not changing. The up-and-down variation of the data is from the noise within your process. From the criteria that you sent me, I expect that you are firefighting about 10% of the time."

Zack said, "Hey, that seems right because we spend about two days a month chasing transactional entry errors that indicate an error rate that's beyond our criterion. Let me see the chart."

Jorge gave Zack the printout and said, "The charts show that with your red-yellow-green scorecard system, you haven't fixed anything. How much do you think that's costing your business?"

Zack shook his head in disbelief and then replied, "You sure know how to use data to hurt a guy's feelings. I don't have a clue how much this is costing the business, but I know it's not pretty!"

Hank suggested, "Zack, if you want to reduce the error rate, you could do some passive analyses as we talked about last month, which might even lead to a DOE."

"DOE? I recall our mentioning that acronym previously but do not remember what DOE means," Zack asked, barely lifting his eyes from the 30,000-foot-level report.

"DOE is short for the design of experiments. I can explain it in more detail after we get some practice putts in. The rain last night probably slowed the greens down," Hank said, eager to play.

Zack had also found some time for a lesson with the pro. Everyone noticed his new swing, even in the warm-ups and on the first tee. His stance was square, his grip was neutral, and his smooth swing now looked more like Wayne's swing than they could ever have imagined. When Zack teed off, it was 250 yards on the fairway, with just a hint of a draw. The others all commented that they might need to adjust handicaps for the group if this continued.

Jorge responded, "Yes, Hank's definition for DOE is correct. We can talk about DOE during our round, but I want to finish up where I left off last time discussing the SmarterSolutions.com/roadmap IEE DMAIC execution details. We still need to address the 'Improve' and 'Control' phases in the roadmap. The IEE DMAIC roadmap includes details of smartly-applied DOE, Lean process improvement, and how to demonstrate 30,000-foot-level metric enhancements. A control system provides techniques for maintaining the gain from process improvement efforts.

"Let's have this discussion after we finish our round."

Waiting at the second tee, Wayne asked, "Did you finish the day sales outstanding (DSO) project yet, Jorge?"

Jorge replied, "Wayne, much has happened since the last time we talked. You may remember, our wisdom of the organization's input led us to examine the amount charged and the customer invoiced. Passive analysis tools from our IEE DMAIC roadmap led us to a statistically significant issue between customers. That is, the customer invoiced was identified as a key process input variable (KPIV) for DSO.

"We then brainstormed about what we might do differently to improve our DSO response. However, to validate these improvement ideas, we needed to execute some tests using the design of experiments or DOE techniques that Hank mentioned earlier.

"We came up with a list of seven factors to evaluate during the DOE. Some of these factors were process-noise-variables, such as from which hospital the invoice originated. We also included things we could change within our process, including billing formats. For the experiment, we set up each of the seven factors with two levels. For example, in the case of the factor-billing department, there were two locations, 1 and 2. From our passive analyses earlier, we thought location number 1 did better, and location number 2 did worse.

"If you consider all combinations of factors and levels, experiments can get to be very large. However, with fractional factorial DOE experimentation, we used a subset of all combinations, and this reduced our number of tests from 128 to 16, while still obtaining valuable information from our process."

"Oh, you get a free lunch for not having to do 128 trials," Zack remarked sarcastically.

Jorge responded, "Not exactly. When we conduct this type of experiment, we confound information about our interactions, but this isn't all bad since it saves us a lot of time. Before I get to that, I should describe the characteristics of an *interaction* between two factors. Remember the old copier machines in the 1970s?"

"That was way before my time," Zack bragged facetiously.

"Sure," Jorge replied dryly, "You're so much younger than the rest of us. Anyway, copier-feed failures were a major problem. Two Xs that could impact a copier's feed-failure-rate were ambient temperature and humidity. If you compared feed failure rates at 68 and 98 degrees at low humidity, no change was noticeable. However, at high humidity, if you compare feed failure rates at either 68 degrees or 98 degrees, a significant change is indicated. Feed failures were higher when both the humidity and the temperature were high, which means that an interaction existed between the two factors temperature and humidity. The real problem source was that the moisture in the air was the highest at this condition, which resulted in water absorption of the paper and feed problems. For this situation, you cannot understand the effect of these factors without looking at both of them together."

Jorge continued, "If an interaction exists within our process, we may never find the solution by changing one factor at a time. A well-structured DOE manages the confounding of two-factor interactions. Anyway, there's too much detail involved with DOE for a productive golf-course conversation. You need much more training to fully understand the benefits of DOE and how to plan them efficiently. But, DOE provides a potent technique that applies to many situations."

As the match progressed, Jorge realized that everyone was playing better today. He was keeping his shots in play and using his short game for a significant effect around the greens. At the turn, he was 38 after nine holes, and Hank thought his way to an intelligent 39 with no penalty strokes. Wayne made several putts wearing his new glasses for a one-under 35, and Jorge wondered what would happen after his laser surgery that would be occurring in a few days. Even Zack demonstrated remarkable variation reduction with his new swing and shot 44 on the front. The match scores for the four friends were the same, but Jorge realized they were all *winning*.

Waiting at the tenth tee box, Wayne asked, "So are DOE techniques applicable to all projects?"

"No," Hank responded. "All Six Sigma and Lean tools have applications, and each of them has situations where their application is most appropriate. However, DOE techniques are very beneficial, both in manufacturing and transactional situations."

Hank continued, "It's like in golf, where there are usually several ways to hit a shot. Some are easier to hit than others. Some have less variation in their outcomes, as Jorge talks about."

"Picking the right tool is always important. For our DSO project, we conducted a DOE where we considered seven factors. During our passive analysis, we found that there were two groups of customers, those who were making timely payments and those who were chronically late. We treated this as one of our seven factors. Another factor we looked at was whether or not we gave the customer a reminder call a week after invoicing."

As they approached the tenth green, Jorge sliced his approach shot more to the right than usual. When they found the ball, it was about four feet directly behind a medium-sized tree with a forked trunk and low-hanging branches. Wayne and Zack feigned disappointment at Jorge's ball lie.

"Looks like that tree has you stymied," said Zack with a heavy dose of mock sympathy.

"Yeah, I guess it's up to you on this hole, partner," Jorge said to Hank.

"Maybe not," said Hank as he looked at the shot more carefully.

Jorge was directly behind the tree, and the base of the eight-inch trunk blocked his path to the hole, while overhanging branches restricted the shot selection to a height of fewer than five feet. However, Hank noticed that the natural *V* in the trunk left an opening to the flag that was almost three feet wide at the top and narrowed down to nothing at ground level.

Hank said, "Look at this! You're back far enough that you can chip right through the fork of this tree with your 5 iron. That should keep it down below the branches, but get it up just enough to go through the *V* in the trunk. Bump it into the face of the green, and it should run right up to the hole."

Zack and Wayne taunted Jorge as he lined up the shot, but their jeers turned to cheers of amazement as he executed an almost perfect bump-and-run shot, exactly as instructed.

"Thanks for the *get out of jail card*, partner. How do you come up with such creative ideas?" Jorge asked with a satisfied grin.

Hank answered, "As the saying goes, 'Judgment comes from experience and experience comes from bad judgment.' My length gets me into a lot of trouble on the course. I've been in so many tough situations that I've learned to be creative. I just used my extensive past wisdom of the organization's inputs to pick the right tool for the job.

"The best thing about being a teacher is that I learn so much!" Hank said as he punctuated his comment by tapping in his miracle par putt.

As they all moved to the next tee, Jorge continued his discussion, "Through the application of DOE techniques we discovered that our late customers were paying sooner, on average, when they received reminder calls a week after they were initially invoiced. The companies that normally pay on time showed no change when they received reminders. This customer payment behavior is an example of the kind of interaction we talked about earlier. Because of this objective data, we were able to motivate change in the process. For our new process, we'll have a reminder call, one week after invoicing, only for those companies that are historically delinquent. As you can imagine, this will save us a lot of time and money. Besides, our good-paying clients won't get frustrated with our phone calls."

Hank added, "In our circuit board defect-reduction project, the passive analysis tools led us to a significant issue of cleanliness within our printed circuit board manufacturing process. Analysis indicated that the cleanliness of the printed circuit board was a significant X for the defect rate Y response. We then brainstormed for what we might do differently to improve cleanliness. To validate these improvement ideas, we need to perform some tests. That's where we'll be using DOE, the way Jorge has been describing."

As the round ended, the match ended up even, but the entire group felt like winners. Everyone had played well, with Wayne shooting par 72, Hank a 79, Jorge 80, and even Zack broke through with an 89. As they drove their golf carts to their cars to deposit their clubs, Jorge thought that this was not just a random combination of unlikely occurrences. This round of golf was more likely an example of a real systemic improvement in everyone's game.

When everyone arrived at their chow-down table, Hank then suggested, "Since both teams won our round of golf-play, neither team is to foot the bill. Because of this, I suggest that we each pay our tab, but split the tab for our teacher, Jorge."

Wayne and Zack together responded in unison, "Agreed!"

Jorge responded, "Thanks. As noted during our golfing round, I wanted to finish walking you through the IEE DMAIC SmarterSolutions.com/roadmap. But, before doing that, I would like to share a thought I had.

"I was thinking about how the DOE techniques that we were discussing could also help Zack improve the effectiveness of a potential project that he has not discussed yet."

"What project is that?" Zack asked.

"Doesn't your financial company send out junk mail to solicit business?" Jorge replied.

Zack tersely responded, "We prefer to view this activity as a mass mailing."

"Given what we've discussed about DOE, don't you think you could use these techniques to improve the response rate from your mass mailings?" Jorge quizzed.

"Maybe it would help and could even improve my standing with our CEO. How would it work exactly?" Zack replied.

Jorge responded, "Well, you would follow the process that we did for our projects. When you get to the point of asking yourself what should be done differently, there'll probably be differences of opinion. Let's consider that one idea was sending a huge postcard instead of an envelope for your mass mailings. This mass-mailing approach would be cheaper than sending a letter and might stand out better against all the other junk mail."

"Mass mail," Zack corrected.

"Anyway," Jorge started laughing, "Before you change to this new marketing strategy, you'd want to test its effectiveness."

"Hey, Jorge," Wayne interrupted, "Why don't you bring a projector so you can do a presentation when we have classes after our golfing rounds?"

Jorge ignored the laughter and continued, "With a traditional approach, we would send out trial postcards and compare the number of responses we get to what we had previously. This approach can cause problems. There is a time delay between the change and response. Also, something else could have happened in the economy to affect our responses. That would be considered a confounding effect. To compare the envelope mailing with the postcard approach, we would have to send out some envelopes and some postcards during the same time frame."

"That would be easy to do and give us valuable information about our process," Zack agreed.

Jorge responded, "Great. We could do this and then compare the responses statistically. However, I believe it would be appropriate to include other factors as part of the experiment for the monthly mailings such as the mailing list source and maybe if the recipient is male or female. You might also include a factor that assesses the marketing effectiveness differences between mass snail-mailings and e-mail blasts. You might also include a cost-effectiveness response."

Zack then said, "All of these factors and some others that I've been thinking about could make a difference."

Jorge responded, "If that's the case, the DOE should consider all these factors in the experiment."

Zack asked, "But won't that mix things up?"

"No, a properly designed DOE does not *mix things up*. I'll talk a little about that when going through the IEE DMAIC roadmap in a couple of minutes. However, when you get back to the office, let's have a conference call. I'll show you a reference that illustrates this point vividly," Jorge responded.

Wayne jumped in, stating, "You know I think that DOE could help within our product development process."

Jorge responded, "That's right. Within the IEE Define, Measure, Analyze, Design, and Verify (DMADV) methodology for development, DOE techniques can be very beneficial in several ways. You could use a DOE to evaluate structurally various combinations of input conditions that might affect a response. You could assess these factors in a structured way, combining manufacturing conditions with customer applications. This DOE approach would help you select the best combination of factor settings to give the best results for your customers. You can also use DOE techniques to develop a test strategy for new products. When I return to the office, I'll call you to tell you about a reference example from our Lean Six Sigma textbook that illustrates how DOE can be useful in development organizations. The bottom line is: Whenever you're considering testing something, consider DOE."

Zack said, "Sounds like DOE can be very useful."

Then Jorge said, "Not to change the subject, but I was thinking about what Hank said last month about Gage R&R. We're not currently taking this issue as a project; however, the execution of many hospital tests and their interpretation do not formally consider the presence of potential testing-result errors. This potential testing issue is especially alarming when a physician states that, for example, tests for AIDS or another virus test are either positive or negative. In either case, if there's an erroneous statement given to patients and their families, the consequences could be devastating."

Hank responded. "I think that all industries should be more sensitive to both Gage R&R and measurement system issues, in general."

Jorge continued, "Hank, I agree. When measurement variation is unsatisfactory or not accurate, one can make the wrong decision. For example, whether we talk about it or not, a measurement system exists in our court system; a trial can reach an inappropriate guilty or not-guilty verdict. Now with DNA testing, the court's measurement system has improved from what it had been in the past. However, in the court system, there can be accuracy-of-results and timeliness-of-delivery DNA testing issues.

A friend, who's involved with DNA testing, told me some horrific stories about DNA testing issues that led to some ugly consequences. Like other situations that we've talked about, DNA testing and its delivery-of-results originate from a process. The DNA testing process overall can gain much when first, there's an overall-performance tracking of its timeliness-of-delivery and accuracy-of-results, from a 30,000-foot-level process-output-response perspective. Secondly, there're both statistical and non-statistical analyses to determine what to do differently to improve the 30,000-foot-level tracking of the delivery of these DNA-process-output responses."

Hank then said, "Jorge, I agree. Measurement system testing issues can be a big deal that's often not considered or candidly discussed. Because of my conversations with you, I've been doing some research and perhaps now have enough knowledge to be dangerous. I don't know, but here goes.

"A manufacturing testing process for incoming-part inspection that Hi-Tech Computers has used in the past and is sometimes still using is acceptable quality level (AQL). AQL is a sampling method that's to help a buyer decide whether to accept or reject a lot of received goods. AQL provides a means for a buyer to determine if a received order meets the quality standards necessary for acceptance without having to test 100% of the units.

"Military Standard (MIL-STD) and American National Standards Institute tables (ANSI/ASQ Z1.4-2003) provide AQL test sampling alternatives for a variety of situations. The use of AQL testing is straight-forward, but my discussions with Jorge got me thinking about whether AQL testing has issues relative to the initiation of the most appropriate behaviors, given the results from a test. My thinking about this AQL question will be different from the norm. I'll be addressing this AQL testing question from a hypothesis test perspective, where a received supplier batch is considered a population from which there are samples selected to determine whether a lot is acceptable or not.

"In the past, Hi-Tech Computers has rejected lots because they failed an AQL test, returning these lots to the supplier. Less than scru-pulous suppliers have simply sent the same lot back to us without any alteration. We've noticed this because sometimes we placed a mark on failed lots in a place that the supplier would not see the markings. When a returned-lot that had this marking was tested again against the orig-inal AQL criteria, the lot often passes. I started investigating why this can occur.

"This investigation led me to the appreciation that an AQL test is fundamentally a statistical hypothesis test. In hypothesis testing, a population sample performance leads to reacting to a null or alternative statement as though it were true. In AQL testing, the null hypothesis is basically that the lot meets a defective-rate-criterion, while the alternative hypothesis is that the lot does not meet the defective-rate-criterion. There's a risk of being wrong when either accepting or rejecting a lot because of how well the sample performs relative to the number of failures that are statistically determined acceptable given a specified number of samples.

"The first kicker with AQL testing alternatives, as provided in one set of commonly referenced tables, is that a sample may need to exhibit a defective rate much worse than a desired test defective-rate criterion for a lot's rejection. Because of this statistical-risk-of-being-wrong-calculation reality, a supplier quality level for a lot may be unsatisfactory, where the resubmission of a failed lot may pass the second-time-around. This second-test passage could occur because of the so-to-speak luck of the draw, where, by just chance, the second-lot sample performed better relative to an acceptable AQL table-determined defective criterion than the first lot's sample.

"It's interesting to note that many on our team think that we should make it a general practice to mark all rejected lots and look for this marking for all received lots. The logic for this practice would be to confront vendors when we receive lots that are marked, telling them that each rejected lot needs to have corrective action. Does the rejected-lot-secret-marking approach fix the fundamental problem? I don't think so. It seems to me that there are some underlying issues with AQL testing.

"The second kicker with AQL testing is that suppliers produce products for our organization from their processes. However, AQL does not assess how well a *process* is performing relative to providing products that meet our specified-requirement needs over many lots delivered to our company. Lot-to-lot variation received from our suppliers should be a potential source of common-cause-variation consideration from the supplier's production process; however, the basis of an AQL sampling statistic calculation is that the population is only the current delivered lot.

"This has two fundamental problems. One problem is that one is starting with basically a *clean sheet of paper* when testing a newly received lot from a supplier. Typically there's no consideration about past-lot performance in the AQL decision-making process as to whether to pass or fail an individual lot. An only-this-lot assessment can lead to a considerable sample size hit when making an informed statistical decision about the sample. Secondly, the underlying philosophy of AQL does not structurally consider that a current lot originated from a process that created previously delivered lots.

"This second point is inconsistent with IEE thinking, which encourages the examination of data from a process-as-a-whole-output point of view to first determine if a process lot-to-lot response is stable and, if so, what's the expected defective-rate performance level of the process. When a delivered non-conformance rate is considered undesirable, there should be process improvement efforts undertaken at the supplier. AQL tests aren't consistent with this form of process-output thinking, and encouragement to make long-lasting processes enhancements whenever an output response is undesirable.

"For this AQL data-set situation, it would have been better to create a 30,000-foot-level report, where the time-series individuals chart horizontal increments are a sequence of lots, and the vertical axis is the proportion of defective sampled units for each lot. When the process output response is considered stable, and the reported expected defective-rate statement is not desirable, process improvement is needed.

"One, perhaps not appreciated benefit, from a 30,000-foot-level examination and reporting of the results of many lots, is first that for this situation the population has expanded from an individual lot test to a process-output evaluation of multiple lots. Secondly, the statement below the report's charting now reflects this shift in population perspective, which inherently can have a much larger sample size, at no additional costs. A benefit of this increased sample size is that any statement below the report's charting will have more confidence in the accuracy of the best-estimate reporting.

"When a supplier's product delivery 30,000-foot-level report is unsatisfactory, this high-level chart should then be discussed with the supplier asking for a process improvement action plan on what they'll be doing to reduce the supplied part's defective rate. The individuals chart in this high-level reporting will provide insight as to whether any process enhancements occurred over time.

"Eventually, a company would probably want its suppliers to take ownership of this 30,000-foot-level metric, its data entry, and then electronically report results to its customer for all delivered products and its key metrics.

"A periodic customer-supplier audit can assess the correct creation of supplier 30,000-foot-level reports and that there was no playing games with the numbers. For organizations that use AQL techniques, I now think that there can be many benefits with a transition from AQL lot testing to 30,000-foot-level process measurement and improvement techniques."

Hank, then said, "I know that this has been a long-winded explanation of one type of testing that occurs in manufacturing. Jorge and Zack may never have seen this form of testing. However, my underlying message is that we need to step back to our overall measurement system to determine if our current approach is the best, relative to addressing the real needs of the business.

"I want to thank Jorge for introducing me to IEE, which has opened my eyes, so I now see that we need to revisit many of our current policies and practices, which may have some fundamental issues. I think that constructively challenging many of these policies and practices in conjunction with executing our IEE enterprise improvement plan (EIP), will provide many more bottom-line benefits than any business enhancement effort that we've undertaken in the past – by far.

"When leadership regularly discusses the status of their EIP's execution, asking for project-execution-status, that's to enhance important 30,000-foot-level performance business metrics, positive actions will inevitably occur. For one thing, process improvement projects will most certainly be completed much faster than what I've seen in past process-improvement programs!"

Jorge responded, "Wow, Hank! I'm very impressed! You're internalizing the concepts of IEE and truly understand how the methodology is much more than a process-improvement program."

Zack then said, "Hank, yes, at Z-Credit Financial, we do not conduct AQL tests, but we do execute audits, which is a type of test. You've got me wondering about the consistency and organizational feedback of these audits. I would suspect that there could be vast differences among the people and organizations conducting the audit.

"However, what just occurred to me is that audits and their feedback can only address simplistic issues and not any business management system issues that may be prevalent. The results from some audits might not be any different than moving chairs on the Titanic as it sinks."

Jorge responded, "Yes, exactly, Zack."

Jorge continued, "An audit could occur in a variety of situations. An examination could be of a supplier, by a customer, for ISO 9001 certification, or a Malcolm Baldrige criteria assessment. For organizational evaluations in general, it should be much simpler and more effective if the audited organizations have implemented the IEE business management system. The reason for making this claim is that all basic auditing desires, from a systematic-framework point of view, are addressed with the implementation of the 9-step IEE framework.

"IEE organizations could benefit if they transition their internal process assessments to the creation of an IEE-system internal audit. This business-management system assessment would give focus on how well their organization is implementing the details of the IEE business management system. A created audit-check-sheet should provide consistent guidance for the details of an IEE system implementation assessment that results in more consistent evaluations between auditors and opportunity for improvement (OFI) feedback from them that provides more value to the organization."

Wayne then stated, "I like what you said about an IEE approach to auditing. I cannot imagine how much our company spends on self-audits and on-site auditing of our suppliers. At times, I've wondered how much all this work and associated expenses lead to true customer benefits and bottom-line benefits."

Hank then interjected, "Boy, do I agree with everything said. On Monday, I'm going to look into how our company is conducting audits and what we might do differently from an IEE perspective to improve our evaluations."

Jorge responded, "Great observations and comments! So good that you appreciate the value of IEE with its hidden nuggets."

Jorge continued, "In a previous outing, I described the 'Design,' 'Measure,' and 'Analyze' phases of the IEE DMAIC methodology. In this conversation, we referenced SmarterSolutions.com/roadmap for implementation details. I would now like to complete this IEE DMAIC execution-details discussion by addressing the roadmap's 'Improve' and 'Control' phases."

Jorge smiled as he saw three thumbs-up signs from his friends.

Jorge then said, "Again, access the SmarterSolutions.com/roadmap on your phone's internet browser.

"A selection of the 'Improve' phase on this web page will show a many-step flowchart with several decision symbols (See Figure 10.1). Not all shown IEE DMAIC improve steps need execution when following this roadmap but should be considered. Included in this 'Improve phase' drill-down are process steps for performing design of experiments (DOE), utilization of Lean concepts, and more.

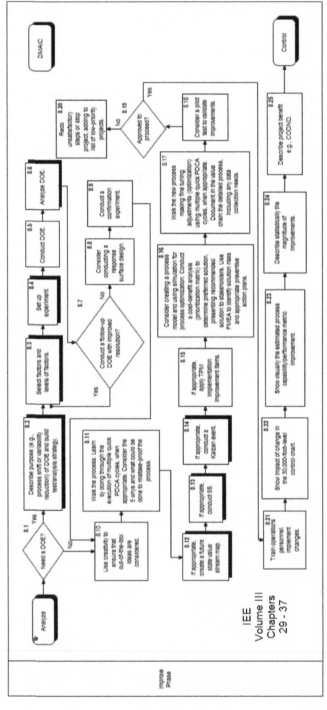

Figure 10.1: IEE DMAIC Roadmap – Improve Phase

"Step 8.1 asks the question, 'Need a DOE?' Earlier today, we talked about DOE, its benefits for improving a process-output response, and that not all improvement projects need a DOE.

"Ron stressed the point that if an improvement manufacturing or transactional project wants to evaluate whether a specific process change enhances a process-output response, a DOE should be considered. As was noted earlier, the structure of a DOE can provide information about the interaction of inputs on the output response of a process, for which a one-at-a-time experimental assessment approach can't.

"Let's now discuss the IEE DOE implementation steps 8.2 through 8.6. Each of these steps has a drill-down that provides more execution details.

"Step 8.2 states, 'Describe the purpose of DOE and build a test and analysis strategy.' For example, the objective of a DOE may be to shift the mean or reduce the variation of a 30,000-foot-level metric identified in an EIP as being essential for overall business enhancement. DOE experiments can be costly; hence, a well-developed upfront plan is vital.

"Step 8.3 states, 'Select factors and levels of factors.' This step is essential since the process-improvement team needs to agree on what factors and their levels to consider in the experiment. We don't want anyone providing so-called Monday-morning-quarterback feedback on what we should have been done differently in the test.

"I need to highlight the importance of choosing the levels of factors in a DOE. I'll use a manufacturing situation to underline this point, but the concept applies equally to transactional DOE tests.

"Consider that a 30,000-foot-level reported dimension on a plastic injected molded manufactured part is not consistently providing a desirable part-dimension. In the IEE DMAIC 'Wisdom of the Organization' phase, a machine processing temperature was an identified factor. Our passive IEE DMAIC analysis did not indicate that this temperature had a significant response impact on the part dimension addressed in our current process operating temperature range.

"This non-significant statistical finding for temperature could, nevertheless, mean that changing temperature either up or down beyond our current operational range might impact the focus dimension of the part. With a DOE, we could structurally increase or decrease the temperature in our DOE experiment beyond current operating conditions, while at the same time evaluating other factors such as injection speed and pressure with potential interactions.

"When selecting factor levels, we need to have our technical process wizards present. We want to be bold in making the difference between high and low settings for the DOE inputs for our statistical significance tests, but not so different in factor-level-settings that the extreme of setting selection creates other issues. Also, it's important to monitor other process-output responses to make sure that these responses aren't negatively impacting something else. By giving focused attention to optimized setting process inputs for one dimension of a part, we might negatively impact something else that's also important to the process output response. Because of this risk, we must exercise care when setting up and exercising an experiment."

Wayne commented, "Jorge, sounds great! I noticed that you linked this DOE effort to an EIP, and it's great not to lose sight of the organization's overall financials; however, could DOE concepts also apply to efforts that aren't strategic?"

Jorge responded, "Glad you brought that point up, Wayne. Yes, other situations besides non-strategic process improvement efforts can benefit from DOEs. One situation that may not be obvious is that DOE can be used within a process to improve it; for example, the use of DOE in product development and then testing the new design for satisfactory performance under various customer situations. A couple of the books listed on the SmarterSolutions.com website provide how-to details of executing a DOE in various situations."

Wayne's response was, "Great to hear, Jorge. I've some homework to do."

Jorge then said, "Let's now look at the web page roadmap steps 8.4 – 8.6, which are 'Set up experiment,' 'Conduct DOE,' and 'Analyze DOE.' Proper execution of these steps is vital to the success of a DOE. Additional DOE steps shown on this web page include considering whether a response surface design should be executed and conducting a confirmation experiment. One thing that I want to highlight is that an

IEE approach for conducting a fractional factorial DOE suggests that one should not exclude factors because of two-level factor confounding concerns. One of the IEE books that I mentioned earlier provides some unique ways to get more information about two-factor interactions with fewer test trials when using wisely applied fractional factorial designs and analysis techniques.

"This IEE DMAIC 'Improve phase' drill-down also includes a step for the 'Use of creativity to ensure that out-of-the-box ideas are considered.' Creativity is an essential consideration for making beneficial process improvement efforts. Generated created ideas might also be included as factors within a DOE to test out idea-theories.

"Hank, I'm sure that you'll see some familiar Lean methodologies in this IEE DMAIC SmarterSolutions.com/roadmap web page view. Included in this IEE DMAIC drill-down are the plan-do-check-act (PDCA) cycle, 5 whys, process mistake proofing, future state value stream map, 5S workplace organization, kaizen event, walking-the-process, and Total Productive Maintenance (TPM)."

Hank responded, "Yes, Jorge, this drill-down looks like a perfect place for these tools to reside for usage consideration. I like how this IEE DMAIC approach emphasizes using the most essential Lean or Six Sigma tool for the enhancement of vital business 30,000-foot-level performance metric reports.

"In time, this IEE DMAIC approach for improvement should reduce contention between our companies' Lean and Six Sigma zealots on what approach and tools should be used for enhancing our processes."

Jorge responded, "Great to hear, Hank.

"Other process steps in this drill-down include showing an enhancement to a project's 30,000-foot-level individuals chart for improved processes, with a quantification of the enhanced performance level. Included also is 'Describe statistically the magnitude of improvements' and 'Describe the project cost of doing nothing differently (CODND)' reduction, when appropriate.'

"Demonstrating the benefit of IEE DMAIC process improvement through the staging of a 30,000-foot-level report is very important, along with a statistical statement of the benefit with a confidence interval and a cost of doing nothing differently reporting. The IEE methodology offers a systems thinking approach to business measurements and improvement. Once there's a resolution to any confusion to the IEE systems thinking approach to business-measurements and improvements, organization leadership will surely appreciate this IEE improvement project deliverable and will be asking for this type of information for their strategic improvement project in general.

"I want to illustrate now how a 30,000-foot-level chart can show the benefits of process improvement efforts. One improvement project that we discussed the other day was reducing lead time, as reported in a 30,000-foot-level chart."

Jorge then handed each of his friends a sheet of paper and said, "Shown on this 30,000-foot-level report is the staging of a metric when a process improvement project transitioned a measurement to an enhanced level of performance (See Figure 10.2).

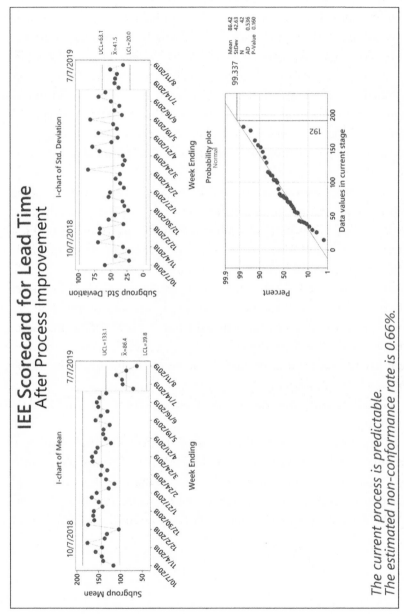

Figure 10.2: 30,000-foot-level Metric: Lead Time (After Process Improvement)

"In this 30,000-foot-level report, the mean and standard deviation individuals charts indicate process-response stability since 7/7/2019. From the included normal-distribution probability plot, the current estimated non-conformance rate is 0.66% relative to meeting a customer-need-lead-time requirement of 192 hours or less. This 30,000-foot-level metric non-conformance rate is much lower than the *before change* estimated rate of 16.4% (Reference Figure 9.8). If this new estimated magnitude for non-conformance, relative to the upper duration specification of 192 hours, is considered acceptable, the improvement project is deemed completed after the establishment of a control plan for maintaining the gain.

"This 30,000-foot-level metric after-process-improvement report provides both a visual and quantification of the benefits from the process-improvement project. The difference in the cost of doing nothing differently (CODND) before and after the change can offer a quantification of the financial benefits from this improvement project."

Zack responded, "Your illustration of how a 30,000-foot-level report can demonstrate the benefits from process-improvement efforts was great. Z-Credit Financial can gain much from 30,000-foot-level reporting. I also like how the IEE DMAIC approach is more than just the usage of process improvement tools individually, but how all the tools can be linked together."

Jorge then said, "Yes, Zack, I like these aspects of the IEE DMAIC system, too.

"Let's now move to the final phase of the IEE DMAIC roadmap. The SmarterSolutions.com/roadmap IEE DMAIC 'Control phase' drill-down (See Figure 10.3) includes the documentation of processes and their performance metrics. Enterprise Performance Reporting System (EPRS) software provides a vehicle for accomplishing this 'Control phase' need."

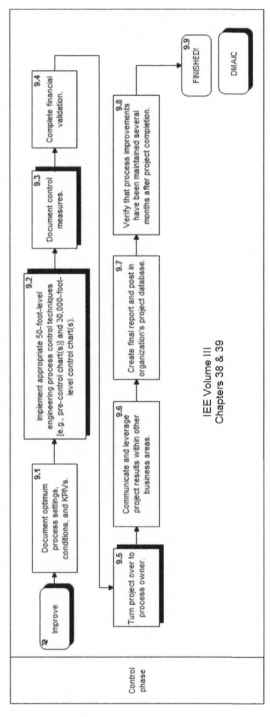

Figure 10.3: IEE DMAIC Roadmap – Control Phase

Wayne stopped Jorge immediately, saying, "What you just said about usage of an EPRS-type software in a 'Control phase' is so essential for the documentation and automated updating of metrics, which are available to all authorized participants!

"In our Lean Six Sigma program, we talk about the 'Control phase' in the DMAIC roadmap. However, it seems like the control measures for our DMAIC improvement projects involve someone's going back to view the process to see if the new process procedures are being followed. Besides being an expensive use of people's time, more often than not, this maintain-the-gain check DMAIC control isn't occurring regularly, if at all in my company.

"In your described EPRS software, I like having the project's new procedures documented so that this information is in alignment with the enhanced IEE value chain 30,000-foot-level metric, which is then automatically updated.

"With this software, everyone can view current information 24/7 relative to up-to-date procedures and high-level performance metrics. This 30,000-foot-level form of reporting provides a high-level means for process-output response monitoring, where timely control measures are undertaken if an individuals chart in a 30,000-foot-level performance metric report indicates a response degradation."

Jorge comments, "Wayne, great observation! I agree!

"I want to highlight a few other aspects of this IEE DMAIC 'Control phase' drill-down. Notice also how there is a step, 'Create final report and post in organization's project database.' This activity could also be undertaken through EPRS software not only for documentation in the current impacted organization but in other organizations as described in the additional step 'Communicate and leverage project results within other business areas.'

"Hope you found this IEE DMAIC wrap-up discussion to be beneficial."

Another smile appeared on Jorge's face when he again saw three thumbs-up signs from his friends.

Wayne then said, "You've sold me. I'm going to discuss the value of an IEE implementation with our CEO."

With that, four happy and relaxed golfers headed home with hopes for continued improvement.

11 MAKING PROGRESS

NOVEMBER

It was a beautiful November day, enjoyable enough that Zack had the top down on his convertible as he pulled into the course parking lot. Today he was looking good and feeling good.

The first thing out of Zack's mouth when he saw Hank at the practice green was, "I expected to see you at the driving range. Are you taking Jorge's advice and practicing your weaknesses instead of your strengths?" When Hank just smiled and ignored him, he said, "From the IEE book Jorge recommended in our conference-call conversation, I understand how the structure of the design of experiments (DOE) techniques that we discussed does not confound individual factor effects."

Hank just smiled again, thinking about Zack, the stylish analytic.

Wayne, who was also putting, said, "Hank, I see now, from the example you pointed out in our conference call, how DOE techniques can be beneficial in the development process. Those real examples were very insightful. I can see how examples from the books used within IEE can help communicate specific application techniques to suppliers and customers who haven't yet experienced IEE and its benefits."

Zack added, "I'm thinking about how so many companies have product recall problems. It's happening in the automobile and computer industries quite regularly. Why aren't they using IEE?"

"Interesting you said that, Zack," said Jorge as he arrived on the scene. "I've wondered the same thing. Many of these companies would

215

say that they're implementing Lean Six Sigma if you ask them. There must be hundreds, if not thousands, of Lean Six Sigma providers now popping up all over. I have to wonder how many of these providers are just jumping on the bandwagon. I wonder how many of these deployments truly address business needs."

Jorge continued, "Let me tell you what happened last month with the two projects that I've been working on. With both projects, we identified some key process input variables that are driving our key process output variables. We changed our processes so that the drivers would give the most consistent response possible. In some cases, we were able to mistake-proof the process. In other situations, there're processes where an important key process input variable (KPIV) to a process will drift, and a timely adjustment to this KPIV is needed to maintain or transition its 30,000-foot-level process output response to within a desired range of responses. In IEE, such a KPIV would be tracked at a 50-foot-level so that timely adjustment interventions occur when appropriate.

"A couple of examples that will need this type of inherent intervention are:

- The periodic redressing of grinding wheels because of operational wear.
- The addition or reduction of available call center operators because of phone volume differences throughout the day.

"A pre-control chart is a methodology that can be useful when tracking a KPIV to determine when to take action. A couple of things to keep in mind is that we need to truly understand the key process input variable (KPIV) to key process output variable (KPOV) relationship, including how much change in a KPIV affects its KPOV. In IEE, pre-control charts are beneficial for KPIV, 50-foot-level reports, but not for KPOV reporting.

"A pre-control chart uses a red-yellow-green color-coding scheme. Documented rules describe when to take action relative to how data points appear in the red-yellow-green colored bands. An internet search and the referenced IEE books describe the details for creating a pre-control chart, with its process adjustment rules for KPIs.

"Grocery store check-out lines are a situation where KPIV 50-foot-level pre-control charting could be used for the management of a process so that there is the achievement of a consistent desired range of KPOV responses. In reality, I've never seen a grocery store formally use a pre-control chart in its operation. Still, grocery stores do follow a similar thought process when managing the number of check-out clerks available at differing times throughout a day.

"To explain this process management approach, consider that for a grocery store that has many check-out lanes, a KPOV is checkout time. From studies, the grocery story strives to achieve a range of times before a cashier begins scanning groceries for a customer to be between one and eight minutes. The reason one minute is the lower limit and not zero is that a zero indicates that a cashier is waiting for someone to check-out, a resource waste from the grocery store's point of view. Instead of waiting for someone to checkout, an idle checkout person could be doing other needed work somewhere else in the store. The high value of eight minutes is the maximum wait time that the grocery store believes customers consider acceptable.

"The store could set pre-control red-yellow-green action criteria to track the average number of people waiting in the grocery lines during check-out. For the pre-control red-colored limits, values for the average number of people in the check-out lines could be four people for the upper red trigger point and one person for the lower red trigger point.

"Conceptually, someone or an in-store-video scanner could monitor the average number of people in the check-out line at a sampling-frequency and with the decision-making-logic add or reduce the number of checkers following traditional pre-control charting rules.

"The basic IEE concept that organizations may need to manage the Xs in a process to achieve the desired range of Y responses is different from attempting to manage a process through Y-output responses, which often happens with traditional scorecards. Not to sound like a broken record, but Y-output management can lead to firefighting common-cause variation as though it were special-cause, which lead to unfavorable, if not destructive, behaviors."

"This makes perfect sense," Hank said. "Not to change the subject, but I wanted to mention something. I haven't mentioned this before, but I found that the soft-skill aspect of IEE also to be advantageous. This effort involved people skills such as team building and change management. We also covered some creativity and project management skills."

Zack then asked, "Do you have any lessons learned from your initial IEE implementation, Jorge?"

Jorge said, "Yes, I do. For one thing, it's essential to have an excellent system for selecting people who are most suited for filling our IEE Black Belt and Master Black Belt positions. Again, these individuals have a much broader skill set and responsibility than traditional Lean Six Sigma Black Belts and Master Black Belts. We needed to replace one person initially selected for our IEE implementation Team since this person was not a good fit.

"Also, our IEE implementation is benefiting from the enterprise improvement plan (EIP) methodology in the sizing and selection of process improvement projects. Through this process, IEE value chain owners achieve operational performance metric enhancements that help the big picture. However, some pet projects did appear in our EIP that were not genuinely benefiting the big picture. After about a month, we removed these projects from our EIP.

"Furthermore, having software that provides automatic updating of 30,000-foot-level metrics that are in alignment with the processes that created them through an IEE value chain is very beneficial to the success of our deployment. Also important is including, as a part of this EPRS software system, a methodology that provides secure, anytime access to the status of IEE improvement projects for all authorized.

"We're finding that the IEE system's visibility and transparency provide project spotlight focus so that there are timely resolutions to any project-completion barriers, and there is prompt completion of project-scheduled tasks. The result of these aspects of IEE is that there is rapid completion of improvement projects, and our organization's culture is making positive enhancements. Employees are feeling less stress, and the financials are experiencing the benefit of our deployment. We're now moving toward having our suppliers more involved with our IEE implementation."

Zack responded, "Where are you going to go from here, Jorge?"

Jorge replied, "Well, as mentioned in an earlier outing, we've created a function called Enterprise Process Management or EPM, which I lead. My team is making significant progress refining our IEE value chain and its automatic metric reporting-updating system.

"Also, if you recall, step nine of the 9-step IEE system loops back to step three, which is 'Analyze.' One of the roles of my team is to work continually within this IEE system loop. In addition to working with others on EIP identified improvement projects, our EPM function is providing leadership both with timely results from enterprise statistical analyses and with what might be done differently by thinking outside of the box. Currently, it appears through this overall effort that our hospital's mean monthly profit is on track to improve by 10%."

Wayne interjected, "Jorge, your financial benefits statement was for your hospital as a whole. We're using a traditional Lean Six Sigma approach that states there was a certain amount of savings from improvement projects. With our approach, we spend a lot of time putting together these numbers. It seems to me that there's often a lot of politics involved in these calculated financial results. In all honesty, I question how much these reported saving are positively impacting the bottom-line."

Jorge responded, "Exactly, Wayne. We wanted to avoid our organization's reporting 100 million dollars in savings, but nobody can find the money.

"The 10% profit improvement benefit that I stated to you is somewhat of a best-estimate, big-picture statistical statement. Leadership was amazed that the common-cause variation in our monthly profit satellite-level metric over five years indicated stability.

"The improvement of this satellite-level, baseline metric became the focus of our EIP efforts. This attentive exertion identified some major low-hanging fruit improvement efforts both for reducing costs and increasing revenue."

Wayne commented, "This makes so much sense to me. Our Lean Six Sigma focus has evolved to getting a so-called hard-savings benefit in a localized business area, which may not benefit the big picture. Increasing revenue in our deployment gets little, if any, consideration."

Zack said, "Guess this is getting your CEO's attention."

Jorge said, "It sure is. Janice has commented that this reported savings are a somewhat small gain when evaluating the overall value of our IEE implementation.

"She is liking that we now have an IEE value chain system and monthly metric reporting that's leading to the right activities at the right time throughout our organization. Our firefighting has most certainly decreased.

"She admits that it was difficult for her to transition initially from table-of-numbers and red-yellow-green scorecard reporting to satellite-level and 30,000-foot-level performance metric reporting. However, now she has internalized the methodology and its benefits.

"She's now requiring anybody that reports a table of numbers or red-yellow-green scorecard to go back and do his or her homework to translate these metrics to 30,000-foot-level performance metrics reporting. She's insisting on the inclusion of these metrics in our IEE value chain using EPRS software.

"The results of Janice's focus on utilization of the IEE system methodologies are cascading throughout Harris. All managers are beginning to have a consistent systems thinking mentality.

"Janice is planning not only to carry the financial savings numbers forward to the board of directors but also to present our overall IEE system and how it has improved how we do business. She plans to put something in our annual report about the system and the benefits we've achieved for our customers and our shareholders."

Zack then said, "You know how I wanted to get some face time with our CEO? Well, I could not get on his calendar. It seems like he was too busy."

Wayne said, "I was able to get in touch with our CEO at Wonder-Chem, but I don't believe that he shared my enthusiasm. He told me to get with the education department to discuss it."

Jorge said, "I want to re-emphasize that I'm delighted we have Janice on board. She's very receptive and listens to our suggestions. She's getting to the point where she's asking us the right questions. As for your point, Wayne, I'm concerned about rollouts through the education department. This type of IEE rollout does not mean that this strategy won't work, but my image of a deployment that originates from the education department is that focus will be on just teaching a bunch of tools. An IEE deployment is most successful when it's a part of managing the business and rolled out through those areas which are doing the operational tasks within a company."

Jorge continued, "And Zack, how about refocusing the intent of your meeting with your CEO? Build a case for IEE by going back and collecting some of your major business metrics. I can help you present the data in a 30,000-foot-level format. We can then make a rough pass at the cost of doing nothing differently. I'll bet that your CEO will have a 180-degree change in perspective after seeing our findings."

Hank responded, "I agree with Jorge. I've learned a lesson about selling IEE, too. Talk the language your CEO likes to hear: money and what relieves his or her pain. I want to elaborate more on this pain point. People may have health issues, and they do not even know it. A physician often asks her patient questions that help uncover un-noticed health issues. When communicating with a CEO or other leaders, I like asking questions about the achievement of the five *Effective Management Attributes* listed on page two of the 'Positive Metric Performance Poor Business Performance' article. These questions can uncover pain issues that he or she has not thought about."

Jorge then said, "Hank, I agree. I think asking questions associated with the achievement of the *Effective Management Attributes* listed at the beginning of the article can get people thinking. What helped set the stage for my initial IEE proposal-meeting to Janice was first to have an IEE-consultant conversation. When proposing something so valuable to the business, I believe that it's vital to utilize the IEE expertise of someone who can provide helpful guidance, perhaps building from past *lessons learned* experiences."

The round of golf that followed was another good one, or, as Jorge would have described it, the second set of scores from an improved process that transitioned scores downward using a 30,000-foot-level performance metric tracking methodology.

For the first time, in a long time, there was no business discussion during the round or lunch that followed.

12 IT WAS GOOD TO RELAX. THE 19TH HOLE

DECEMBER

Zack was running to catch up with the others at the first tee. He called ahead excitedly, "As you suggested, Jorge, I worked with Ron, your IEE consultant, to build a CEO-conversation strategy. When we presented the metrics to our CEO and showed him how the cost of doing nothing differently (CODND) was running at least 20% of our gross income, he suddenly got interested. Now I've a new job. I'll be leading the corporation's new IEE Deployment. Our rollout starts next month. Deploying IEE is going to be fun!"

Jorge responded, "I'm looking forward to hearing your story in the upcoming months. I must warn you, though, that my consulting fees will be going up considerably if you get promoted."

"If so, that'd be worth it!" Zack smiled. "Now, I've some control over my game's key process input variables (KPIVs). You know, my grip, stance, and swing basics—we'll win enough golf bets to pay for them."

Zack's first tee shot backed up his boast, a gentle draw about 240 yards in the left-center of the fairway.

Stepping up to the tee, Wayne said, "I had a similar experience when I set up another meeting with our CEO and started speaking his language. When I put the advantages in terms of overall financial money and pain relief, he bought it immediately. We're setting up the infrastructure to start our IEE rollout next month as well."

Hank smiled, "Ah yes, the universal language of business executives has always been money. But pain relief also needs to be ranked up there with the presentation of organizational money using an IEE approach."

Wayne continued, "I agree with Zack. After my eye surgery, I see so much better reading the greens and judging distances. We'll be winning more bets and collecting more of that money portion of the universal language from you two."

Wayne followed up his comments with monotonous precision. His drive was another ho-hum performance off the tee, 265 yards straight down the middle in the perfect location.

Jorge commented, "Looks like we better step it up, partner."

Hank teed his ball. With plenty of room to work within the fairway, he hit a monster drive that airmailed Wayne and Zack, leaving him in perfect birdie position.

Hank said, "You may want to check your credit limits to see if they can handle a lunch tab after all."

Jorge then hit his soft fade down the middle a few yards behind Zack's ball. He was the short hitter off the tee. But, from this position in the fairway, Jorge knew that he was actually ahead of the game. He hit first from the fairway, putting his 5 wood on the green, and the pressure was firmly back on the others in the group.

Jorge commented, "You know, I just realized that we're all enjoying our game much more. We all seem to be under a lot less stress."

Hank had resolved his Mexican production problems and had moved on to bigger, new cost savings and revenue enhancements from his IEE program, making Hi-tech very competitive on price, while still trading on its high-quality reputation. Hank had just been named senior vice president with new corporate-wide IEE enterprise process management responsibilities. It meant fewer day-to-day headaches and more time for golf and maybe even a family life again.

Wayne had leveraged IEE at Wonder-Chem, building on the previous Lean Six Sigma training, to create a definite competitive advantage in over-the-counter health care products. Now he was excited about executing the Design for Six Sigma (DFSS) portion of the IEE roadmap and its potential to improve R&D and reduce product development times.

The IEE DFSS process follows a Define, Measure, Analyze, Design, and Verify (DMADV) roadmap. It had turned out that not only was money a universal language component for CEOs, but time was also money.

Zack was also making personal progress as the corporate IEE director for Z-Credit. He was finding a fertile market for business improvement in the financial sector and was beginning to build a reputation as a fast tracker again. He was even getting home most evenings before his wife and kids went to bed!

As for Jorge, he was proud that he had been able to improve Harris Hospital's performance in such a short time. It seemed that there was more orchestration of activities. He had kept his promise to provide his patients with the best care possible at the lowest possible cost. Now he spent most of his time coaching teams on applying the IEE methodology instead of fighting managerial fires. "Isn't it great to love your job!" he thought.

At the end of the round, when the group met at Jorge's SUV in the parking lot, everyone looked at Jorge as Hank asked, "So when is our next golf date?"

Wayne and Zack chimed in, "Yes, and what's our next lesson, *Professor* Jorge?"

13 EPILOG

The previous chapters of this book described the Integrated Enterprise Excellence (IEE) business management and its benefits.

The Appendix of this book offers additional information about IEE and the implementation of its methodologies:

- Appendix A provides more than 20 website links for further details about the IEE methodology and its use.
- Appendix B provides information about the book's datasets, scorecards, and companies.
- Appendix C describes how-to-implement IEE books and assistance.

The book *Leadership System 2.0: Implementing Integrated Enterprise Excellence* (Breyfogle 2020b) (Reference Appendix A, Web page 20) provides in a novel-book format:

- Description of an IEE deployment, including gaining the sponsorship of Janice Davis, Harris Hospital's CEO (Chapter 4)
- Description of EPRS software implementation at Harris Hospital (Chapter 6)
- IEE application illustrations in a non-profit organization, school, mining company, and government (Chapter 9)
- Over eighty application examples of IEE techniques (Appendix A)

Often people do not have time to read a recommended book. For readers and listeners of this book who believe that their organization could benefit from IEE, they might suggest that their manager or others listen to this book when commuting to-and-from work or while exercising. If the book described concepts appear beneficial to this person, he or she could suggest this audiobook to others.

One initial casual book-listening suggestion could lead to an audiobook organizational dissemination of IEE concepts and its benefits. In time, the CEO, or another organization leader, could receive a recommendation that he or she listens to this audiobook. After listening to this book, those organizational leaders who want to investigate IEE further should then be asking for the book-described IEE one-on-one leadership meeting.

For additional thoughts on how to present the IEE business management system to others, see Appendix A, Web page 18.

14

APPENDIX A: WEB PAGES FOR IEE ARTICLES, VIDEO, AND SOFTWARE

The resource center at SmarterSolutions.com provides information on various aspects of IEE and its implementation details (Reference Appendix A, Web page 21).

The following web pages are a subset of this website's resource center. Provided is a video link and other material, where many of these pages offer a linked-to-PDF article at the bottom of the page that contains additional details.

Web page 1: Integrated Enterprise Excellence (IEE)
One-minute Referenced Video

- Summary: Provides a one-minute video that describes the benefits of the IEE system with its performance metric tracking methodology over traditional scorecards.
- Web page: SmarterSolutions.com/iee-one-minute-video

Web page 2: Integrated Enterprise Excellence (IEE) Overview
Referenced Article

- Summary: Provides the "Positive Metrics Poor Business Performance: How Does this Happen?" article, which summarizes the 9-step IEE system, in a PDF format.
- Web page: SmarterSolutions.com/iee-article

Web page 3: Examples – Converting Company Scorecards to 30,000-foot-level Performance Metric Reports

- Summary: Provides links to eight actual-company-dataset examples that illustrate the conversion of various traditional business scorecards to 30,000-foot-level performance metric reports and the additional insight gained through these conversions.
- Web page: SmarterSolutions.com/iee-scorecard-conversions

Web page 4: The Improvement of Scorecard Management: Comparing Deming's Red-Bead Experiment to Red-Yellow-Green Scorecards

- Summary: Describes how common-place organizational red-yellow-green scorecards have the same issues that Deming illustrated in his 1980's training with his red-bead experiment and how a 30,000-foot-level reporting resolves this RYG scorecard reporting issue.
- Web page: SmarterSolutions.com/red-bead-experiment

Web page 5: Business Goal Setting and Process Improvement – Is there a Conflict?

- Summary: Describes the advantages of converting from a next month or quarter financial specified-value-goal-setting methodology to giving focus to the improvement of a mean monthly response such as organizational profit margins or EBITDA.
- Web page: SmarterSolutions.com/iee-goal-setting

Web page 6: Diabetes Measurement Tracking at the 30,000-foot-level

- Summary: Illustrates the transition of a diabetic's physician-visit and individual-daily readings to a 30,000-foot-level format and the benefits of this transition. Included is an IEE Analysis of

Means (ANOM) that provides insight for making improvements so that future reported diabetic-measurements could be enhanced. The concepts in this diabetes-metrics-tracking example are not unlike many personal and business-metric situations.

- Web page: SmarterSolutions.com/iee-diabetes-metrics

Web page 7: A System to Capture and React to Voice of the Customer

- Summary: Provides a methodology for capturing actionable VOC information in an IEE value chain, which can have whole-enterprise benefits.
- Web page: SmarterSolutions.com/iee-voc

Web page 8: Reports to reduce the Risk of Organizational Problems

- Summary: Provides a methodology for reducing organizational risks as part of an IEE business management system.
- Web page: SmarterSolutions.com/iee-risk-management

Web page 9: Beyond Lean Six Sigma – Why Lean and Six Sigma Deployments Fail and What You Can Do to Resolve the Issue

- Summary: Describes why traditional Lean Six Sigma deployments are not typically long-lasting and how the IEE system addresses this issue by improving functional 30,000-foot-level metrics that benefit the business as a whole.
- Web page: SmarterSolutions.com/iee-lean-six-sigma-issues-resolution

Web page 10: Organizational Business Management System Issues – Examples of Managing to the Ys Where Unfavorable or Destructive Behaviors Resulted

- Summary: Describes how an IEE implementation and usage might have prevented the publicized, unfavorable, and destructive issues that occurred in many well-respected companies.
- Web page: SmarterSolutions.com/iee-y-management-issues-resolution

Web page 11: IEE Business Management and Process Improvement Theory

- Summary: Provides over 30 links to IEE implementation details and applications theory
- Web page: SmarterSolutions.com/iee-theory

Web page 12: Integrated Enterprise Excellence (IEE) Blog

- Summary: Provides past and current thoughts about business management and process improvement in IEE blogs. Included in this discussion are the concepts and methodologies of IEE and more.
- Web page: SmarterSolutions.com/iee-blog

Web page 13: EPRS-Metrics Software – 30,000-foot-level and Satellite-level Performance Metrics Reporting

- Summary: Provides software for the creation of 30,000-foot-level and satellite-level performance metric reports for various types of time-series data, using EPRS-metrics software. The author intends to have a *no-charge* licensing fee for this software.
- Web page: SmarterSolutions.com/eprs-metrics-software

Web page 14: EPRS-IEE Software – IEE System

- Summary: Describes EPRS-IEE software (i.e., IEE software) that, among other things, can automatically update 30,000-foot-level and satellite-level metrics, which have a structural linkage through an IEE value chain to the processes that created them. One approach for an organization to accomplish this automatic metric updating is to install EPRS software on a server that is behind the organization's firewall. For each 30,000-foot-level and satellite-level metric, the IEE implementation team determines an appropriate spreadsheet format that the EPRS software will access nightly for updating all IEE performance metrics. Someone in the organization who is very familiar with the organization's databases will create queries that access the organization's databases to fill in the 30,000-foot-level metric spreadsheets in the appropriate formats before the EPRS software nightly updating.
- Web page: SmarterSolutions.com/eprs-iee-software

Web page 15: Characteristics of Successful IEE Master Black Belts and Black Belts

- Summary: Describes the characteristics of successful IEE Master Black Belts and Black Belts.
- Web page: SmarterSolutions.com/iee-belt-characteristics

Web page 16: IEE Implementation Books

- Summary: Provides information about the books that show the how-to details for implementing IEE at both the enterprise and process-improvement level. *Integrated Enterprise Excellence Volume II* describes the particulars for implementing the 9-step IEE business management system. In its 1100+ pages, *Integrated Enterprise Excellence Volume III* provides the details for executing the IEE Define, Measure, Analyze, Improve, and Control

232

(DMAIC) process improvement roadmap. *Lean Six Sigma Project Execution Guide* is a tabbed reference that provides IEE DMAIC roadmap drill-downs that can be quickly accessed.

- Web page: SmarterSolutions.com/iee-books

Web page 17: IEE Training

- Summary: Describes IEE training offerings.
- Web page: SmarterSolutions.com/iee-training

Web page 18: IEE Explanation to Others

- Summary: Provides options on how the IEE business management system can be explained to others so that they appreciate its benefits and understand the basics.
- Web page: SmarterSolutions.com/iee-explanation-to-others

Web page 19: IEE Audio Books

- Summary: Provides access to IEE audiobooks.
- Web page: SmarterSolutions.com/iee-audio-books

Web page 20: IEE Two-book Novel Description

- Summary: Provides access to IEE novel description books in all formats; i.e., *Management 2.0: Discovery of Integrated Enterprise Excellence* (Breyfogle 2020a) and *Leadership System 2.0: Implementing Integrated Enterprise Excellence* (Breyfogle 2020b).
- Web page: SmarterSolutions.com/iee-novel-books

Web page 21: IEE Resource Center

- Summary: Provides articles, videos, and other information about the IEE business management system and process improvement methodologies.
- Web page: SmarterSolutions.com/iee-resource-center

Web page 22: Post-Book-Publication IEE Information

- Summary: Provides post-publication information about the methodologies described in this IEE book.
- Web page: SmarterSolutions.com/iee-post-publication-information

15 APPENDIX B: DATASETS, SCORECARDS, AND COMPANIES

The organizations presented in this book, Harris Hospital, Hi-Tech Computers, Z-Credit Financial, and Wonder-Chem, are fictitious. The author created situations that these companies' employees, Jorge, Hank, Zack, and Wayne, encountered and needed to resolve. The book's storyline presents fabricated scenarios; however, the author has observed all the described conditions at some point in time in his career.

Except for the four scorecards shown in the "Positive Metrics Poor Business Performance" article, figures presented in this book are from randomly-generated datasets that represent what an organization might experience. A website link provides the conversion and benefits of transitioning the article's four scorecard reports to 30,000-foot-level metrics (Reference Appendix A, Web page 3).

The fabricated IEE 30,000-foot-level and satellite-level report book figures originated from randomly-generated datasets from a normal distribution. The associated book figures illustrate the basic concepts of IEE metric reporting using an easy-to-understand presentation format.

One significant difference between the simulated data used to create these book-figures and what the expectation is for some hospitals and other transactional measurements is the normality of data. Often real data for a hospital or another organizational 30,000-foot-level metric situation could be more accurately represented by a non-normal distribution, such as a log-normal distribution.

EPRS-metrics software (Reference Appendix A, Web page 13) can efficiently address non-normal data-distribution circumstances but is beyond the scope of this book (Reference Appendix A, Web page 11).

16 APPENDIX C: HOW-TO-IEE BOOKS AND ASSISTANCE

16.1 IEE IMPLEMENTATION BOOKS

An Integrated Enterprise Excellence (IEE) five-book series (See Figure 16.1) describes the details of implementing IEE both at the enterprise and improvement-project level (Reference Appendix A, Web page 16). These books are a follow-up to the author's ASQ Crosby Medal award-winning book, *Implementing Six Sigma* (Breyfogle 2003).

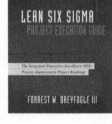

Figure 16.1: Integrated Enterprise Excellence (IEE) Five-book Set

1. *The Integrated Enterprise Excellence System: An Enhanced, Unified Approach to Balanced Scorecards, Strategic Planning, and Business Improvement* (Breyfogle 2008a): This book describes, from a high-level perspective, the IEE system and its benefits over traditional business scorecard, strategic planning, and process improvement methodologies.

2. *Integrated Enterprise Excellence Volume I – The Basics: Golfing Buddies Go Beyond Lean Six Sigma and the Balanced Scorecard* (Breyfogle 2008b): This book describes in a golfing-novel format the IEE system and its benefits over the traditional organizational deployments of Lean, Lean Six Sigma, and the Balanced Scorecard.

3. *Integrated Enterprise Excellence Volume II – Business Deployment: A Leaders' Guide for Going Beyond Lean Six Sigma and the Balanced Scorecard* (Breyfogle 2008c): This book describes the details of implementing the 9-step IEE business management system.

4. *Integrated Enterprise Excellence Volume III – Improvement Project Execution: A Management and Black Belt Guide for Going Beyond Lean Six Sigma and the Balanced Scorecard* (Breyfogle 2008d): This book's 1100+ pages describe the details for executing an enhanced Lean Six Sigma Define, Measure, Analyze, Improve, and Control (DMAIC) improvement project roadmap. In this DMAIC roadmap, there is an integration of Lean and Six Sigma tools so that the right tool is used at the correct time.

5. *Lean Six Sigma Project Execution Guide: The Integrated Enterprise Excellence (IEE) Process Improvement Project Roadmap* (Breyfogle 2010): This book provides, through its tabbed-book structure, quick access to the implementation detail steps of the enhanced IEE DMAIC project execution roadmap.

16.2 IEE IMPLEMENTATION ASSISTANCE

To schedule an IEE implementation conference-call discussion, contact Smarter Solutions, Inc. at info@SmarterSolutions.com.

17 ACRONYMS

5S	Sort, Set in order, Shine, Standardize, and Sustain
AD	Anderson-Darling (test for normality)
ANOVA	Analysis of variance
ANOM	Analysis of means
ANSI/ASQ	American National Standards Institute; American Society for Quality
AQL	Acceptable quality level
BB, IEE	Black Belt, IEE
BPIE	Business process improvement event
CEO	Chief executive officer
COPQ	Cost of poor quality
CODND	Cost of doing nothing differently
DNA	Deoxyribonucleic acid
DFSS	Design for Six Sigma
DMADV	Define, Measure, Analyze, Design, and Verify
DMAIC	Define, Measure, Analyze, Improve, and Control
DOE	Design of experiments
DPMO	Defects per million opportunities
DSO	Days sales outstanding
EBITDA	Earnings before interest, taxes, depreciation, and amortization
EIP	Enterprise improvement plan
EPM	Enterprise process management
EPRS-metrics	Enterprise Performance Reporting System metrics (software); Reference Appendix A, Web page 13

EPRS-IEE	Enterprise Performance Reporting System IEE (software); book also references IEE implementation software as 'EPRS software;' Reference Appendix A, Web page 14
GLM	General linear model
GM	General manager
HIV	Human immunodeficiency virus
HR	Human resources
IEE	Integrated Enterprise Excellence
IMS	Integrated management system
IT	Information technology
KPI	Key performance indicator
KPIV	Key process input variable
KPOV	Key process output variable
LOS	Length of stay
LCL	Lower control limit
LSS	Lean Six Sigma
MBA	Master of business administration
MBB, IEE	Master Black Belt, IEE
MIL-STD	Military standard
MSA	Measurement system analysis
N	Sample size
OKR	Objectives and key results
PDCA	Plan-do-check-act
PGA	Professional Golfers Association
PPM	Parts per million
QHSE	Quality, Health, Safety and Environment (Management)
QMS	Quality management system
R	Range
R&D	Research and development
RYG	Red-yellow-green (scorecard)
s	Standard deviation of a sample
SMART (goals)	Specific, measurable, actionable, relevant, and time-based

SPC	Statistical process control
TOC	Theory of constraints
TPM	Total Productive Maintenance
TPS	Toyota Production System
TQM	Total quality management
VOC	Voice of the Customer
UCL	Upper control limit
VP	Vice president
VSM	Value stream mapping
WIP	Work in progress
WOTO	Wisdom of the organization
XmR	X (individuals), mR (moving range)
$\bar{X}$	Sample mean
YTD	Year to date (measurement response)
μ	Mu, population true mean
σ	Sigma, population true standard deviation

18 GLOSSARY: GOLF TERMINOLOGY

Address: The final position, stance, and actions just before the golf swing begins.

Alignment: The position of the golfer's body and clubface to the target line.

At the turn: After the 9th hole, or the halfway point on an 18-hole golf course, is the *turn* for home point.

Away: The ball or golfer farthest from the hole is *away* and usually the next golfer to shoot.

Best ball: Team competition format in which the best score of any team member is recorded on each hole.

Big dog: A slang term for the driver, the longest golf club that hits the ball the farthest.

Birdie: A hole completed in one shot under par.

Bite: Describes a ball hit with backspin, which stops or backs up on the green.

Blind hole: Any hole where the golfer cannot see the desired target area for a shot.

Bogey: A hole completed in one shot over par.

Break: The turn of a putt to the right or left as it rolls. Also, the contour of the green that causes the putt to turn.

Bump-and-run: An approach shot to the green purposely played to hit into the face of a hill to reduce speed and then run (roll) to the hole.

Bunkers: Grass bunkers are areas on the course with severe terrain that serve as natural obstacles but are not treated as hazards. Sand or pot bunkers filled with sand are treated as hazards.

Casual water: Temporary accumulation of water on the course that is not part of the course design, as from rain or sprinklers. Balls may be lifted from casual water without penalty.

Carry: The distance a shot flies in the air. Also, to clear a hazard successfully.

Chip: Short approach shot to the green that is hit low and carries just onto the putting surface and then bounces and rolls to the hole. Also, chip and run.

Dead: A shot right at the hole, especially if it stops close to the hole.

Divots: The piece of turf taken by a proper iron swing.

Dogleg: A hole where the fairway bends to the right or left. Also, the area where a fairway bends.

Double bogey: A hole completed in two shots over par.

Drop area: When a ball is hit into a hazard and cannot be played as it lies, it may be dropped and played from designated drop areas, with an appropriate penalty.

Draw: A shot that turns slightly from right to left in flight for a right-handed golfer. Also, the deliberate attempt to play a controlled shot that has a *draw*. Not to be confused with a *hook*, a shot with an extreme right to left movement, for a right-handed golfer.

Fade: A shot that turns slightly from left to right in flight for a right-handed golfer. Also, the deliberate attempt to play a controlled shot that has *fade*. Not to be confused with a *slice*, a shot with an extreme left to the right movement, for a right-handed golfer.

Fat: A shot that strikes the ground before impacting the ball. Such a shot often takes too much turf, too big a divot, and ends up short of the intended target.

Free drop (or relief): Slang for allowance to move the ball to an unobstructed position without penalty; e.g., from casual water or ground under repair.

Fringe: The close-cut grass surrounding the green. Also known as the apron, frog hair, or collar.

Green, fast vs. Slow: Greens that are cut short or are dry and hard are typically *fast*. Putts will go farther than normal and break more on fast greens. Greens that grow longer, or are wet and soft, are often *slow*. Putts will go shorter than normal and break less on slow greens. Putts may also be referred to as *fast* or *slow*.

Grain: The direction that the grass grows, which may affect the speed and break of putts. Putts hit with the *grain* will roll farther and break less than putts against the *grain*.

Ground under repair: Marked areas of the course where maintenance is being performed. Balls landing in these areas may be dropped without penalty out of the marked area but no nearer the hole.

Handicap: A system to rank golfers according to their skill levels, allowing them to engage fairly in even competition.

Hazard: Lakes, streams, ponds, creeks, ditches, bunkers, or nature areas on the golf course may be marked as hazards. Balls may be played from within the hazards or dropped out of the hazards with appropriate penalties.

Hole out: To complete the final stroke into the cup or hole.

Home: A shot that lands on the green is said to get home; e.g., get home in two.

Honor: The player with the lowest score on the previous hole plays first on the next hole. When ties occur, honors carry over from the previous hole.

In regulation: The ideal score (par) on a hole minus two putts; that is, the ideal number of strokes allowed to reach the green in regulation. For example, on a par four hole, getting on the green in two shots would be in regulation.

Lag: A conservative attempt to get close enough to (often short of) the hole so that the next putt can be made. The opposite of a bold putt that may go far past the hole and require a difficult second putt.

Lay up: A strategic shot played short of the green or hazard intended to leave a safe play on the next shot.

Left edge, right edge: The left or right edges of the hole or green may be used as aiming targets when allowing for the break or the wind.

Lie: The position of the ball in the grass (good, buried, tight, fluffy) or relative to the terrain (level, uphill, downhill, sidehill).

Links: The term has two meanings in golf. Links is generally used to refer to the course that golf is played on. It also has a more technical definition, referring to a particular type or style of golf course.

Long irons: Typically 1, 2, 3, and 4 irons. Long irons can project a golf ball farther than short irons. A 1-iron has less of an angled club face than a 4-iron. A 1-iron can project a golf ball with less height and a longer distance than a 4-iron.

Matches: Games, league competitions, or wagers.

Match play: Competition format in which the winner is determined by the number of holes won, rather than by total strokes (stroke play).

Net: Score on a hole or round after the handicap has been deducted from the gross score.

Nineteenth hole: Slang term for a pub, bar, or restaurant on a golf course. A standard round of golf has only eighteen holes of play.

Obstructions: Man-made objects such as cart paths, benches, etc. that are not part of the course design. Typically, a free drop may be given when an obstruction impedes a golfer's ball, stance, or shot path.

Out: The ball or player farthest from the hole. Also away.

Out-of-bounds (OB): A ball that has gone beyond the designated area of play for the hole, which is normally marked by white stakes. When a ball is hit OB in tournament competition, the golfer must play another ball from the original spot with a one-stroke penalty. In recreational play, it is customary for the new ball to be dropped just inside the fairway closest to where the ball left the fairway with a one-stroke penalty.

Pairing: Players scheduled to play together as competitors or partners.

Par: The regulation number of strokes set for a hole played perfectly, determined by yardage and hole design.

Pin: An alternative golf term used for the flagstick that marks each hole on a course.

Pin placement: Hole location on the green. A pin placed in the middle of a large green may be called an easy pin placement, while one hidden close behind a bunker is called a tough or sucker pin placement.

Pitch: A short, high approach shot into the green, which lands softly and doesn't roll too far.

Pitch in or chip in: A pitch or chip shot that goes directly into the hole from an off-the-green shot.

Putt out: To putt the ball into the hole. Also, to continue putting after the first putt, even if the golfer is not away.

Putting line: The line a putt follows to the hole on the green, determined by the slope and contour of the green.

Reading a putt: The act of estimating the speed and line of a putt before putting.

Relief: Shots that come to rest in an obstruction or ground under repair may be entitled to relief. *See* Free drop.

Rough: The area of the course off the fairway, not in a hazard, where the grass is often allowed to grow taller.

Sand traps: Hazards filled with sand. They are often positioned close to landing areas either near the fairway or the green.

Scramble: A team competition in which all team members hit their shot and choose the best ball position from which to shoot their next round of shots. This best-ball selection process is repeated until the team holes out.

Scratch: A term used to describe a golfer who shoots par or has a zero handicap.

Scoring: The grooves on the face of the club, especially irons. It may also refer to the act of shooting low scores.

Short game: Approach shots and putts. The part of the game that is typically inside approximately 100 yards from the hole.

Short hitter: A player who doesn't hit the ball far or hits shortest off the tee.

Short irons: Typically, the 7, 8, and 9 irons, and the pitching, gap, sand, and lob wedges. Short irons can project a golf ball a shorter distance than long irons. A 9-iron has more of an angled club face than a 7-iron. A 9-iron can project a golf ball higher, traveling a shorter distance than a 7-iron.

Skin: A game in which an amount is bet on each hole; e.g., dime skins. The lowest score on a hole wins, but if two players tie, all tie, and the pot rolls over until someone records a skin.

Snowman: Scoring an eight on any single golf hole.

Starter: Course employee in charge of tee times.

Thin: A shot that catches the ball with the sole of the club. Thin shots may damage the ball or produce uncontrolled low shots.

Tee, golf: A thin wood or plastic peg two or three inches in height on which a golf ball sits, raising the golf ball off the ground when playing the first stroke of a hole from the tee box.

Tee box: The tee area at the start of each hole.

Tees: Red, White, or Blue: Within a tee box, red tees indicate positions from which ladies tee off. White tees are commonly used by average players. Blue tees may be championship tees. Other colors may be used, depending on local course convention. Tee colors indicate the starting position for players who have different skill levels. The terms tee, tee box, and teeing ground are synonymous.

Two-putt: The standard allowance for putting when computing par. Two putts are considered the norm to complete the hole once the ball reaches the green.

Unplayable lie: A ball in a position that cannot be played, as determined by the player. Standard rules for relief with penalty apply.

19 GLOSSARY

30,000-foot-level metric: Reporting of a process output response or business metric from a high-level viewpoint. In this elevated performance report, short-term variation from the natural variation of input variables will result in an individuals chart or charts that views these fluctuations as common-cause variations. This metric has no calendar boundaries, and data from the latest region of stability are used to provide a predictive statement for stable processes. An undesirable 30,000-foot-level prediction statement suggests that the associated metric's process needs improvement. Evidence that a 30,000-foot-level response has improved is that its individuals chart response has a demonstrated enhancement to an improved level of performance. If this new process response level is considered statistically stable, EPRS-metrics 30,000-foot-level performance metric reporting software will use raw data from the individuals chart staging to calculate a new prediction statement for this reporting. Firefighting often occurs in organizations when there is a reaction to all unsatisfactory outputs as if they had a special cause. The incorporation of 30,000-foot-level performance metric reporting methodology can improve the understanding of process variation and redirect firefighting activities to fire-prevention activities; that is, using a team to systematically improve the underlying process through an IEE process improvement methodology. In IEE, a 30,000-foot-level metric is used for establishing a process response baseline before beginning a project and then for tracking the project-response progress.

50-foot-level metric: A KPIV metric that impacts a 30,000-foot-level response; e.g., process temperature when manufacturing plastic parts. This type of chart can involve frequent sampling since special-cause or process-drift-input issues need timely identification so that problems or process shifts can be quickly resolved without jeopardizing the quality or timeliness of the outgoing product or service. A pre-control chart can be used to monitor 50-foot-level process-input variables.

5S: Refers to five Japanese terms used to describe the steps of the 5S workplace organization method. In Japanese, the five S's are Seiri, Seiton, Seiso, Seiketsu, and Shitsuke. In English, the five S's are translated as Sort, Set in order, Shine, Standardize, and Sustain.

5 Whys: An iterative interrogative technique for exploring a particular problem's cause-and-effect relationships. By repeating the question 'Why?', the technique objective is to determine the root cause of a problem or defect. Each 'Why?' response forms the basis of the next question.

Acceptable quality level (AQL): A sampling method used to define a production order sample to find whether or not the entire product order has met the client's specifications relative to an AQL testing criterion. Based on the sampling data, the customer can make a decision to accept or reject the lot.

Accuracy: Accuracy and precision are two perspectives that should be considered when evaluating the *drive to a target* of a golfer's swing or business-metric-target achievement. Accuracy refers to how close a measurement is to the true or accepted value. Precision refers to how close measurements of the same item are to each other. To illustrate accuracy versus precision in golfing terms, consider that someone is at a driving range and is targeting his golf-swing for hitting a flag on the range, which is to simulate a golf-course pin location. For this situation, if he takes ten shots and then estimates that the mean of these shots was twenty yards short of the pin, this mean shortage distance from the pin target would be an accuracy estimate for the person's shot. Variation of golfing shot distance around a mean shot distance would represent the precision of a

golf swing. In business, an IEE 30,000-foot-level report out probability plot quantifies both measurement accuracy and precision on
an overall high-level metric's response – in one chart.

Analysis of means (ANOM): A statistical hypothesis testing procedure
for assessing the equality of the mean of each group in a population to the overall population mean.

Analysis of variance (ANOVA): A procedure to test statistically the
equality of means of discrete factor inputs.

ANSI/ASQ Z1.4-2003: Sampling procedures and tables for inspection
by attributes is an acceptance sampling system used in AQL testing.

Attribute response: See Response.

Average: See Mean.

Balanced scorecard (the): Initially, the balanced scorecard (Kaplan
and Norton 1992) was to track business organizational functions
in the areas of financial, customer, and internal business process
and learning & growth. In this system, an organization's vision
and strategy can also lead to the cascading of objectives, measures,
targets, and initiatives throughout the organization. This book
describes issues with this system and an alternative IEE approach
that overcomes these shortcomings.

Baldrige Award (Malcolm Baldrige National Quality Award): rec-
ognizes U.S. organizations in the business, health care, education,
and nonprofit sectors for performance excellence.

Benchmark: A standard in judging quality, value, or other essential
characteristics.

Benchmarking: Provision of a standard against which something can
be assessed.

Best estimate: An estimate calculated from sample data without a confidence interval.

Black Belt (BB), IEE: Full-time IEE implementation practitioner that
focuses on improving processes so that organizational IEE value
chain 30,000-foot-level metrics are enhanced and the enterprise as
a whole and its customers benefit.

Bottom-line: The final profit or loss that a company experiences.

Box plot: Describes various aspects of data pictorially. The box contains the lower and upper quartiles. The median appears as a horizontal line within the box. A box plot is sometimes called a box-and-whisker plot.

Brainstorming: Consensus building among experts about a problem or issue using group discussion.

Business process improvement event (BPIE): Functional process improvement effort that is to enhance an associated 30,000-foot-level metric but has not been identified as being an organizational strategic effort and an EIP component.

Capability, process: See Process capability.

Categorical variable: A variable that can be considered in one of a number of possible groups. Examples of categorical variables are gender, race, age group, and educational level.

Cause-and-effect diagram: Also called the fishbone or Ishikawa diagram, the C&E Diagram is a graphical brainstorming tool used to organize possible causes (KPIVs) of a symptom into categories of causes. Standard categories considered are materials, machine, method, personnel, measurement, and environment. These are branched as required to additional levels. It is a tool used for gathering wisdom of the organization.

Cause-and-effect matrix: A tool used to help quantify team consensus on relationships thought to exist between key input and key output variables. The results can lead to other activities such as FMEA, multi-vari charts, ANOVA, regression analysis, and DOE.

C-chart: In SPC, a c-chart is to be the control charting methodology that is used when monitoring subgroups of count data over time. For this type of IEE-metric reporting situation, an individuals chart, not a c-chart, is used to determine if a 30,000-foot-level count-data response is considered stable or not. The reason for using an individuals chart instead of a c-chart for a count-response data situation is that, for a c-chart, common-cause variation between subgroups, there is no mathematical impact on calculated UCL and LCL values. This mathematical truism is an important issue; in a vast majority of high-level 30,000-foot-level tracking responses there will be Y-output common-cause variation between subgroups. Because of this between-subgroup-variation occurrence, a c-chart count data chart could indicate many false special-cause signals that lead to wasteful firefighting common-cause variation as though it were special-cause (Reference Appendix A, Web page 11).

Common cause: In IEE, common-cause variation is viewed from a high-level 30,000-foot-level or satellite-level process-output perspective. Natural or random variation is inherent in most processes over time, affecting response measurement from the process. In IEE 30,000-foot-level reporting, if an individuals chart has no data points beyond statistically calculated UCL and LCL values, the process is presumed to have only common-cause variation. When this condition occurs, the processes are said to be stable and predictable. In IEE, this stability assessment is made using an individuals chart, not a $\bar{X}$ and R chart, p-chart, or c-chart. When a process experiences this high-level common-cause variation but does not meet customer needs, the process is said not to be capable. For non-capability process response situations, there is a need for process enhancements, or input variable changes to improve the condition; that is, this metric improvement need creates a *pull* for an improvement project creation.

Confidence interval: The limits or band of a parameter that contains the true parameter value at a specified confidence level. The confidence band can be single-sided to describe an upper and lower limit, or double-sided to describe both upper and lower bounds.

Continuous data response: See Response.

Control chart: See Individuals chart.

Control plan: A written document created to ensure that processes are run so that products or services meet or exceed customer requirements. It should be a living document, which is updated with both additions and deletions of controls based on experience from the process.

Cost of doing nothing differently (CODND): Unlike COPQ, a CODND monetary value does not require a specification. An example CODND value for a response that has no true specification is work in progress (WIP), where a CODND value could be determined for mean monthly expense cost to the business. In IEE, a CODND monetary value could be determined before beginning a process improvement project and then compared to a post-project value to determine the value of the process enhancements to the business.

Cost of poor quality (COPQ): Traditionally, the cost of quality issues has been given the broad categories of internal failure costs, external failure costs, appraisal costs, and prevention costs. IEE gives focus to determining CODND instead of COPQ.

Customer: Someone for whom work or a service is performed. The end-user of a product is a customer of the employees within a company that manufactures the product. There are also internal customers in a company. When an employee does work or performs a service for someone else in the company, the person who receives this work is a customer of this employee.

Cycle Time: Frequency that a process completes a part or product. Also, the time it takes for an operator to go through work activities before repeating the activities. Also, cycle time can be used to quantify customer order to delivery time.

Dashboard: *See* Scorecard.

Days sales outstanding (DSO): In accountancy, a company determines days sales outstanding to estimate the size of their outstanding accounts receivable. The DSO metric quantifies the size not in units of currency, but average sales days. Typically, days sales outstanding is calculated monthly as a mean value. However, for a DSO measurement from a 30,000-foot-level point of view, one needs to include the variation from individual payments, in addition to a central tendency mean response. This 30,000-foot-level response format for DSO provides individual duration-of-payment days, even if only from a sample of transactions over time. This form of reporting offers much more insight than a simple mean response.

Defect: A nonconformity or departure of a quality characteristic from its intended level or state.

Defective: A nonconforming item that contains at least one defect, or having a combination of several imperfections causing the unit not to satisfy intended requirements.

Design for Six Sigma (DFSS): A structured approach that can utilize both Six Sigma and Lean tools within the development process for both product and processes. DFSS can lead to a significant reduction in development cycle time and the likelihood of reworks while maximizing customer satisfaction.

Design of experiments (DOE): In the IEE DMAIC 'Improve phase,' DOE can be used as proactive analysis methodology where process input variables are changed in a structured fashion to assess whether an evaluated input level has a statistically significant effect on an output response. Factor levels can be assessed in a fractional factorial experiment or in a full factorial experiment structure.

Discrete data: Count information that only has a certain number of values. Examples include the number of attendees in a meeting and number of questions answered correctly.

Distribution: A pattern that randomly collected numbers from a population follows. In IEE, the normal and log-normal distributions are frequently used to model a process output response for determining a predictive statement when a process is determined to be stable in a 30,000-foot-level report. With this high-level reporting for a continuous response, a probability plot provides a data-fit visualization to the distribution where a process capability statement relative to the needs of the business could be determined.

DMAIC roadmap, IEE: An IEE project Define, Measure, Analyze, Improve, and Control roadmap for improvement project execution, which contains a true integration of Six Sigma and Lean tools.

DMADV: The five IEE design project steps are:

Define—Define internal and external customer needs.

Measure—Determine customer measurement needs and specifications.

Analyze—Assess process options to address customer needs.

Design—Create the product, process, or IT project to meet customer needs.

Verify—Test the created product, process, or IT project for its performance and ability to satisfy customer needs.

DMAIC, IEE: The five IEE DMAIC phases are:

Define—Define and scope the project.

Measure—Establish current, high-level 30,000-foot-level performance metrics for the process. Consider measurement system analysis (MSA) and the use of Lean tools. Wisdom of the organization (WOTO) assessments are also a part of this phase.

Analyze—Use IEE analysis tools to passively uncover root causes. Evaluate relationships between input factors and output responses and model processes.

Improve—Optimize processes, including the application of Lean and DOE tools.

Control—Institutionalize and maintain gains.

DNA: Deoxyribonucleic acid is a self-replicating material present in nearly all living organisms and the carrier of genetic information.

DPMO (defects per million opportunities): Number of defects that, on average, occur in one million opportunities. Care should be taken to assure that all defects, including touch-ups and reworks that previously may not have been recorded, are included in this calculation. Also important is an agreed-upon standard method for counting opportunities.

EIP (Enterprise improvement plan): A system for drilling down from business goals to specific projects (Reference Figure 7.12).

Elephant in the room: An obvious problem or difficult situation exists that people do not want to talk about.

Enterprise Performance Reporting System (EPRS) software: EPRS-metrics software provides a means to easily create 30,000-foot-level metric reports (Reference Appendix A, Web page 13). EPRS-IEE software (also referenced as EPRS software) can, among other things, create an organizational IEE value chain with 30,000-foot-level metrics that are automatically updated (Reference Appendix A, Web page 14).

Failure: A device is said to fail when it no longer performs its intended function satisfactorily.

Failure rate: Failures/unit time or failures/units of usage. Sample failure rates can be presented as 0.002 failures/hour, 0.0003 failures/auto miles traveled, 0.01 failures/1000 parts manufactured.

Failure mode and effects analysis (FMEA): A proactive method of improving or minimizing failures in a product or service. For a process FMEA, wisdom of the organization inputs can be used to list what can go wrong at each step of a process that could cause failures or customer problems. Each item is evaluated for its importance, frequency of occurrence, and the probability of occurrence detection. In an FMEA, this information is used to prioritize the items that most need improving. Recognized items are then assigned a corrective action plan to reduce their risk of occurrence— the opposite of fault tree analysis.

False negative: A test result that incorrectly indicates a particular condition or attribute is absent.

False positive: A test result that incorrectly indicates a particular condition or attribute is present.

Fault tree analysis: A top-down, deductive failure analysis in which an undesired state of a system is analyzed using logic to combine a series of lower-level events.

Firefighting: An expression used to describe the process of performing emergency fixes to problems where often the reactions are the result of common-cause variation rather than special cause.

Fractional factorial experiment: Design of experiments (DOE) strategy that assesses several factors/variables simultaneously in one test, where only a partial set of all possible combinations of factorial levels is tested to identify important factors more efficiently. This type of test is much more efficient than a traditional one-at-a-time test strategy.

Full factorial experiment: Factorial experiment where all combinations of factor levels are tested.

Functions, IEE value chain: An organizational or business function is a core process or set of activities carried out in a company or its departments. Common functions include operations, marketing, human resources (HR), information technology, customer service, and finance.

Flow chart: Path of steps of work used to produce or do something.

Gage R&R (repeatability and reproducibility): A methodology used in measurement system analysis (MSA). It is the evaluation of measuring instruments to determine their capability to provide a precise response. It determines how much of the observed process variation is due to measurement system variation. Gage repeatability is the variation in measurements using the same measurement instrument several times by one appraiser's measuring the identical characteristic on the same part. Gage reproducibility is the variation in the average of measurements made by different appraisers using the same measuring instrument when measuring the identical characteristics on the same part.

Gemba Walk: The action of observing the actual process, understanding the work, asking questions, and learning what really is happening during process execution.

General linear model (GLM): A statistical linear regression model for a continuous response variable given continuous and/or categorical predictors.

Governance, corporate: The system by which business corporations are directed and controlled. The corporate governance structure specifies the distribution of rights and responsibilities among different participants in the corporation, such as the board, managers, shareholders and other stakeholders, and spells out the rules and procedures for making decisions on corporate affairs. This system also provides the structure through which company objectives and the means of attaining those objectives and monitoring performance are set. IEE delivers a structured system for corporate governance.

Green Belt (GB), IEE: Part-time IEE implementation practitioner that focuses on improving processes so that organizational IEE value-chain 30,000-foot-level metrics are enhanced and the enterprise as a whole and its customers benefit.

Green Belts (GBs): Part-time Lean Six Sigma practitioners.

Hard savings: Savings that directly impact the bottom-line.

Histogram: A graphical representation of the sample frequency distribution that describes the occurrence of grouped items.

Hoshin kanri: A process used in strategic planning where strategic goals are to be communicated throughout the company and then put into action.

Hypothesis testing: Consists of a null hypothesis (*H0*) and alternative hypothesis (*Ha*) where, for example, a null hypothesis indicates equality between two process outputs, and an alternative hypothesis indicates non-equality. Through a hypothesis test, a decision is made whether to reject or not reject a null hypothesis. When a null hypothesis is rejected, there is α risk of error. Most typically, there is no risk assignment when we fail to reject the null hypothesis. However, an appropriate sample size could be determined such that failure to reject the null hypothesis is made with β risk of error.

Incapable process: A process that does not produce results consistent with specification requirements or customer expectations.

In control: The description of a process where variation is consistent over time; that is, only common causes exist. In IEE, an individuals chart is used to determine whether a process is in control; that is, stable from a high-level point of view. When an IEE 30,000-foot-level individuals chart has no data points beyond the chart's statistically determined UCL and LCL values, the process is said to be stable, and the process response is considered predictable.

Individuals control chart: A control chart of individual values where between-subgroup variation mathematically affects calculated UCL and LCL values. For this type of control chart, the difference between the data-calculated UCL and LCL value increases when there is more between-subgroup variation. In IEE, the individuals chart is used to assess process stability in a 30,000-foot-level report. In an individuals chart, when there are no plotted data outside data-calculated UCL and LCL limits, and there are no patterns in the plotted data, the process is considered to be stable and predictable. Mathematically determined UCL and LCL values from the data are independent of specification limits or targets. In IEE, $\bar{X}$ and R chart, p-chart, and c-chart techniques are not used to determine whether a process response is stable or not. *See* $\bar{X}$ *and R chart, p-chart, and c-chart.*

Inferential statistics: Statements made about a population from the analysis of samples; that is, properties of the population are inferred from the analysis of samples.

Infrequent subgrouping/sampling: Traditionally, rational sub-grouping issues involve the selection of samples that yield relatively homogeneous conditions within the subgroup for a small region of time or space, perhaps five in a row. For a given situation, differing sub-grouping methodologies can dramatically affect the measured variation within subgroups, which in turn affect the distance between the UCL and LCL lines for an SPC chart. For the high-level metrics of IEE, an infrequent subgrouping/sampling approach is needed so that short-term variations caused by KPIV fluctuations are viewed as common-cause issues. A 30,000 foot-level individuals chart created with infrequent subgrouping/sampling can reduce the amount of organizational firefighting; however, this does not mean a problem does not exist within the process. For example, when an accompanying 30,000-foot-level predictive response is unsatisfactory for a stable process output response, this improvement need can *pull* (using a Lean term) for the creation of an IEE improvement project.

Integrated Enterprise Excellence (IEE, I double E): A 9-step roadmap for the creation of an enterprise process system in which organizations can significantly improve both customer satisfaction and their bottom-line. IEE business management techniques can help manufacturing, development, and service organizations become more competitive and/or move them to new heights. The IEE system is a structured approach that guides organizations through the tracking and attainment of organizational goals. IEE goes well beyond traditional Lean Six Sigma and the balanced scorecard methods. IEE integrates enterprise process measures and improvement methodologies with tools such as Lean and TOC in a never-ending pursuit of excellence. IEE becomes an enabling framework, which integrates, improves, and aligns with other initiatives such as TQM, ISO 9001, Malcolm Baldrige Assessments, and the Shingo Prize. IEE is the organizational orchestration that moves toward the achievement goal of the three Rs of Business; that is, everyone is doing the Right things and doing them Right at the Right time.

Integrated Management System (IMS): Combines all related components of a business into one system for easier management and operations. Quality, Environmental, and Safety management systems can be combined and managed in IMS. The IEE business management system can provide a foundation for implementing IMS.

Interaction: The effect of one causal variable on a response depends on the state of a second causal variable.

ISO 9001: An international standard that specifies requirements for a quality management system (QMS) for organizations to use to demonstrate the ability to consistently provide products and services that meet customer and regulatory requirements.

ISO 45001: An international standard that specifies requirements for an occupational health and safety management system with guidance to proactively improve performance in preventing injury and ill-health.

ISO 14001: An international standard that specifies the framework requirements for an effective environmental management system for organizations to follow.

Kaizen event (or kaizen blitz): Kaizen is a Japanese term meaning gradual unending improvement by doing little things better and setting and achieving increasingly higher standards. Kaizen events are short duration improvement projects with a specific aim for improvement. A facilitator leads events, with the implementation team being members predominantly from the area in which the kaizen event is being conducted plus a few additional people from support areas.

Kanban: Pulling a product through the production process. This method of manufacturing process-flow-control only allows the movement of material by pulling from a preceding process. Kanban keeps inventory low, and, when quality errors are detected, less production is affected.

Key performance indicator (KPI): A type of performance measurement that evaluates the success of an organization or of a particular engaged activity such as projects, programs, products and other initiatives.

Key process input variable (KPIV): Factors in a process correlated to an output characteristic(s) important to the internal or external customer. Optimizing and controlling these factors are vital to the improvement of a key process output variable (KPOV).

Key process output variable (KPOV): Characteristic(s) of the output of a process that are important to the customer. Understanding what is important to the internal and external customers is essential to identifying KPOVs.

Lean: Improving operations and the supply chain with an emphasis on the reduction of wasteful activities like waiting, transportation, material hand-offs, inventory, and overproduction.

Level 5 system: Jim Collins' book, *Good to Great* (Collins 2001), describes Level 5 Leaders as leaders who display a potent mixture of personal humility and indomitable will. Level 5 Leaders are incredibly ambitious, but their ambition is first and foremost for the cause, for the organization and its purpose, not for themselves. IEE provides a means to create not only Level 5 leaders but also a Level 5 system that offers a culture that can be formulated, which is long-lasting and works effectively even when Good-to-Great organizational Level 5 leaders leave an organization.

Low-hanging fruit: Refers to an action that takes almost no effort.

Marginal plot: Permits the visualization of the distribution of data in both the x-axis and y-axis directions.

Master Black Belt (MBB), IEE: IEE expert who is skilled in both understanding and implementing all aspects of the 9-step IEE system in an organization.

Mean: The mean of a sample ($\bar{x}$) is the sum of all the responses divided by the sample size. The mean of a population (μ) is the sum of all responses of the population divided by the population size. For a random sample of a population, $\bar{x}$ is an estimate of a population's mean (μ).

Measurement system analysis (MSA): Assessment of an overall measurement system, including gage repeatability and reproducibility (R&R).

Median: For a sample, the number that is in the middle when all observations are ranked in magnitude. For a population, the value at which the cumulative distribution function is 0.5.

Military standard (MIL-STD): United States defense standard that is used to help achieve standardization objectives by the U.S. Department of Defense. These standards are also used by other non-defense government organizations, technical organizations, and industry.

Mistake proofing: The use of a methodology that either makes it impossible for an error to occur or makes the error immediately obvious once it has occurred.

Muda: A Japanese term indicating efforts that do not add value (waste). Some categories of muda are defects, overproduction or excess inventory, idle time, and poor layout.

Multi-vari chart: A chart that displays the measurement differences within units, between units, between samples, and between lots. It is useful in detecting variation sources within a process.

Null hypothesis: See hypothesis.

Normal distribution: A bell-shaped distribution that is often useful to describe various physical, mechanical, electrical, and chemical properties.

Objectives and key results (OKR): Framework for defining and tracking objectives and their outcomes.

Out of Control: Control charts exhibiting one or more special-cause conditions. When an IEE 30,000-foot-level individuals chart has one or more points beyond statistically calculated UCL and LCL values, a default statement in the report will state that the process output response is not predictable.

Pareto chart: A graphical technique used to quantify problems so that effort can be expended in fixing the *vital few* causes, as opposed to the *trivial many*. Named after Vilfredo Pareto (born 1848), an Italian economist.

Pareto principle: 80% of the trouble comes from 20% of the problems; that is, the vital few problems.

Parts per million (PPM): Number of units of mass of a contaminant per million units of the total mass. In Six Sigma, PPM can be used to describe a defective rate; e.g., a PPM rate of 10,000 would equate to a 1% defective rate.

Passive analysis: Data collected and analyzed as the process is currently performing to determine potential KPIVs. Process alterations are not assessed.

P-chart: In SPC, a p-chart is to be the control charting methodology used when monitoring the proportion of nonconforming units in a sample, where the sample proportion nonconforming is the ratio of the number of nonconforming units to the sample size. For this type of IEE-data situation, an individuals chart, not a p-chart, is used to determine if a 30,000-foot-level non-conforming proportion response is considered stable or not. The reason for using an individuals chart instead of a p-chart for non-conformance 30,000-foot-level rate data tracking is that for a p-chart any Y-response common-cause-between-subgroup variation that is occurring would have no mathematical impact on calculated UCL and LCL values. This is an essential issue in that, for a vast majority of high-level 30,000-foot-level tracking responses, there will invariably be some level of common-cause, output-response variation between subgroups. Because of this between-subgroup-variation occurrence, a p-chart for this type of data could show many false special-cause signals that can lead to wasteful firefighting common-cause variation as though it were special cause (Reference Appendix A, Web page 11).

Plan-do-check-act (PDCA): An iterative four-step business management method for continuous process improvement. PDCA is also referenced as the Deming cycle, Shewhart cycle, or plan-do-study-act (PDSA).

Poka-yoke: A Japanese term indicating a mechanism that either prevents a mistake from occurring or makes a mistake evident at a glance.

Precision: See Accuracy.

Prediction statement: In IEE, when a satellite-level or 30,000-foot-level performance metric reporting is considered stable, it is said to be predictable. Data from the chart's recent region of stability is used to determine a best estimate prediction statement provided below the report's charting. When a specification exists, and the process is considered predictable, the report provides a best estimate non-conformance rate statement. When there is no specification, and the process is deemed stable, a mean (or median) and 80% frequency of occurrence rate is reported below the graphs of the 30,000-foot-level performance-metric reporting. This reporting 80% statement provides the chart-reader a quantification of the expected amount of variation from the process; that is, there is the expectation that four out of five reported occurrences will be in the stated 80% frequency of occurrence range.

Probability plot: Data are plotted on a selected probability-plot coordinate system to determine if a particular distribution is appropriate; that is, plotted data follow a straight line. When data follow a probability plot distribution such as normal or log-normal, statements about percentiles of the population can be made from the probability plot. In IEE 30,000-foot-level and satellite-level reports for continuous data, a probability plot is used to determine for stable processes a predictive statement.

Population: The totality of items under consideration.

Pre-control chart: An approach to monitor processes over time, which involves the classification of product measurements into one of three groups depending upon the relative position of the measurement to specification limits. The process is to be adjusted when specific patterns occur in the plot. In IEE, a pre-control chart can be used to manage the Y-response impact from drifting or changing X process inputs at a 50-foot-level.

Problem-solving: The process of determining the cause from a symptom and then choosing an action to improve a process or product.

Process: A method to make or do something that involves several steps.

Process capability/performance indices (Cp, Cpk, Pp, Ppk): For process capability indices, Cp is a measurement of the allowable tolerance spread divided by a short-term 6σ data calculated spread. Cpk has a similar ratio to that of Cp except that this ratio considers the shift of the mean relative to the central specification target. For process performance indices, Pp and Ppk calculations are similar to Cp and Cpk calculations, except the calculation is from a long-term viewpoint, instead of a short-term perspective. A 6σ calculated data spread is used in the calculations (Reference Appendix A, Web page 11).

Pull: A Lean term that results in an activity when a customer or downstream process step requests the action. A home builder that builds houses only when an agreement is reached on the sale of the house is using a pull system. *See* Push.

Pull for project creation: This term is derived from the Lean term, pull. An IEE implementation objective is that performance metric ownership is assigned through the business IEE value chain, where functional performance metric tracking is at a 30,000-foot-level. In the 9-step IEE system, the enterprise is analyzed as a whole in step 3 to determine what performance metrics need improvement and by how much so that whole-organizational satellite-level goals can be met. A metric improvement need would then create a *pull for project creation*. An EIP shows a summary of an organization's *pull for project creation* efforts. *See* Push for project creation.

Push: A Lean term that results in an activity that a customer or downstream process step has not explicitly requested. This activity can create excessive waste and/or inventory. A home builder that builds houses on the speculation of sale is using a push system. If the house does not sell promptly upon completion, the homebuilder has created excess inventory for the company, which can be very costly. *See* pull.

Push for project creation: This term is derived from the Lean term, push. Lean Six Sigma (LSS) deployments are to create and execute projects that are to be beneficial to the business. When assessing the typical Lean Six Sigma project selection process, either a deployment steering committee or some level of management selects projects from a list that they and others think is important. For this type of deployment, there is often a scurry to determine projects for attendees to work on during their LSS training that starts next week. This system could be considered a push for project creation; that is, people are hunting for projects because they need to work on a defined project during LSS training. With this deployment system, there can be initial successes since agreed-to low-hanging fruit projects can often be readily identified and provide significant benefits; however, this system of project determination is not typically long-lasting. After a while, people usually have a hard time defining and/or agreeing to what projects should be undertaken. Besides, this project creation system does not typically look at the system as a whole when identifying projects to undertake. This system of project selection can lead to sub-optimization, which can be detrimental to the enterprise as a whole. Finally, this LSS deployment system typically creates a separate function entity that manages the deployment, which is separate from operational scorecards and functional units. In time, people in these functions can be very visible on the corporate radar screen when downsizing forces occur, or there is a change in executive management, even though the LSS function has been claiming much past success. *See* Pull for project creation.

p-value: A statistical analysis output. The null hypothesis is rejected when this value is equal to or less than the desired level of significance; e.g. 0.05.

Quality, cost, and time metrics: A frequently referenced description of performance metric for IEE value chain functions. These three categories are to encompass process efficiency, productivity, and customer satisfaction.

Quality, Health, Safety and Environment Management (QHSE): A system for implementing organizational quality, health, safety, and environmental management.

Quality management system (QMS): Collection of business processes focused on consistently meeting customer requirements and enhancing their satisfaction.

Random: Having no specific pattern.

Range: For a set of numbers, the absolute difference between the largest and smallest value.

Red-yellow-green (RYG) Scorecard: Used by organizations to track individual performance metrics relative to goals. A RYG scorecard colored response assesses how well a metric response performs relative to its goal, where green indicates being on track, yellow is an at-risk indicator, and red suggests attention is required. Sometimes a RYG scorecard is referenced as a stoplight scorecard.

Regression analysis: Data collected from an experiment are used to empirically quantify, through a mathematical model, the relationship that exists between the response variable and influencing factors. In a simple linear regression model, $y = b0 + b1x + \varepsilon$, x is the regressor, y is the expected response, $b0$ and $b1$ are coefficients, and ε is random error.

Response: Two basic types of process-output responses are continuous and attribute. A continuous response could also be referenced as variables data. A response is said to be continuous if any value can be taken between limits; e.g., 2, 2.0001, and 3.00005. An attribute response is a measure of the presence or absence of a characteristic. Attribute data focus on numbers; variable data focus on measurements. For example, data on defective products simply classify a process output unit as defective or not defective. This type of measurement could be translated into a failure rate proportion output; e.g., 1 out of 1000 sheets of paper on the average jam when fed through a copier. Continuous response examples include weight, distance, and voltage measurements.

Risk Management: Process of identifying possible risks, problems, or disasters before they happen. IEE includes a means to have a business risk management system that allows leadership to set up procedures to avoid the risk, minimize its impact, or, at the very least, help cope with its implications.

Robust process: A process is considered robust when its output variation is not sensitive to the normal variation from its input variables. For example, a manufacturing process step is robust to different operators who regularly execute the operation step.

Rolled throughput yield (RTY): For a process that has a series of steps, RTY is the product of yields for each step.

Sample: A selection of items from a population.

Satellite-level metric: Similar to a 30,000-foot-level metric except that the satellite-level metric tracks financial metrics, such as profit margins or EBITDA. *See* 30,000-foot-level metric.

Scatter plot: Assessment of the relationship between two continuous variables with the intention of determining a cause-and-effect relationship.

Scorecard: A major difference between the dashboards and scorecards is that a scorecard focuses on a given metric and compares it to a forecast or target, whereas a dashboard will present multiple numbers in different ways. Performance measurement is generally considered to be a regular measurement of outcomes and results, which generates reliable data on the effectiveness and efficiency of programs. Performance metrics are used to measure the behavior, activities, and performance of a business. Satellite-level and 30,000-foot-level metrics track and report performance metrics regularly from a process-output point of view that provides a predictive statement when responses are considered stable. In IEE documentation, satellite-level and 30,000-foot-level metrics are sometimes referenced as a scorecard/dashboard.

Shingo Prize: An international award for operational excellence that assesses: vision and strategy alignment; employee empowerment; continuous improvement; innovation and development; quality and sustainable results.

Sigma: The Greek letter (σ) is often used to describe the standard deviation of data.

Sigma level: A metric calculated by some to describe the capability of a process relative to its specification. A six-sigma level is said to have a 3.4 DPMO rate. A three-sigma level is about 66,800 DPMO. A four-sigma level is about 6210 DPMO, while a five-sigma level is about 233 DPMO. Sigma level is sometimes referred to as sigma quality level. The IEE system does not use and report sigma level metrics (Reference Appendix A, Web page 11).

Significance: A statistical statement indicating that the level of a factor causes a difference in a response with a certain degree of risk of being in error.

Six Sigma: A term coined by Motorola that emphasizes the improvement of processes to reduce defect rates, decrease variation, and to make general improvements.

SMART goals: Not everyone uses the same letter descriptors for SMART. In IEE, referenced descriptors are italicized in the following list: S—*specific*, significant, stretching; M—*measurable*, meaningful, motivational; A—agreed upon, attainable, achievable, acceptable, action-oriented, *actionable*; R—realistic, *relevant*, reasonable, rewarding, results-oriented; T—*time-based*, timely, tangible, trackable.

Soft savings: Savings that do not directly impact the financial statement as hard savings do. Possible soft savings categories are cost avoidance, lost profit avoidance, productivity improvements, profit enhancement, and other intangibles.

Soft skills: A person who effectively facilitates meetings and works well with other people has good soft skills.

Special cause: Variation in a process from a reason that is not an inherent part of that process; that is, it is not a common cause.

Specification: A criterion that is to be met by a part or product.

Stable process: In satellite-level and 30,000-foot-level performance metric tracking, individuals charts are used to assess process stability. An individuals chart of a process-output that has no data points beyond the chart's UCL and LCL lines is considered stable.

In IEE, when a process is deemed stable, a prediction statement is provided below the report's charting for both a satellite-level and 30,000-foot-level reports. EPRS-metrics software offers an option for the chart's creator to override the technicality of any point being beyond the UCL or LCL line because of the belief that the occurrence was by chance.

Stakeholders: Those people who are key to the success of an IEE project; e.g., finance, managers, people who are working in the process, upstream/downstream departments, suppliers, and customers.

Standard deviation (σ, s): A mathematical quantity that describes the variability of a response. It equals the square root of variance. The standard deviation of a sample (s) is used to estimate the standard deviation of a population (σ).

Statistical process control (SPC): The application of analytical techniques in the control of processes.

Test: Assessment of whether an item meets specified requirements by subjecting it to a set of physical, environmental, chemical, or operating actions/conditions.

The balanced scorecard: *See* Balanced scorecard (the).

Three Rs of business: Everyone doing the Right things and doing them Right at the Right time.

Theory of constraints (TOC): The TOC described by Goldratt (Goldratt 1992) presents a systems-thinking process where the focus is on the system's bottlenecks. TOC thinking provides a viewpoint for continual improvement of the performance of the entire system, rather than viewing the system in terms of discrete processes. TOC addresses the larger systematic picture as a chain or grid of interlinked chains. The performance of its weakest link determines the performance of the whole chain. In IEE, TOC is a step 3 consideration in the IEE 9-step business management system.

Total Productive Maintenance (TPM): The TPM process is to increase the Overall Equipment Effectiveness (OEE) of plant equipment. OEE is the resulting product from the multiplication of three equipment factors; that is, performance, availability, and quality.

Tribal knowledge: Any unwritten information that is not commonly known by others in an organization. This term often references information that may need to be known by others for producing quality products or services.

TRIZ: A problem-solving tool based on the study of patterns of inventions in global patent literature.

Total quality management (TQM): Describes a management approach that is to have long-term success through customer satisfaction. In TQM effort, all members of an organization are to participate in improving processes, products, services, and the culture in which they work.

Toyota Production System (TPS): Integrated socio-technical system developed by Toyota that comprises its management philosophy and practices. TPS organizes manufacturing and logistics for the automobile manufacturer, including interaction with suppliers and customers.

Value added (VA) time: The execution time for the work elements that a customer is willing to pay for.

Value chain, IEE: Describes in flowchart fashion, both primary and support organizational activities and their accompanying 30,000-foot-level or satellite-level performance metrics. An example of primary activity flow is: develop product—market product—sell the product—produce the product—invoice/collect payments—report satellite-level metrics. Example support activities include IT, finance, HR, labor relations, safety & environment, and legal.

Value stream mapping: A Lean manufacturing technique for the analysis, design, and management of the flow of materials and information required to bring a product to a customer. Standard symbols depict various work streams and information flows.

Variance: Has more than one meaning in business. In accounting, a variance is a difference between an actual amount and a pre-determined standard amount or amount budgeted. In a statistical sense, a variance is a measure of the amount of spread in a distribution.

Wisdom of the organization (WOTO): Structured conversations and dialog with people who know a process intimately to describe what is currently being done in the process and what might be done to improve processes. An end goal is to solicit improvement ideas using brainstorming tools such as cause-and-effect diagrams. In IEE WOTO is within the IEE DMAIC's 'Measure phase' drill-down.

Work in progress (WIP): The partially finished goods of a company, which are waiting for completion and eventual sale, or the value of these items. WIP items are either just being fabricated or waiting in a queue or storage buffer for further processing.

$\bar{X}$ **and R chart (pronounced X-bar and R chart):** In SPC, an $\bar{X}$ and R chart is to be the control charting methodology used when monitoring the mean ($\bar{X}$) and range (R) of process samples, which were collected and measured at regular subgroup-time intervals. For this type of IEE-data situation, two individuals charts, not an $\bar{X}$ and R chart, are used to determine if a 30,000-foot-level process-output response is stable or not. One of these individuals charts tracks the subgroup's mean ($\bar{X}$) response, while the other individuals chart tracks the subgroup's standard deviation response. The reason for using individuals charts, instead of an $\bar{X}$ and R chart pair, is that for both of the $\bar{X}$ and R chart subgroup responses any common-cause-between-subgroup variation which occurs will have no mathematical impact on calculated UCL and LCL values. This calculation reality is an essential fact in that, for a vast majority of high-level 30,000-foot-level tracking responses, there will invariably be some level of Y-response common-cause variably between subgroups. Because of this, an $\bar{X}$ and R chart of this type of data could show many false special-cause signals, which can lead to wasteful firefighting common-cause variation as though it were special-cause occurrences (Reference Appendix A, Web page 11).

XmR chart: In SPC, an XmR chart is to be the control charting methodology used when monitoring single data items with X indicating observations and mR indicating moving range. For this type of IEE-data situation, only the individuals chart, not the moving range chart, is used to determine if a 30,000-foot-level non-conforming individual-value response is considered stable or not. The reason for not using the moving range chart of this two-chart pair is that the moving range chart would add unnecessary complexity to 30,000-foot-level reporting since moving range charting tracking is somewhat redundant to the tracking of the individual values. *See* Individuals control chart.

Y-response management: For a process, the output or its Y is dependent upon the inputs that occur in the process's execution; that is, Y=f(X). Organizational management to the Ys through the setting of measurement-value goals that are to be met at some point in time, utilizing techniques such as red-yellow-green scorecards or table-of-numbers reporting, can lead to very unfavorable, if not destructive, organizational behaviors.

20 REFERENCES

Axelrod, J and Rand E. (2015), "How investigators cracked the Blue Bell listeria outbreak case," CBS News, https://www.cbsnews.com/news/how-investigators-cracked-blue-bell-listeria-outbreak-case/.

Bloomberg (2019), "Charting GE's Historic Rise and Tortured Downfall," https://www.bloomberg.com/graphics/2019-general-electric-rise-and-downfall/.

Breyfogle, F. W., Enck, D. Flories, P, Pearson, T (2001), *Wisdom on the Green: Smarter Six Sigma Business Solutions*, Smarter Solutions, Austin, TX.

Breyfogle, F. W. (2003). *Implementing Six Sigma: Smarter Solutions Using Statistical Methods*. 2d ed. Wiley, Hoboken, NJ.

Breyfogle, F. W. (2008a), *The Integrated Enterprise Excellence System: An Enhanced, Unified Approach to Balanced Scorecards, Strategic Planning, and Business Improvement*, Citius Publishing, Austin, TX.

Breyfogle, F. W. (2008b), *Integrated Enterprise Excellence Volume I—The Basics: Golfing Buddies Go Beyond Lean Six Sigma and the Balanced Scorecard*, Citius Publishing, Austin, TX.

Breyfogle, F. W. (2008c), *Integrated Enterprise Excellence Volume II—Business Deployment: A Leaders' Guide for Going Beyond Lean Six Sigma and the Balanced Scorecard*, Citius Publishing, Austin, TX.

Breyfogle, F. W. (2008d), *Integrated Enterprise Excellence Volume III—Improvement Project Execution: A Management and Black Belt Guide for Going Beyond Lean Six Sigma and the Balanced Scorecard*, Citius Publishing, Austin, TX.

Breyfogle, F. W. (2010), *Lean Six Sigma Project Execution Guide: The Integrated Enterprise Excellence (IEE) Process Improvement Project Roadmap*, Citius Publishing, Austin, TX.

Breyfogle, F. W. (2020a), *Management 2.0: Discovery of Integrated Enterprise Excellence*, Citius Publishing, Austin, TX.

Breyfogle, F. W. (2020b), *Leadership System 2.0: Implementing Integrated Enterprise Excellence*, Citius Publishing, Austin, TX.

Broder, J. (2011), "BP Shortcuts Led to Gulf Oil Spill, Report Says," The New York Times, https://www.nytimes.com/2011/09/15/science/earth/15spill.html.

Collins, J. (2001), *Good to Great: Why Some Companies Make the Leap... and Others Don't*, HarperCollins Publishers Inc., New York, NY.

Colvin, G. and Wahba, P. (2019), "Sears' Seven Decades of Self-Destruction," Fortune, https://fortune.com/longform/sears-self-destruction/.

Deming, W. Edwards (1986), *Out of the Crisis*, Massachusetts Institute of Technology, Cambridge, MA.

Egan, M. (2015), "Kmart's sales have fallen off a gigantic cliff," CNN Business, https://money.cnn.com/2015/06/08/investing/kmart-sales-decline-sears-eddie-lampert/.

Galuszka, P (2008), "Eight Reasons Why Circuit City Went Bankrupt," CBS News, https://www.cbsnews.com/news/eight-reasons-why-circuit-city-went-bankrupt/.

Goldratt, E. M. (1992), *The Goal*, 2d ed., North River Press, Great Barrington, MA.

Grove, A. S. (1983), *High Output Management*, Random House Inc., New York, NY.

Hess, E. (2010), "Stark Lessons From The Dell Fraud Case," Forbes, https://www.forbes.com/2010/10/13/michael-dell-fraud-leadership-governance-sec.html#48d2a97c6d6a.

Kaplan, R. S. and D. P. Norton (1992), "The balanced scorecard – measures that drive performance," *Harvard Business Review*, Jan.–Feb.

Porter, M. (1985), *Competitive Advantage: Creating and Sustaining Superior Performance*, Free Press, New York, NY.

Senge, P. M. (1990), *The Fifth Discipline: The Art and Practice of the Learning Organization*, New York: Doubleday/Current.

Sinek, S., (2019), *The Infinite Game*, Penguin Random House LLC, New York, NY.

Sullivan, J. (2017), "Ouch, 50% of New Hires Fail! 6 Ugly Numbers Revealing Recruiting's Dirty Little Secret," https://www.ere.net/ ouch-50-of-new-hires-fail-6-ugly-numbers-revealing-recruitings-dirty-little-secret/.

Wiersema, M. (2002), "Holes at the Top: Why CEO Firings Backfire," Harvard Business Review, https://hbr.org/2002/12/holes-at-the-top-why-ceo-firings-backfire.

Wolff-Mann, E., (2019), "Wells Fargo scandals: The complete list," Yahoo Finance, https://finance.yahoo.com/news/wells-fargo-scandals-the-complete-timeline-141213414.html.

21 ACKNOWLEDGMENTS

I want to thank the many people who helped in differing ways with the creation of this book. I need to first thank my wife, Becki, for her support of my IEE passion over the years and for my continual refinement efforts of how to best convey the benefits of IEE to others.

I do have the concern that I missed someone in this acknowledgement section of the book. If so, I am sorry.

Over many years, I have worked with Rick Haynes, Doug Wheeler, Chinh Tran, and Tri Pham to develop the Enterprise Performance Reporting System (EPRS) software that supports IEE metric reporting and its organizational implementation. This team did a great job creating the software coding for EPRS-metrics (Reference Appendix A, Web page 13) and EPRS-IEE (Reference Appendix A, Web page 14).

The conversations and dialog that I had about general hospital situations and measurement reporting practices with Tim Jones, Earl Maxwell, and Bob Spurck made the book's storyline and situations consistent with what could occur in a hospital.

I mailed draft copies of this book at different stages of this book's development to over fifty people. Some feedback was extensive, but all feedback was valuable! What I thought was interesting is that there was virtually no overlap in the responses. All comments were from a different perspective, which was great! Everyone who gave feedback impacted this book in a positive way.

Detailed draft-copy reviews and many helpful improvement suggestions were provided by Bob Ashenbrenner, Peter Courtois, Mike

Harkins, Andrew Lux, Brian Mitchell, Michael Parrillo, Tony Perez, and Mike Whitescarver.

Others who provided book-improvement suggestions that were very valuable are Manny Barriger, Jim Bennett, Scott Berman, Steven Bonacorsi, Jim Bossert, Fred Bothwell, Evaristo Campos, Rachele Collins, Mark Feller, Ralph Fulwood, Russ Gale, Carrie Green, Jesse Hamilton, Janet Hammill, Cheryl Holden, Arch Holder, Elaine Jennings, John Jennings, Elizabeth Keim, Joe Knecht, Ric Love, Jerry Mairani, Todd Minnick, Lawrence Mossman, Steve Mundwiller, Andy Paquet, Bill Pugh, Dan Rand, Alexander Sasfrass, Janice Shade, Doug Shifflett, Frank Shines, Jerel Walters, and Doug Wheeler.

Thanks go to Adam Hough and his team who assisted with Amazon's launch of this book. Thanks also to Grant Tharp for his narration of the audio version of this book.

For many years, Dorothy S. Stewart has edited my books and articles. Again, Dorothy did a great and timely edit of this book. She also gave much phone guidance for specific conventions to use in the book's text.

30,000-foot-level and satellite-level metric figures were created using a Smarter Solutions, Inc. developed add-in to Minitab*.